An American Vision

An American Vision
Policies for the '90s

edited by
Edward H. Crane
and David Boaz

CATO
INSTITUTE
Washington, D.C.

Library of Congress Cataloging-in-Publication Data

An American vision.

  1. United States—Economic policy—1981–   .
2. United States—Social policy—1980–   3. United
States—Politics and government—1981–   I. Crane, Edward H.,
1944–   . II. Boaz, David, 1953–
HC106.8.A453   1989   338.973   88-35280
ISBN 0-932790-72-0
ISBN 0-932790-73-9 (pbk.)

Printed in the United States of America.

CATO INSTITUTE
224 Second Street, S.E.
Washington, D.C. 20003

Contents

1. Introduction

Edward H. Crane and David Boaz

During the primaries of the late but not lamented presidential campaign it was often noted that despite a plethora of candidates, none seemed to project a compelling vision for America. Indeed, many of the candidates seemed to grate at the suggestion that such a vision was even desirable. Republican senator Bob Dole's views were perhaps representative of (if expressed a bit more candidly than) the majority of the 14 or so "serious" candidates in both parties who sought the presidency:

> I've been advised by people I have a lot of respect for not to play the vision game. Not yet. As soon as you have your vision, the press is going to dismantle it for you. And then, "Oh, this is the guy's vision." So, then you say, "Well, then, I'm going to get another vision."

That such an attitude should exist among politicians is all the more remarkable in the wake of Ronald Reagan's political success in offering a vision to the electorate. It earned him "mandate"-level landslides in 1980 and 1984. One can question Reagan's administrative ability to translate those mandates into policy, or even the depth of his understanding of the implications of the vision he set forth (as we and others have done). But when Ronald Reagan spoke of getting the government off the backs of the American people, of limited government, lower taxes, individual rights, and the spirit of enterprise, he struck a resonant chord with the electorate. He projected the image of a man who had a positive sense of what kind of society Americans desired and therefore what specific public policies should be pursued.

Political vision, at bottom, is an ideological concept. It is not a program, as such, or a collection of randomly selected policy prescriptions. Rather, it is an integrated, internally consistent set of

1

proposals that work as a *process*, rather than as discrete solutions to what generally are systemic problems.

In Great Britain ideology and its nuances are of great interest to intellectuals, from academia to the media. Their American intellectual counterparts are less preoccupied with ideology. Paradoxically, Americans in general, we would argue, are notably *more* ideological than the majority of Englishmen. The American ideology is almost visceral—what the subjectivist economists refer to as "inarticulate knowledge." It is more the result of a cultural assimilation, a kind of wisdom that passes through the generations, than an openly proclaimed national dogma.

But inarticulateness does not preclude profundity. And, indeed, the American ideology—the American vision—traces its roots to some very profound thinking during our colonial period. Its intensity reflects the intensity of a very open and articulate debate over ideology that characterized the colonial and revolutionary periods in American history.

So Gov. Michael Dukakis's political handlers were too clever by half when they inserted into his acceptance speech at the Democratic National Convention the admonition that "this campaign is not about ideology." By saying it wasn't, they reminded everyone—including, perhaps, the camp of Vice President George Bush—that it was. That anyone should have to be reminded of the need for political vision so soon after Reagan's stunning success in projecting it is a telling commentary. Politicians in this country shy away from political principles like a vampire from the cross, which may explain the oft-noted alienation average Americans feel toward them.

If the roots of the American vision are to be found in our 18th-century heritage, then that vision is one that sees man as free by his nature, by right. It is one that sees government's legitimate role as, primarily, protector of our liberties. It is a vision that in the 19th century came to be known as liberal. But that was when the "L-word" was respected throughout the world as a symbol of the average man's liberation from the domination of the state. Today, neither liberalism nor conservatism can lay legitimate claim to that original liberal tradition, though both make the attempt.

What that tradition demands is scrupulously limited government. What we have is recklessly expansive government. As recently as 1920 government spending at all levels (federal, state, and local)

2

amounted to just 10 percent of national income. By 1950 that percentage had skyrocketed to 26 percent. Ominously, today, after eight years of conservative control of the White House, government spending is at 44 percent of national income. None of which even speaks to the massively intrusive role government now plays in our lives: selecting the books our children learn from, strangling our financial institutions with archaic regulations, taxing our savings, denying terminally ill individuals experimental drugs—there is no area of our lives where bureaucrats fear to tread.

But why, if the American vision is one of strictly limited government, has all this and much more come to pass? Political scientists, media commentators, and other court apologists would have it that Big Government exists because that's what Americans want. We categorically reject that answer. In our view there exists a systemic bias toward government growth, which, while well-documented, is nevertheless greatly underestimated. Concentrated benefits and diffuse costs create strong incentives for Congress to pass more laws, create more "entitlements," and generally bow to pressure from the special interests. The self-interest of bureaucrats, unencumbered by consumer constraints or a bottom line, leads to ever more rationales for new programs or expansion of existing ones. And once created, government programs take on a life of their own—what Milton Friedman refers to as the "tyranny of the status quo."

Add to this systemic pressure the benign neglect of the American people (who have always tended toward a healthy lack of interest in government) and one has a powerful recipe for government growth. And while the philosophical opposition to that growth remains integral to the American psyche, Congress sticks to its profligate ways, isolated by its incumbent-protection perks and legislation. How else can we reconcile a recent CBS News/New York Times poll that showed some 83 percent of Americans supporting a balanced budget through spending cuts with a 98 percent-plus reelection rate for House incumbents?

Ronald Reagan's spirited call for individual rights, lower taxes, less regulation, and more entrepreneurship had a decidedly ideological ring to it—something Americans hadn't heard put forward so eloquently in this century. The call awakened a seemingly dormant popular ideology, and voters responded with enormous

3

enthusiasm. The pundits were amazed, and the Washington establishment braced for what the media had warned them would be nothing short of a revolution. As was documented in Cato's book *Assessing the Reagan Years*, for the most part, it wasn't to be.

A Policy Blueprint

Nevertheless, an ideological public policy revolution of sorts was accelerated by the Reagan landslide of 1980. It occurred mainly outside of government, and despite setbacks in Congress it continues to grow to this day. This book, intended as a policy blueprint for the incoming Bush administration and those in Congress—of both parties—with the courage to challenge the status quo, is indicative of this trend. We have recruited some of the nation's most thoughtful policy analysts in an effort to offer an American vision that is consistent with our nation's heritage of limited government and individual rights.

The book has been divided into three general sections on the economy, foreign policy, and domestic policy and a small concluding section on the Constitution and liberty. An overriding theme that weaves its way through each section is what Nobel laureate and Cato Distinguished Fellow F. A. Hayek refers to as the "unintended consequences" of government intervention. No matter how benign the intentions, government intervention—in the domestic economy, overseas, or dealing with personal choices—involves coercively structuring human relations. While some such intervention may be warranted, it more often than not runs counter to the interests of a free and prosperous society. It inhibits the "spontaneous order" (to quote Hayek again) that is the mark of an open and peaceful society. It is the reason the Founders of this nation had a vision for America predicated on the idea that "that government is best which governs least."

It is important to recognize that the Founders were not naive romanticists who simply spouted clichés, oblivious to the functioning of the real world. They were, in fact, unusually sophisticated men—giants when compared to the vast majority of today's political leaders. So we should not be surprised that the careful analysis undertaken on these pages confirms their worldview. Each of the chapters in this book avoids the myopia of so much policy work in Washington. The authors stand back from their subject matter far enough to gain a rational perspective on how we've come to the current situation and to offer policy prescriptions that, if innovative and even radical, are nonetheless realistic and achievable.

The Economy

In the opening chapter of the section on the economy, Daniel J. Mitchell, the bright young fiscal expert at Citizens for a Sound Economy, lays out an optimistic scenario for getting control over the federal spending crisis. "Deficits are bad," he writes, but "spending is the problem, and the goal of fiscal policy should be to minimize the level of federal spending."

"Fisher Simons," a prominent Washington tax analyst, complements Mitchell's piece with a chapter on tax policy that punctures the various arguments for higher taxes. "Higher taxes," he concludes, "will only have the effect of reducing the pressure to cut spending and will lead to higher spending."

The Cato Institute's chairman, William Niskanen, one of the nation's leading trade experts, takes up the subject of trade and, after giving the Reagan administration a low grade for having "turned sharply protectionist," argues, "We now need to develop an offensive strategy to reduce trade restraints." Niskanen offers a five-point approach to implementing such a strategy.

Fred Smith, the irrepressible head of the Competitive Enterprise Institute, extends the argument for reducing government's role in the economy by addressing the question of deregulation. The new administration, he writes, should "devote the necessary resources to ensure that past deregulation gains are preserved and future deregulation efforts better implemented." His thoughtful chapter offers interesting insights into both the politics and economics of deregulation and covers transportation, telecommunications, financial services, and antitrust reform, each an area where well-intended federal intervention has hampered economic performance and consumer choice.

Efficient capital markets are critical to economic growth, especially in the global marketplace. Tulane University business professor S. David Young is an expert in this field, and his chapter demonstrates the fundamentally positive role played by the securities exchanges on "Black Monday" in 1987. Most proposals to "fix" the system, he argues, either ignore market corrections that have already occurred or would rigidify equity and debt markets, thereby reducing their efficiency.

The final chapter in the section on the economy, written by Cato's director of regulatory studies, Catherine England, deals with the looming thrift crisis. England emphasizes that the problem can be directly traced to federal regulation and says that any solution must place much more reliance on the free market. Specifically, she cites the perverse incentives of federal deposit insurance and the need for financial institutions to "mark to market" their investment portfolios, allowing for market monitoring of financial soundness.

Foreign and Defense Policy

Often overlooked in discussions of the philosophy of the Founders is their profound wariness of foreign adventurism and "entangling alliances," as they called them. Since the days of the republic's founding, American foreign policy has strayed markedly from that advice. Our self-appointed role as the world's policeman has both proven enormously costly and in many instances—Iran, the Philippines, Nicaragua, and Vietnam, to name a few—created more enemies than friends. Our section on foreign policy offers a rational alternative to our current costly approach of extended deterrence, one that would both increase our national security and reduce the tremendous burden placed on the economy by a $300 billion military budget.

In the first chapter in this section, Cato senior fellow and Georgetown University School of Foreign Service professor Earl C. Ravenal discusses the "price of defense." Perhaps more than any other single individual, Ravenal has drawn attention to the fact that the cost of the Pentagon is ultimately a function of our foreign policy commitments. He offers a fascinating look at what that $300 billion is actually being spent for and suggests significantly less expensive alternatives.

Next, Cato adjunct scholar Christopher Layne looks at the future of NATO and concludes that geopolitical realities are going to dictate a reduced role for the United States in that alliance, which is estimated to account for some 40 percent of our military budget. Layne believes there is a "window of opportunity" for the United States to gain a diplomatic advantage over the Soviets in Europe by initiating plans for a strategic withdrawal from that theater by both

6

superpowers. "Far from being a radical idea," he writes, "devolution and Europeanization [of NATO] would mark a return to the original vision of the alliance's architects."

In a chapter on the Pacific Basin consistent with Layne's analysis, Cato's director of foreign policy studies, Ted Galen Carpenter, argues that allies such as Korea and Japan should take on a much greater share—eventually all—of the burden of defending themselves. "Clinging to an obsolete policy of U.S. paternalism," he writes, "entails both excessive risks and costs to the American people."

Alan Tonelson focuses on the Caribbean and Central America, areas of far greater strategic interest to the United States than those for which the bulk of our defense budget is allocated. He recommends a new policy of nonintervention, both military and political, based on an understanding that we will not tolerate military ties to nations outside the hemisphere deemed unfriendly to the United States.

Finally, Cato senior fellow Doug Bandow concludes the foreign policy section with an analysis of the detrimental effect that so-called aid has had on Third World nations. By strengthening government control of the economy and undermining indigenous industries (particularly agriculture), foreign aid, argues Bandow, has done much more harm than good over the decades. "Aid," Bandow writes, "as a largely government-to-government transfer, reinforces the primary cause of Third World poverty: statist domestic economic policies."

Domestic Policy

One could write a hundred chapters on domestic policy, of course, and still not have a comprehensive survey of the issues involved. We have selected seven issues that we believe are of major importance and immediate concern. In each instance the authors are seeking private, voluntary solutions to government interventions that have led to undesirable circumstances.

Peter J. Ferrara, who after years as an adjunct scholar recently joined Cato's staff as a senior fellow, opens the domestic policy section with an analysis of his specialty, social security. A classic case of unintended consequences, social security began as a modest "safety net" program for the indigent elderly but has become the

7

major source of income for the majority of retired Americans. In the process, as a pay-as-you-go system, social security has also drained capital from the economy and become a greater tax burden than the income tax for most Americans. Ferrara offers innovative proposals to provide for heavier reliance on the private sector for both health care and retirement income.

No issue is more timely than that of education. After decades of declining test scores and soaring expenditures, more and more Americans are coming to recognize that our educational problem is a systemic one that cannot be cured by tinkering or throwing more money at it. A leader in the choice-in-education movement, former Delaware governor Pete du Pont, has written a forceful chapter on this subject. "Competition will reward good schools," he writes, "force bad schools to get better, and provide every family in the United States with choices it does not have today."

An important part of the growing market-oriented policy school in America is privatization, popularized in large part through the efforts of the Heritage Foundation and the Reason Foundation. In our chapter on privatization, analyst Peter Young, who has been actively involved in the issue here and in Great Britain (with the Adam Smith Institute), provides a state-of-the-art case for privatizing government services, ranging from the U.S. Postal Service (a favorite of ours) to airports and the air traffic control system. Invariably, he argues, privatization means lower costs, more attention to consumer demands, and improved services.

In the past year, a heretofore unmentionable policy proposal, legalization of drugs, has been gaining a respectful, if skeptical, hearing. As journalist Jeff Riggenbach points out in his chapter on "the drug prohibition problem," such distinguished commentators as Baltimore mayor Kurt Schmoke, Princeton political scientist Ethan Nadelmann, and columnist William F. Buckley, Jr., have argued that this "new Prohibitionism" is rewarding criminals, creating violent crime, and doing little if anything to stem the availability of drugs. Legalization, he claims, would cut crime, protect our civil liberties, and allow us to concentrate on the important job of educating Americans, particularly young people, on the dangers of drugs.

Coeditor and Cato vice president David Boaz has written a chapter on how to improve life in the inner city. This is an issue that

8

apparently will have a high priority in the Bush administration, and Boaz offers five specific proposals to get the job done. "For 20 years we have tried flooding the poor with money and social programs," he says. "That approach has not only failed to eliminate poverty, it has created a seemingly intractable problem of dependency."

Agricultural policy in the United States has grown into a $20 billion fiasco, according to James Bovard, author of our chapter on agriculture. Bovard has written widely on agricultural policy— including in the *New York Times* and the *Wall Street Journal*—and is convinced that federal policies have made the American farmer less competitive and the American consumer less wealthy. Bovard makes a strong case for abolishing price supports and acreage allocations and returning to a free market in agriculture.

The final chapter in the domestic policy section deals with the environment, an area too long ignored by free market advocates. But not all free market advocates. For years a growing "new resource economics" school of free market environmentalists has been publishing research in this field. A major figure in that movement, Cato adjunct scholar Terry Anderson, has written this chapter, which should receive special attention in light of the heightened awareness of federal ecological mismanagement in the wake of the Yellowstone Park fire disaster.

Toward Liberty

The brief final section of the book, on the Constitution and liberty, contains two thoughtful and provocative chapters that address broader themes than the previous chapters. *Cato Journal* editor James Dorn makes an incisive case for the new school of "principled judicial activism." Eschewing both the "living Constitution" concept of the left and the "judicial restraint" of the right, Dorn argues that the Framers viewed a watchful Supreme Court as essential to controlling the growth of government—*provided* its activism was grounded in the Lockean natural rights tradition on which the Constitution was premised. As Dorn writes, the new president's "success in constraining the growth of government and protecting individual rights will largely determine whether we remain in a state of constitutional chaos or restore the Framers' vision of constitutional order and freedom."

In our book's concluding chapter, George Gilder, who has played

such an important role in the renaissance of respect for entrepreneurship, ties things up on an encouragingly optimistic note. New
microchip technologies, he argues, are creating vast new frontiers
for capitalism. More important, he writes, "The old industrial technologies favored control. The new technologies favor freedom.
Governments cannot take power by coercing people or raising taxes,
by mobilizing men or heaping up trade surpluses, by seizing territory or stealing technology." Gilder's enthusiasm is infectious,
and we believe his optimism is warranted.

The Cato Institute is pleased and proud to be publishing this
important book as the Bush administration begins its first days.
And we would add a note that, like the Cato Institute itself, the
policy proposals contained here are not partisan. It seems to us that
the overwhelming majority of Americans share the same fundamental policy goals: We desire peace, freedom, prosperity, and the
opportunity to pursue happiness. These proposals are put forward
in that spirit. We hope the strength of their logic will appeal to
independents, Republicans, and Democrats alike. Thomas Jefferson
once wrote that "the natural progress of things is for liberty to yield
and government to gain ground." It is important that we counter
that "natural progress" of bureaucratic encroachment over our lives
and our prosperity. To do so will require vision—an American
vision.

PART I

THE ECONOMY

2. Stemming the Flow of Red Ink: How to Stop the Federal Spending Crisis

Daniel J. Mitchell

Conventional wisdom suggests that deficit spending is here to stay. The federal budget deficit is over $100 billion for the eighth straight year. Federal spending has supposedly been cut to the bone, and yet the deficit still remains at dizzying heights. Congress is deeply divided between those who would raise taxes and those who favor spending control. The chances of enacting a consensus package that would significantly reduce the deficit seem increasingly remote.

At first glance there is little reason to dispute this gloomy scenario. Spending has increased by more than $535 billion since 1980, an increase of 90 percent. The rate of growth of spending has easily outraced what would have been necessary to keep pace with inflation and population growth, and federal spending as a percentage of gross national product has hit record peacetime highs. The national debt has tripled in the last nine years, will soon pass $3 trillion, and now equals more than $10,000 for every man, woman, and child in the country.

Many observers believe this bleak outlook will continue into the future. Although this is certainly a possible outcome, it need not become reality. Indeed, there is strong evidence that the situation has improved dramatically in recent years. Furthermore, the new president, if he has the political courage that will be required, already has the tools to force dramatic reductions in the deficit.

This chapter begins with an examination of the recent history of deficit spending, followed by a look at the evidence that the trend is abating. The next section discusses the relationship between taxes and spending, and then explains why the new president will be in a very strong position to force Congress to produce responsible budgets. Finally, reforms and policies are proposed that would ensure that deficit spending is eliminated in a way that enhances economic growth.

Deficits: A Legacy of Overspending

One of the most powerful and enduring myths of the Reagan years is that federal spending has been brought under control. Notwithstanding this common misperception, federal spending has risen faster during the 1980s than at any other point in U.S. history. It is this unprecedented increase in spending that is the sole cause of the budget deficit.

Federal spending was $591 billion in 1980. In 1989 the overall level of federal spending reached $1.127 trillion, an increase of $536 billion. The 90 percent increase was nearly double what would have been necessary to keep pace with inflation. Some might contend that the increase was concentrated in defense, while spending was slashed in other parts of the budget. Spending, however, increased in all parts of the budget, defense and domestic. Defense spending did rise substantially, up $166 billion since 1980. Interest payments also rose rapidly, accounting for $111 billion of the $536 billion. The largest increase, though, was for domestic programs. From $402 billion in 1980 to $664 billion in 1989, spending on domestic programs jumped over $250 billion.

Government spending has grown by all measures. The budget now consumes an estimated 22.1 percent of the nation's output, as measured by gross national product. Federal spending has averaged over 23 percent of GNP in the 1980s. In contrast, federal spending averaged 20.45 percent of GNP in the 1970s and 19.04 percent of GNP in the 1960s. The figures are even more discouraging considering that federal spending should naturally fall as a percentage of GNP over time if it is assumed that spending should do no more than simply keep pace with inflation and population growth.

Indeed, other than substantial growth in overall spending, little has changed in the budget during the 1980s. Defense accounts for a slightly higher percentage of total outlays than it did in 1980, though defense is still considerably below its postwar average. Payments for individuals have remained virtually unchanged, consuming 47 percent of total outlays in 1980 and 47 percent in 1989. Interest payments are up, while discretionary domestic spending is down. Of course, actual spending in all categories has increased

14

even if the percentage of outlays accounted for by the category has decreased.

Given the tremendous growth in federal spending, it is not surprising to find large deficits. Despite the evidence showing spending to be responsible for the deficit, there are those who believe the problem is that the American people are not taxed heavily enough. This argument is bolstered by confusion between cuts in tax rates and cuts in taxes.

Much to his credit, President Reagan did initiate dramatic reductions in tax rates, with the top bracket down to 28 percent today from 70 percent in 1980. Total tax collections, however, have soared from $517 billion in 1980 to an estimated $980 billion in 1989. As was the case with spending, the increase in tax revenues has been much higher than needed to keep pace with inflation and population growth.

The Economic Recovery Tax Act of 1981 did reduce the amount of money the government could take out of the productive sector of the economy in the form of taxes compared with what would have been collected, but even before the final stage of the tax cut went into effect in early 1983, other taxes were being increased. All told, Congress has enacted and Reagan has signed 14 tax increases into law. Combined with the hidden tax increase of bracket creep, which continued until indexing was implemented in 1985, these changes in the tax law mean the government is collecting more under the current tax code than would have been collected under the laws existing in 1980.

Other measures of the tax burden confirm that government has not relaxed its grip on the economy. The Tax Foundation has computed that the average taxpayer had to work until May 5 just to pay taxes in 1988. This is the latest date upon which "Tax Freedom Day" has fallen in history, exceeding the previous record of May 4, which took place in 1981. Tax collections as a percent of GNP also depict a growing tax burden. Tax collections were 19.4 percent of GNP in 1987, the same as they were in 1980. More revealing is the fact that tax collections as a percent of GNP in 1987 were over a full percentage point higher than the 18.31 percent average for the decade of the 1970s.

The surge of tax revenues has done nothing to balance the budget, even though each tax increase has been sold as a "deficit-reduction" measure. Unfortunately, legislators have used the bulge in tax revenues to boost spending to record levels. For all the bad news, however, two factors—fewer tax increases and Gramm-Rudman-Hollings—have combined to begin slowing down the growth of spending in the last four years.

Gramm-Rudman-Hollings: Backdoor Spending Control

The Balanced Budget and Emergency Deficit Control Act, better known as Gramm-Rudman-Hollings, was passed in the fall of 1985 as a means of putting a cap on yearly federal deficits. The act dramatically altered the budgetary decisionmaking process. Although the law does not guarantee fiscal responsibility, it has made it much harder for Congress to increase spending without restraint. In the hands of an effective president, Gramm-Rudman-Hollings could be used as a tool to balance the budget by reducing the growth of federal spending.

Originally passed in part as a consequence of the inability of Congress and the White House to agree on a substantive deficit-reduction plan, the law initially required that the federal deficit be eliminated by 1991. Unlike previous statutory efforts to control deficit spending, though, it contained an enforcement mechanism, sequestration, to prevent legislators from ignoring the law. Should Congress produce a budget with a deficit projected to exceed the Gramm-Rudman-Hollings target, automatic, across-the-board reductions are to be made in the eligible parts of the new budget's spending levels. Sequestration did occur in the first year that Gramm-Rudman-Hollings was in effect, but the sequester was limited to $11.7 billion.

The Supreme Court ruled in the summer of 1986 that the sequestration provision was unconstitutional. Even without an enforcement device, however, the law still imposed discipline on the process, in that 60 votes were (and still are) needed in the Senate to waive points of order that could be raised when legislation was being considered that would violate the law's deficit provisions. Without sequestration, however, Gramm-Rudman-Hollings would not have its maximum impact. As part of a deal that stretched out the deficit targets, sequestration was restored in 1987. The law presently calls for a balanced budget in 1993. Table 2.1 depicts the original and current Gramm-Rudman-Hollings deficit targets. With

Table 2.1

GRAMM-RUDMAN-HOLLINGS: PAST AND PRESENT DEFICIT TARGETS

Category	Target ($ Billions)							
	1986	1987	1988	1989	1990	1991	1992	1993
Original Law	172	144	108	72	36	0		
Present Law			144	136	100	64	28	0
Deficit	221	150	155	148*				

*Estimate based on Congressional Budget Office projection.

the exception of 1993, a sequester will not take place as long as the deficit is within a $10 billion "margin of error" of the deficit target.

Gramm-Rudman-Hollings has sharply cut back on the growth of federal spending. In the five years prior to Gramm-Rudman-Hollings, outlays grew at an annual rate of nearly 10 percent. In the four years since Gramm-Rudman-Hollings, annual spending growth has fallen to 4.5 percent. Other factors, such as disinflation, have contributed to the slowdown of spending growth, but the growth of spending—even in inflation-adjusted terms—has fallen from almost 4 percent to slightly more than 1 percent.

The effect of Gramm-Rudman-Hollings is also seen in the decline of federal spending as a percentage of GNP. From 24 percent of GNP in 1985, spending has fallen to an estimated 22.4 percent of GNP in 1988 and could fall to under 22 percent in 1989.

The often-overlooked key to Gramm-Rudman-Hollings is that the legislation is just as much a spending-control provision as it is a deficit-reduction device. The fact that there is a cap on the deficit also means there is a cap on overall spending. When Congress enacts a budget under Gramm-Rudman-Hollings, legislators can spend no more than the sum of projected tax revenues plus the allowable deficit target.

The effect of the Gramm-Rudman-Hollings spending cap was demonstrated during the enactment of the 1989 budget. Using administration economic assumptions, the Congressional Budget Office estimated that tax revenues would be $980 billion. Since the 1989 deficit target is $136 billion (plus the $10 billion "margin of error"), Congress could only spend a maximum of $1,126 billion.

Although Gramm-Rudman-Hollings is remarkably well-crafted,

there are ways in which Congress and the president can either evade or unjustly increase the spending limit without violating the letter of the law. Selling government assets, which is a good step in and of itself, is often done just to make it possible to spend more because most revenues from asset sales are actually counted as "negative spending." Shifting government paydays into preceding or succeeding fiscal years is another way of meeting a spending limit without actually controlling spending. Some steps have been taken to control these and other budget gimmicks, but politicians can be ingenious when it comes to finding ways to spend taxpayers' money.

The most tempting way for Congress and the White House to escape Gramm-Rudman-Hollings' fiscal discipline is to use optimistic economic assumptions. Because no one has ever found even a remotely successful way to predict the economy, budgets are enacted using estimates of how the economy will be performing next year. Such economic growth estimates significantly affect budget options. Most importantly, if economic growth is assumed to be higher, then tax revenues will be higher. Every dollar of additional revenue the government expects to collect because of higher growth estimates means an additional dollar that politicians can spend.

Indeed, Congress chose to use the administration's economic estimates for the 1989 budget because higher growth projections meant that revenues—and therefore spending—could be about $10 billion higher. Unfortunately, there is no way to objectively prove that politicians are using rosy numbers just to increase spending. By the time actual economic growth figures become available, it is too late. Gramm-Rudman-Hollings only limits projected deficits. No provisions exist to reduce the deficit once the sequestration deadline has passed. Notwithstanding these limitations, Gramm-Rudman-Hollings has done more to reduce the rate of growth of federal spending than most observers of the budget process expected.

Gramm-Rudman-Hollings: Putting an End to Tax-and-Spend?

Gramm-Rudman-Hollings has completely changed the budget process. Prior to the law, politicians would decide how much they wanted to spend and how much they wanted to tax, and the deficit was simply the difference between the two. There was pressure, of course, to balance the budget or have a lower deficit, but decisions were not driven by a deficit number. Now, however, the entire budget debate revolves around what will be necessary to meet the Gramm-Rudman-Hollings deficit target.

Furthermore, by limiting the total level of spending, Gramm-Rudman-Hollings has forced interest groups to compete against each other in dividing up a "fixed pie" of dollars instead of being able to gang up on the taxpayers or drive the government deeper into debt. This competition forced the privatization of Conrail and the termination of the general revenue-sharing program. Most recently, Gramm-Rudman-Hollings' fiscal discipline compelled legislators to largely defund the pork-laden Urban Development Action Grant program, something the Reagan administration had been unsuccessfully trying to get Congress to do for seven years.

Instead of being able to simply increase spending across the board, politicians are now forced to set priorities. Increasing spending on politically popular programs may now necessitate cutting back on other parts of the budget. Another way of saying that Gramm-Rudman-Hollings places a cap on the overall level of spending is to note that the law limits the growth of spending. When preparing a budget for a new fiscal year, Congress can increase spending by no more than the expected growth of revenues minus the difference between the present year's deficit and the deficit target for the new year.

Recognizing that Gramm-Rudman-Hollings limits total spending in any given fiscal year, which is just another way of saying that the law limits annual spending growth, leads to a very important conclusion: Tax increases will have no effect on the deficit. Every single dollar of a tax increase will simply lead to another dollar of federal spending. Only in the narrowest and most unlikely of circumstances is it possible for a tax increase to result in a lower deficit.

As shown, when Congress enacts a new fiscal year's budget under Gramm-Rudman-Hollings, overall spending is limited to the sum of projected tax revenues plus the allowable deficit target. For 1989 that meant spending was limited to about $1,126 billion, in that revenues were projected to be $980 billion and the deficit target is $146 billion (assuming, quite safely, that Congress will take advantage of the $10 billion margin of error). What would have been the effect, however, if Congress had raised taxes by $20 billion?

Projected revenues would have increased to $1 trillion, meaning that total spending would have increased to $1,146 billion. It is theoretically possible that Congress might not have increased spending by the full $20 billion, but the chances of that not happening are so remote as to be nonexistent.

The only way a tax increase would result in a lower deficit is if Congress deliberately enacted a budget with a projected deficit below the Gramm-Rudman-Hollings target. Although this may not sound like an impossible task, political dynamics make it exceedingly unlikely. Tax increases are politically unpopular. Few politicians, as Walter Mondale can attest, find success when they publicly make tax increases part of their agenda. Politicians raise taxes only if the benefits they receive from having more money to spend outweigh the costs of upsetting taxpayers. This noncontroversial axiom of political behavior helps explain why a tax increase would not reduce the deficit under Gramm-Rudman-Hollings.

The so-called budget summit agreement between the White House and Congress in 1987 is a clear example of why tax increases do not result in a lower deficit. At the time, 1988 revenues were estimated to be $897 billion and the deficit target was $144 billion, so total spending was limited to $1,041 billion. Spending could increase by only $39 billion since 1987 outlays were projected to be $1,002 billion. It appeared as if there would be a stalemate between Congress and the White House over taxes, ultimately leading to a sequester. The dramatic fall in the stock market broke the stalemate, however, as the administration reneged on its no-tax-increase commitment after allowing itself to be convinced that the financial markets would not recover unless politicians were given more money to spend. The final agreement, largely the package passed by the House of Representatives shortly after the market fell, raised taxes by $12 billion. With revenues now estimated at $909 billion, Congress was able to spend $1,053 billion, $12 billion more than would have been possible without the tax increase. As with almost all budget numbers, actual figures differed from projections, but the underlying relationship—higher taxes lead to a proportional increase in spending—stands true.

Notwithstanding the pronouncements of politicians who supported the package, the tax increase did not reduce the deficit. Gramm-Rudman-Hollings set the deficit; raising taxes simply allowed

Congress to meet the deficit target at a higher level of spending. There was some interest in Congress in enacting a package that would have resulted in a deficit below the Gramm-Rudman-Hollings target, meaning that some of the additional tax revenues would have gone for deficit reduction. However, even with the environment created by the stock market fall, the political pressures to spend the maximum amount of money possible derailed the effort. This action conclusively demonstrated that although theoretically tax increases could be used to reduce the deficit, in practice they will be used only to increase spending.

The law can be changed so that a tax increase would be used for deficit reduction. If the Gramm-Rudman-Hollings law was amended so that the deficit targets were reduced for every dollar that taxes were raised, 100 percent of the additional tax revenues would be used to lower the deficit. For instance, if Congress raised taxes by $20 billion next year, the 1990 deficit target would automatically fall from $100 billion to $80 billion. The option of spending the additional money, which is all but certain under current law, would be removed. If proponents of tax increases sincerely wanted to reduce the deficit, they would agree to this proposition. Waiting for an answer, however, will have all the suspense of a Soviet election.

The relationship between taxes and spending under Gramm-Rudman-Hollings dramatically increases the power of the president to limit the growth of spending. As long as the president is committed to veto any tax increase, Congress has no choice but to limit the growth of spending unless legislators can override the veto in both the Senate and House. The only other way Congress can exceed the spending cap imposed by Gramm-Rudman-Hollings is to change the deficit target. That would also require legislation that could be vetoed. Congress could pass a budget with a deficit exceeding the target, but that would be a futile gesture since it would result in a sequester.

Indeed, if the president, along with at least one-third of one house of Congress, was committed to opposing any tax increase and to protecting the integrity of the deficit targets, there is no reason why the budget would not be balanced by 1993. Gramm-Rudman-Hollings would be suspended if there was a recession, but an economic downturn would be less likely if spending growth was limited and there were no tax increases.

21

Gramm-Rudman-Hollings does not guarantee responsible budget decisions, and it does not prevent politicians from raising taxes. The 1987 budget summit demonstrated how legislators can avoid making the tough fiscal choices Gramm-Rudman-Hollings was designed to elicit. Furthermore, as important as Gramm-Rudman-Hollings is to the budget process today, there are other ways to successfully reduce the burden of government spending on society.

Economic Growth versus Government: Winning the War on Spending

The first objective of economic policymakers should not be a balanced budget. Deficits are bad, but they are only a symptom, not the disease. Government spending is the problem, and the goal of fiscal policy should be to minimize the level of federal spending. Regardless of how government spending is paid for, whether through taxes or borrowing, resources are being taken out of the productive sector of the economy. Each means of payment exacts a toll on economic growth. Taxes limit production by reducing the rate of return on the activity being taxed. It does not matter whether the tax is levied on income, savings, consumption, or wealth. Nor does it matter whether the tax is broad-based or narrow. Taking money out of the pockets of individuals and businesses and giving it to politicians reduces economic growth. The primary victims of tax policies are the poor, who are most dependent on economic growth to provide them with the opportunities enjoyed by the more fortunate in society.

Government borrowing, however, is equally damaging to the economy. Deficits drive up interest rates. Because the government is able to satisfy its borrowing needs regardless of how high interest rates climb, the major effect of government borrowing is to crowd out legitimate loans. A family trying to purchase a home, a consumer seeking to finance a car, a business person seeking funds to expand a factory, or anyone else seeking a loan is going to feel the impact of high interest rates caused by federal deficits.

For any given level of government spending, it is preferable to finance those outlays through taxes. There are moral, as well as economic, problems with shifting part of the burden of today's government spending onto future generations. Politicians, however, should not be able to exploit well-meaning concern about the deficit as a ruse to raise taxes.

Beginning with President Reagan's final budget in early January 1989 and followed by the new president's revisions shortly thereafter, the battle over the 1990 budget will be a pivotal exercise. To promote economic growth, increase opportunity, and encourage production, investment, and savings, the new president and Congress should adopt the following policies:

No Tax Increases

There is a serious threat of a tax increase in 1989. Without additional revenues, politicians will be forced to limit the growth of spending to $30–40 billion in 1990. The current services budget—a baseline projection showing how much spending would have to increase to keep pace with inflation, fund already legislated increases, and meet the commitments of entitlement programs—is likely to call for a $70–80 billion increase. Although politicians will doubtless argue that a tax increase is needed to reduce the deficit, the real purpose would be to allow them to increase spending at a much faster rate.

The only effect of a tax increase under Gramm-Rudman-Hollings is higher spending. Government revenues are already projected to increase $74 billion annually through 1993. It will not require draconian budget cuts to meet the Gramm-Rudman-Hollings deficit targets without tax increases. Indeed, even with the Congressional Budget Office's relatively modest economic growth projections, it will be possible to meet the deficit targets without raising taxes and still have enough revenue to increase spending by over 3 percent annually between 1990 and 1993. Taxes will not lower the deficit; nor is more revenue required to protect the budget from being cut, even though actual budget cuts are long overdue.

The nation is experiencing its longest period of peacetime economic growth in history. There is no need to risk that growth simply to give politicians more money to distribute to interest groups. Far better to leave the money in the hands of individuals and businesses, where it can be used to create jobs, improve living standards, and strengthen the country's competitive position. Indeed, according to CBO projections, if policymakers simply limit the growth of spending to what would be allowed under Gramm-Rudman-

Hollings without tax increases through 1993, federal spending would fall to under 20 percent of GNP for the first time since 1974.

Freeze Federal Spending

Blocking any and all tax increases would be sufficient to limit the growth of federal spending to 3 percent. The economy would be better off, however, if the overall level of spending was not allowed to grow at all. Because revenues are expected to grow so quickly, a spending freeze would produce a budget surplus in as little as two years, considerably ahead of the Gramm-Rudman-Hollings deadline. A spending freeze would result in lower interest rates because the deficit would fall even faster than it would under Gramm-Rudman-Hollings. Lower interest rates would spur investment, encourage the creation of additional jobs, and increase economic growth.

A spending freeze need only limit total spending in an upcoming fiscal year to the amount being spent in the current fiscal year. One way of accomplishing that is by using an across-the-board freeze in all budget categories. If, however, politicians want to increase spending in politically sensitive areas such as social security, AIDS research, or military pay, they would be free to do so as long as they cut spending someplace else to compensate for the increases. In effect, the spending freeze would be like Gramm-Rudman-Hollings in that it would encourage policymakers to decide which programs are most important.

Enforce "Truth in Budgeting" by Reforming the Current Services Budget

The current services budget provides projections both for overall spending and for specific budget categories. If it were separated from the rest of the budget process, there would be nothing wrong with the current services budget. Indeed, it contains much useful information.

Congress has decided, however, that the current services budget should serve as a benchmark against which all other budget proposals are judged. In other words it is automatically assumed that spending should increase. Furthermore, since Congress has become quite adept at increasing spending in future years, the current services baseline rises at a rapid rate. In practical terms use of this benchmark has a great impact on voters' perception of the budget. A large percentage of the electorate, even among those who closely follow the budget debate, is convinced that the budget was cut during the Reagan years. This misperception is a result of the current services budget.

Assume, for instance, that the president submits a budget calling for a $35 billion spending increase. If the current services budget says spending could increase $75 billion, however, that $35 billion increase suddenly becomes a $40 billion cut. In the parlance of Washington budgets, the word "cut" has been redefined. Everyone else in the country understands that to cut spending means to spend less in a given time period than one did in the preceding time period. In Washington, though, to cut spending means to not increase spending as fast as one wanted to.

The president's 1989 budget demonstrates how the current services budget is used to distort public perception. The president requested that Congress spend $1.094 trillion in 1989, $38 billion more than the $1.056 trillion the administration estimated 1988 spending would be. Because the current services budget called for $1.102 trillion in spending in 1989, however, the $38 billion increase became an $8 billion cut. The same principle is evident on the individual program level. Medicare spending, for instance, has skyrocketed from $32 billion in 1980 to over $80 billion in 1989. According to the current services budget, however, Medicare spending has been cut by $49 billion in the same time period.

Interest groups, quite naturally, have exploited the definition of "cut" to protest the "bone-wrenching" cuts of the Reagan administration. A confused media has added to the problem by accepting the politicians' terminology and reporting stories about nonexistent budget cuts. The current services budget will doubtless play a large role in the battle over the 1990 budget. Because it will likely call for an increase of over $70 billion, if the president requests a spending increase of only $30 billion, there will be widespread stories about the president's call for a spending cut of $40 billion. Advocates of higher spending will say that a tax increase is needed to keep the safety net together and maintain the country's defenses. The new president, as well as others with a stake in honest and responsible fiscal policy, should work to repeal the requirement that the current services budget be used as the starting point for each year's budget debate. Should Congress prove unwilling to enact a "truth in budgeting" law, the president should seek opportunities to expose the dishonest uses of the current services budget. Indeed, by advocating a spending freeze, the president would partially avoid the pitfalls of the current services budget by focusing attention on year-to-year changes in actual spending.

Aggressively Veto Spending Bills

One of the surprising shortcomings of the Reagan administration was the president's reluctance to veto bad legislation. Repeated promises to veto budget-busting bills were more often than not hollow threats. Reagan vetoed fewer bills than any president in modern history. Furthermore, by failing to follow through on veto threats, the president undercut his own agenda because Congress quickly learned that the White House was often more concerned with short-term public perception than with long-term economic growth.

Most importantly, by failing to veto bills, especially those adding to the deficit, Reagan allowed the public to become confused as to who is responsible for the deficit. Most opinion polls indicate that the president and Congress are held equally responsible for the deficit, even though Congress spent well over $150 billion more than the president requested between 1982 and 1989. Additionally, the few times Reagan vetoed legislation, the debate focused on the bill itself, thus allowing the president to be portrayed as an opponent of clean water, highways, or civil rights. On the other hand, if the president consistently vetoed legislation, public perception would begin to see the White House as the last line of defense against a profligate Congress.

Finally, efforts to secure line-item veto power for the president should continue. In particular, the line-item veto power should be crafted to allow the president to use it as an item-reduction veto, which means he could replace excessively high spending numbers with lower numbers as part of an effort to control spending. For instance, if Congress appropriated $400 million for the Legal Services Corporation, the president could substitute $200 million with an item-reduction veto instead of having to make an all-or-nothing choice.

The arguments for any form of line-item veto are well-known. Congress has learned to protect wasteful, pork-barrel spending by attaching it to politically important pieces of legislation. A line-item veto would allow the president to strike out offensive items in a bill without jeopardizing entire pieces of legislation. Nor would the line-item veto upset the balance of power between the executive and legislative branches since Congress would retain the right to override any and every line-item or item-reduction veto the president makes.

Means-Test Entitlement Programs

The fastest growing part of the budget is entitlements. Programs such as social security and Medicare have risen much quicker than needed to keep pace with inflation and are projected to continue rising at a rapid rate. Something must be done with entitlement programs if long-term spending control is to be possible, yet any effort to control these programs is quickly attacked as an assault on the poor. A large portion of these expenditures, however, go to individuals who have above-average incomes, and the bulk of the money goes to people above the poverty line. While doubtless still difficult, it does seem that a proposal to institute some sort of income or wealth requirement as a condition of receiving taxpayer funds would have a chance—particularly, in the case of Medicare and social security—if it was packaged as a way of restoring long-term stability to the system.

Protect and Strengthen Gramm-Rudman-Hollings

It is very likely that Gramm-Rudman-Hollings will come under attack in 1989. The $100 billion deficit target in 1990 may require more spending control than Congress is capable of demonstrating. While Congress's first instinct will be to raise taxes, should that option appear unfeasible, the only other way Congress could spend more money is by raising the deficit target. Just as the president should be committed to veto any tax increase, he should also be prepared to defend the integrity of the deficit targets. Congress will probably raise the specter of sequestration if the president refuses to accommodate its spending demands, so the president should also be prepared to accept a sequester if Congress is not capable of passing a budget. Opponents of spending restraint may claim that a sequester will impose deep and arbitrary cuts in spending. Such cuts, however, are a creation of the current services budget. Even under a sequester, spending will increase on an annual basis. Nor are the cuts arbitrary, given that Congress specifically chose which programs would be eligible for a sequester. Furthermore, there is nothing to stop Congress from changing the sequester guidelines whenever the legislators so desire.

Not only should Gramm-Rudman-Hollings be protected against assault, there are several ways the legislation could be strengthened. Currently, large sections of the budget, particularly entitlements, are immune from sequester. Defense, which accounts for less than 30 percent of outlays, must bear 50 percent of the sequester. Fairness demands that the entire budget, other than interest on the national debt, be made eligible for sequestration and that all categories be equally affected. Other positive reforms could include restrictions on Congress's ability to waive Gramm-Rudman-Hollings. Presently the Senate can waive the act if 60 senators agree, while the Rules Committee in the House routinely waives the law's requirements. Gramm-Rudman-Hollings should be amended to prohibit Congress from evading the spirit of the law.

Finally, Gramm-Rudman-Hollings should be amended to prevent politicians from using optimistic economic estimates to avoid budget discipline. As the law currently stands, there is no mechanism to control spending if the actual deficit turns out to be higher than the projected deficit, an event made likely if Congress uses unrealistically positive economic assumptions. Changes should be made that would require quarterly reestimates of the deficit. If, after any reestimate, the deficit is above the target, a sequester can then be applied.

Enact a Tax-Limitation/Balanced-Budget Amendment

A permanent solution to the spending crisis requires either that the incentives of policymakers be changed or that their powers to make bad decisions be limited. Many of the recommendations discussed above are designed to increase incentives for policymakers to make responsible budgetary choices. The coercive nature of government, however, makes it possible for powerful individuals to use the power of the state for purposes that are not in the national interest. Our founding fathers recognized this problem and attempted to strictly limit the powers of the government. Over time, however, the wisdom of the founding fathers has been forgotten as interest groups have learned to use the political system to enrich themselves at the expense of the average citizen.

A tax-limitation/balanced-budget amendment would limit the ability of politicians to use the power of the purse to engage in special-interest politics. By permanently limiting the size of government, such an amendment would help enhance the possibilities for long-term economic growth and individual opportunity. A tax-limitation/balanced-budget amendment should not be seen as a panacea; the amendment would do nothing to limit government's ability to make poor regulatory and monetary decisions. Indeed, it is likely that pressures for additional regulation would increase because interest groups would seek new ways to transfer wealth in their direction once the fiscal gravy train was derailed. Just because an amendment would not solve all the problems created by government, however, does not mean it would not be a step in the right direction. A tax-limitation/balanced-budget amendment would significantly limit at least one of the ways in which politicians inhibit economic prosperity.

Conclusion

Government spending takes resources out of the productive sector of the economy. Whether the spending is paid for through taxes or borrowing, money is being taken from individuals and business people who would use the funds more wisely. At one point in history, government spending was viewed as a stimulus to economic growth. We now know that government cannot spend money unless it takes it away from someone first. Special-interest politics, however, has given government spending its own momentum. Controlling that spending will be one of the greatest challenges of the 1990s. If the battle can be won—and it does appear that the tools are there to accomplish that in the short run—it will truly be an example of the public interest prevailing over the special interests.

3. An Agenda for Tax Policy

Fisher Simons

The next Congress is almost certain to enact a major tax increase. Although new taxes are neither justified nor desirable, the political pressure for new revenues to expand government spending is likely to be inexorable. Nevertheless, for three major reasons, the people opposed to higher taxes should not remove themselves completely from the tax-policy debate. First, some taxes are worse than others, and there may well be certain proposed taxes that should be resisted most strongly. Second, any major tax bill offers opportunities as well as dangers; it may be possible to enact specific tax cuts even in legislation designed to raise revenue, which could help offset some of the potential damage of such legislation. Third, there may be methods of raising revenue that actually further the goal of reducing government intrusion in the economy. The purpose of this chapter is to examine and illuminate these issues.

Higher Taxes Unnecessary

The pressure for higher taxes stems from several widely held beliefs. One is that federal budget deficits impose an unacceptable economic burden on the economy. Another is that such deficits result largely, if not entirely, from the 1981 tax cut. Lastly, even those politicians who do not ascribe to the above two beliefs do think that the continuing federal deficits impose uncomfortable political pressure on them to hold down spending for popular programs and to impose a severe constraint on new spending.

With regard to the effects of budget deficits, it is difficult to find evidence that they have imposed an unacceptable burden on the economy. Historically the two principal costs attributed to deficits have been inflation and higher interest rates. As Table 3.1 indicates, though, both inflation and interest rates fell even as budget deficits reached unprecedented levels. Such casual observation is sup-

Table 3.1
Budget Deficits and Inflation and Interest Rates, 1970–87

Year	Budget Deficit ($ Billions)*	GNP Deflator (%)	Treasury Bill Rate (%)
1970	12.4	5.5	6.5
1971	22.0	5.7	4.3
1972	16.8	4.7	4.1
1973	5.6	6.5	7.0
1974	11.6	9.1	7.9
1975	69.4	9.8	5.8
1976	53.5	6.4	5.0
1977	46.0	6.7	5.3
1978	29.3	7.3	7.2
1979	16.1	8.7	10.0
1980	61.3	9.0	11.5
1981	63.8	9.7	14.0
1982	145.9	6.4	10.7
1983	176.0	3.9	8.6
1984	169.6	3.7	9.6
1985	196.0	3.2	7.5
1986	204.7	2.6	6.0
1987	151.4	3.0	5.8

*NIPA basis.

ported by academic research, which finds no relationship between federal budget deficits and inflation or interest rates.[1]

This is not to say that budget deficits impose no costs. However,

[1]On inflation, see William A. Niskanen, "Deficits, Government Spending, and Inflation," *Journal of Monetary Economics* 4 (August 1978): 591–602; Gerald P. Dwyer, Jr., "Inflation and Government Deficits," *Economic Inquiry* 20 (July 1982): 315–29; and R. W. Hafer and Scott E. Hein, "Further Evidence on the Relationship between Federal Government Debt and Inflation," *Economic Inquiry* 26 (April 1988): 239–51. On interest rates, see Charles I. Plosser, "Government Financing Decisions and Asset Returns," *Journal of Monetary Economics* 9 (May 1982): 325–52; William G. Dewald, "Federal Deficits and Real Interest Rates: Theory and Evidence," Federal Reserve Bank of Atlanta *Economic Review* (January 1983): 20–29; Brian Motley, "Real Interest Rates, Money and Government Deficits," Federal Reserve Bank of San Francisco *Economic Review* (Summer 1983): 31–45; Gregory P. Hoelscher, "Federal Borrowing and Short Term Interest Rates," *Southern Economic Journal* 50 (October

the principal cost of budget deficits is to create a fiscal illusion that causes overall government spending to be higher than it would be otherwise. The higher spending, in turn, absorbs real resources from the economy. Consequently, to the extent that such resources are used in ways that are less productive than if they had remained in the private sector, the nation as a whole is worse off.

The real cost of government, therefore, is the burden of total spending, irrespective of the deficit. Moreover, the method of financing can create an additional economic burden—a deadweight loss—if revenues are raised so as to discourage production. Government borrowing also imposes costs, but they are much lower than many methods of raising taxes. Thus the only way to be sure that a reduction in the deficit does not have negative economic effects is to cut spending. Raising taxes, even if they are dedicated exclusively to deficit reduction, may impose greater burdens on the economy than the cost of deficit financing.

With regard to the effects of the 1981 tax cut, much of the handwringing in Congress and the press about the evils of budget deficits is really directed at the tax cut itself rather than deficits per se. It is often asserted that the tax cut caused the triple-digit budget deficits—the implication being that the tax cut should be rescinded and marginal tax rates returned to their pre–1981 levels.

Such assertions are entirely without basis. The truth is that the 1981 tax cut only held the tax burden constant. As Figure 3.1 indicates, federal revenues as a share of gross national product are about the same as they were in the 1970s and are rising, not falling. In fact, real federal revenues increased 19.4 percent between 1980 and 1987 despite the tax cut. The deficit resulted not from lower revenues but from higher spending that resulted largely from the recession of 1981–82 and significantly higher interest payments—both principally a consequence of Federal Reserve policy.[2]

1983): 319–33; Treasury Department, The Effect of Deficits on Prices of Financial Assets: Theory and Evidence (Washington: Government Printing Office, 1984); Paul Evans, "Interest Rates and Expected Future Budget Deficits in the United States," Journal of Political Economy 95 (February 1987): 34–58; and idem, "Do Budget Deficits Raise Nominal Interest Rates?" Journal of Monetary Economics 20 (September 1987): 281–300.

[2]See Michael R. Darby, Accounting for the Deficit: An Analysis of Sources of Change in the Federal and Total Government Deficits (Washington: Treasury Department, Office of the Assistant Secretary for Economic Policy, 1987).

34

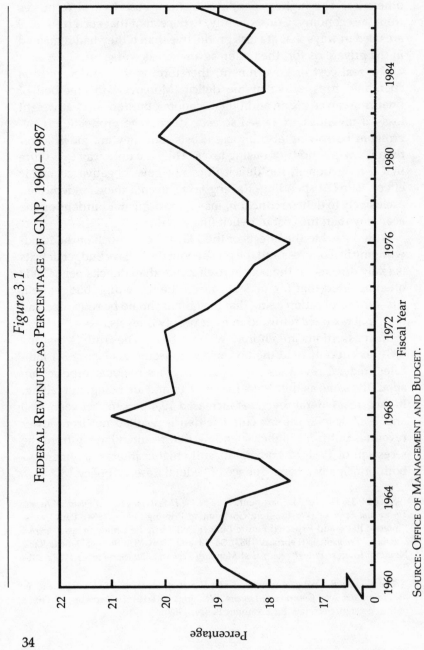

Figure 3.1

FEDERAL REVENUES AS PERCENTAGE OF GNP, 1960–1987

Fiscal Year

Percentage

SOURCE: OFFICE OF MANAGEMENT AND BUDGET.

That federal revenues have risen despite the tax cut should not be surprising given the significant number of tax increases enacted during the 1980s. According to the Office of Management and Budget, 14 major tax bills were enacted between 1982 and 1987, and they caused federal revenues to rise by $124.2 billion over the five-year period. In short, over 50 percent of the 1981 tax cut was taken back through higher taxes.[3]

It should also be noted that there was a supply-side response to the tax-rate reductions—a response that raised federal revenues. According to economist Lawrence Lindsey of Harvard University, the increased incentives created by the lower marginal tax rates led to increased realizations of taxable income, thereby recouping as much as 25 percent of the static revenue loss of the 1981 tax cut.[4] Moreover, according to Internal Revenue Service data, these higher revenues came largely from the wealthy, who received the largest reduction in their marginal tax rate, when the top rate fell from 70 percent to 50 percent. As Table 3.2 illustrates, between 1981 and 1986 the wealthy substantially increased their tax payments, both in dollar terms and percentage terms.

For these reasons it is disingenuous to blame the 1981 tax cut for the budget deficit. Those who do so simply want to raise taxes to fuel additional spending. Because federal revenues as a percentage of GNP were the same in 1987 as they had been in 1980, it is clear that any recision of the tax cut and a return to pre-1981 tax rates would constitute a massive tax increase.

In any case, even a tax increase of $100 billion per year—equivalent to abolishing the 1981 tax cut—would be unlikely to eliminate the budget deficit. One reason is that the negative economic impact would be so great that the government would never get anything close to the $100 billion it expected. Another reason is that any additional revenue would fuel additional increases in spending—a point that has recently sparked considerable academic interest. Several studies have concluded that higher revenues cause higher

[3]Office of Management and Budget, *Budget of the United States Government, Fiscal Year 1989* (Washington: Government Printing Office, 1988), p. 4–4.

[4]Lawrence B. Lindsey, "Individual Taxpayer Response to Tax Cuts: 1982–1984," *Journal of Public Economics* 33 (July 1987): 173–206.

Table 3.2
TAX PAYMENTS BY PERCENTILE AND INCOME CLASS, 1981–86

Category		Taxes Paid	
Percentile	Percent of Total: 1981	Percent of Total: 1986	1981–86 Change (%)
Lowest 50 percent	7.5	6.4	−15
51–95 percent	57.6	49.3	−14
95–99 percent	16.8	18.2	+ 8
Top 1 percent	18.1	26.1	+44

Adjusted Gross Income Class	1981		1986	
	$ Billions	Percent of Total	$ Billions	Percent of Total
Under $50,000	189.9	66.8	172.4	45.7
$50,000–$100,000	51.1	18.0	89.1	23.7
Over $100,000	43.2	15.2	115.4	30.6

SOURCE: Internal Revenue Service.

spending.[5] This conclusion suggests that the way to control government spending is to hold down tax revenues.[6]

It is often asserted that the main purpose of the 1981 tax cut was

[5]Neela Manage and Michael Marlow, "The Causal Relation between Federal Expenditures and Receipts," *Southern Economic Journal* 52 (January 1986): 617–29; idem, "Expenditures and Receipts: Testing for Causality in State and Local Government Finance," *Public Choice* 53, no. 3 (1987): 243–55; Paul Blackley, "Causality between Revenues and Expenditures and the Size of the Federal Budget," *Public Finance Quarterly* 14 (April 1986): 139–56; Douglas Holtz-Eakin, Whitney Newley, and Harvey Rosen, *The Revenues-Expenditures Nexus: Evidence from Local Government Data*, NBER Working Paper no. 2180 (Cambridge, Mass.: National Bureau of Economic Research, March 1987); and Rati Ram, "Additional Evidence on Causality between Government Revenue and Government Expenditure," *Southern Economic Journal* 54 (January 1988): 763–69. For a contrary view, see George M. von Furstenberg, R. Jeffrey Green, and Jin-Ho Jeong, "Tax and Spend, or Spend and Tax?" *Review of Economics and Statistics* 68 (May 1986): 179–88; William Anderson, Myles Wallace, and John Warner, "Government Spending and Taxation: What Causes What?" *Southern Economic Journal* 52 (January 1986): 630–39; and Congressional Budget Office, *The Relationship Between Federal Taxes and Spending: An Examination of Recent Research* (Washington, July 1987).

[6]This is consistent with the theoretical view set forth in Geoffrey Brennan and James M. Buchanan, *The Power to Tax: Analytical Foundations of a Fiscal Constitution* (New York: Cambridge University Press, 1980).

precisely to create a budget deficit so large that it would force spending cuts through Congress.[7] This is not true. There was every expectation both in 1977, when the original Kemp-Roth tax bill was introduced, and in 1981, when the Reagan tax cut took effect, that higher revenues from faster economic growth combined with spending restraint would lead to a balanced budget.[8] Nevertheless, it is true that without the deficit, federal spending would be far higher than it already is.

The fact is that federal spending growth has been very low during the 1980s, and virtually no major spending programs outside the defense area have been enacted, although significant parts of the budget have been cut for the first time. Because spending is the basic function of Congress, this fiscal restraint has created severe tensions within Congress. Instead of focusing on the distribution of federal largess as they used to, the members of both houses now devote much of the year to wrestling with a seemingly intractable budget. Indeed, their frustration has reached such a high level that they have increasingly resorted to automatic spending control devices such as the Gramm-Rudman-Hollings legislation. Thus it is clear both to the members of Congress and the spending constituencies they represent that if there are ever to be funds available for big-ticket spending programs, taxes must be increased.

Although taxes are likely to be raised, it is important to note that it is quite possible to raise taxes in such a way that the burden of the tax greatly exceeds its revenue yield, by imposing an excess burden in addition to the tax. It is also possible to impose taxes that are so detrimental to production that they actually reduce revenues rather than raise them. A prime example of detrimental taxation is the increase in the tax rate on long-term capital gains in 1969. Before the rate increase the capital gains tax raised over $5 billion; after the increase the yield fell to a little over $3 billion.[9]

Economic theory is fairly clear on the kinds of taxes that do the least harm to the economy: The heaviest taxes should be on those things that are least able to escape taxation and the lightest should

[7]Sen. Daniel Patrick Moynihan (D-N.Y.) often makes this point.

[8]See Paul Craig Roberts, *The Supply-Side Revolution* (Cambridge, Mass.: Harvard University Press, 1984).

[9]Treasury Department, *Report to Congress on the Capital Gains Tax Reductions of 1978* (Washington: Government Printing Office, 1985), p. 154.

be on those things that are best able to escape taxation.[10] This approach suggests light taxation of such things as profits, savings, and capital gains because they are very sensitive to the after-tax rate of return. By contrast, heavy taxation of wages, rents, and consumption is less likely to reduce the tax base and hence the tax yield.

This taxation approach is largely accepted by tax policymakers today. As a consequence there has been a growing movement toward lower marginal income tax rates, reduced taxes on capital income, and consumption-based tax systems throughout the industrialized world and even in developing countries.[11] Table 3.3 illus-

Table 3.3

TOP INDIVIDUAL AND CORPORATE TAX RATES IN 11 COUNTRIES,
1984 and 1990 (%)

| | Individual | | Corporate | |
Country	1984	1990	1984	1990
Australia	60	49	46	39
Canada	51	45	51	44
Denmark	73	68	40	50
France	65	57	50	42
Italy	65	60	36	46
Japan	88	76	53	37
Netherlands	72	60	43	35
Sweden	82	75	52	52
United Kingdom	60	40	45	35
United States	50	33	46	34
West Germany	56	53	56	50

SOURCE: Joseph A. Pechman, ed., *World Tax Reform: A Progress Report* (Washington: Brookings Institution, 1988), pp. 4–5; supplemented by press reports.

[10]See F. P. Ramsey, "A Contribution to the Theory of Taxation," *The Economic Journal* 37 (March 1927): 47–61.

[11]See Joseph A. Pechman, ed., *World Tax Reform: A Progress Report* (Washington: Brookings Institution, 1988); Organization for Economic Cooperation and Development, *Personal Income Tax Systems under Changing Economic Conditions* (Paris, 1986); and Ved P. Gandhi, ed., *Supply-Side Tax Policy: Its Relevance to Developing Countries* (Washington: International Monetary Fund, 1987).

trates the trend toward lower marginal tax rates on both individuals
and corporations in major countries.

The Value-Added Tax

If Congress decides to seek a major tax increase, therefore, it will
be compelled to look at the value-added tax. From an economic
point of view the VAT is said to be almost the perfect tax. Those in
favor of the VAT believe it can raise large revenues at very low
rates—the Congressional Budget Office has estimated that a 5 percent VAT with no exemptions would raise $77 billion the first year,
rising to almost twice that amount within four years.[12] As a tax on
consumption it would leave profits and savings entirely free of tax.
It would not involve increases in marginal tax rates, which could
hamper incentives, and it allegedly would improve the trade balance because it would be levied at the border on imports and rebated
on exports. Those against the VAT argue principally that it would
be regressive and inflationary.

Actually, both sides overstate their cases. The alleged benefits of
a VAT, for example, usually assume that it is imposed as a replacement for some existing tax, such as the corporate tax or social
security tax. However, if a VAT is imposed by Congress, it will
most likely be a new tax on top of all the others. Accordingly, many
of the efficiency gains from a VAT would evaporate. Proponents
also generally assume that the tax would be imposed on a broad
base with no exemptions. However, this would make the tax highly
regressive. Consequently it is virtually inevitable that a VAT would
contain many exemptions for food and other necessities, thus
requiring higher rates to obtain the same revenue and adding enormous complexity and administrative costs to the use of the VAT.[13]

It should also be noted that the assumed benefit to savings from

[12]Congressional Budget Office, *Reducing the Deficit: Spending and Revenue Options*
(Washington, March 1988), p. 342.

[13]On the efficiency cost of VAT exemptions, see Charles L. Ballard and John B.
Shoven, "The Value-Added Tax: The Efficiency Cost of Achieving Progressivity by
Using Exemptions," in Michael J. Boskin, ed., *Modern Developments in Public Finance*
(New York: Basil Blackwell, 1987), pp. 109–29.

a VAT is speculative at best.[14] Imposition of VATs in Europe, for example, did not increase saving and investment.[15] Also, the argument that a VAT would improve the trade balance is completely wrong. Actually, a border tax and rebate mechanism would merely allow foreign and domestic goods to compete on the same basis. It would have no impact whatsoever on the trade balance.[16]

As for arguments against the tax, the regressivity of the VAT can be redressed with exemptions, although at a cost to efficiency. Furthermore, the inflationary impact of the tax is very much overstated. It would depend a great deal on whether the VAT replaced or came on top of other taxes, as well as on monetary policy and other factors. It probably would not be much of a problem.[17]

More serious criticism of a VAT should focus on the compliance and administrative costs, which could be very high, and on the potential of the tax to raise revenue too easily, thus leading to far higher spending and taxation than we have today.

The administrative and compliance costs of a VAT have two parts: the cost to the government and the cost to business. The cost to government was estimated by the IRS in 1984 to be $700 million per year (in 1984 dollars) and to require the hiring of 20,000 additional

[14]See Robert DeFina, "Increasing Personal Saving: Can Consumption Taxes Help?" *Federal Reserve Bank of New York Quarterly Review* (Autumn 1980): 21–27; Paul Davidson, "Can VAT Resolve the Shortage of Savings (SOS) Distress?" *Journal of Post-Keynesian Economics* 4 (Fall 1981): 51–60; and Robert E. Hall, "Consumption Taxes versus Income Taxes: Implications for Economic Growth," in *1968 Proceedings of the 61st Annual Conference on Taxation of the National Tax Association* (1969), pp. 125–45.

[15]Henry Aaron, ed., *The Value-Added Tax: Lessons from Europe* (Washington: Brookings Institution, 1981), p. 13; and Stephen M. Brecher et al., *The Economic Impact of the Introduction of VAT* (Morristown, N.J.: Financial Executives Research Foundation, 1982), p. 48.

[16]Treasury Department, *Tax Reform for Fairness, Simplicity and Economic Growth: The Treasury Department Report to the President*, vol. 3, *Value-Added Tax* (Washington: Government Printing Office, 1984), p. 22. See also Harry Johnson and Mel Krauss, "Border Taxes, Border Tax Adjustments, Comparative Advantage, and the Balance of Payments," *Canadian Journal of Economics* 3 (November 1970): 595–602; and Mel Krauss and Peter O'Brien, "Some International Implications of Value-Added Taxation," *National Tax Journal* 23 (December 1970): 435–40.

[17]See Alan A. Tait, "Is the Introduction of a Value-Added Tax Inflationary?" Departmental Memorandum no. 80/75 (Washington: International Monetary Fund, November 3, 1980); and idem, "Is the Introduction of a Value-Added Tax Inflationary?" *Finance & Development* (June 1981): 38–42.

IRS agents.[18] However, it should be noted that this cost assumed a flat-rate VAT on a comprehensive base. Obviously, differential rates and bases would greatly increase the cost of administration.

The cost of compliance to business would be far higher, with costs being considerably higher for small businesses than larger ones.[19] For example, in 1978 it was estimated that the compliance cost for the smallest 69 percent of traders in Great Britain exceeded 100 percent of the tax revenue collected.[20] Of course, small businesses could be exempted from the tax, but this would just increase the complexity of the tax, increase opportunities for evasion, and create confusion for consumers.[21]

The most serious problem with a VAT, however, is that it could easily become a "money machine," in that high revenues can be raised at low rates and the tax itself is hidden in the cost of goods, rather than paid directly. Indeed, this is one of the main reasons that people support consumption taxes. As early as the 18th century, for example, David Hume declared that "the best taxes are such as are levied upon consumptions . . . because such taxes are least felt by the people."[22]

Although reducing the cost of paying taxes to the taxpayer is obviously a desirable goal of tax policy, there is the danger that such a tax would more easily be raised to finance low-priority government spending. The experience in Europe confirms such fears. As a Treasury Department study concluded,

[18]Treasury Department, *Tax Reform for Fairness*, p. 113.

[19]See Phyllis A. Barker, "The Value-Added Tax—The Cost to the Businessman," *Journal of Accountancy* 134 (September 1972): 75–79; Seth Parker, "Compliance Costs of the Value-Added Tax," *Taxes—The Tax Magazine* 54 (June 1976): 369–80; James M. Bickley, *The Effect of a Value-Added Tax on Small Business*, committee print, Committee on Small Business, U.S. House of Representatives, 100th Cong., 2d sess. (Washington: Government Printing Office, 1988); and John Blundell, "Britain's Nightmare Value Added Tax," Heritage Foundation International Briefing no. 16 (Washington, June 13, 1988).

[20]Graham Bannock, *VAT and Small Business: European Experience and Implications for North America* (Washington: National Federation of Independent Business Research and Educational Foundation, 1986), p. 64.

[21]For a discussion of the confusion created by Britain's VAT, see John Blundell, "Rolls Royces and Canned Carrots," *Reason* (February 1984): 45–46.

[22]David Hume, "Of Taxes," in *Essays: Moral, Political, and Literary* (1752; reprint, Indianapolis: Liberty Classics, 1985), p. 345.

> Foreign experience indicates that those countries with value-added taxes tend to be high-tax, and presumably high government spending countries. . . . For nearly all European countries with value-added tax, total taxes have increased as a percentage of national output since the introduction of the value-added tax.[23]

This point is confirmed by Henry Aaron of the Brookings Institution, who points out that "the value-added tax in Europe was intended as a substitute for other taxes, but it has been associated with an increase in taxation."[24] The experience in Michigan, which has a form of VAT, also supports the view that a VAT fuels higher spending and taxation.[25]

Tables 3.4 and 3.5 present some evidence on this point. It is evident that total tax revenue as a percentage of gross domestic product increased in every country listed. In all but two of the dozen countries, value-added taxes also increased—in many cases sharply. The contribution of higher VAT revenues to the growth of total revenues varied from less than 2 percent to over 100 percent. Although this does not prove that the VAT caused an increase in overall taxation, it does strongly suggest that the VAT made raising taxes easier.

There is certainly dispute on this point. A 1985 study by J. A. Stockfisch, for example, found no relationship between the institution of a VAT and the growth of government spending. He reached this conclusion by comparing the growth of spending in countries with VATs to that in countries without VATs.[26] However, as Charles McLure, a VAT supporter, has pointed out:

> All the countries included in Stockfisch's sample of countries adopting a VAT already had a national sales tax (that is, they already had a money machine, though perhaps a less efficient one). Stockfisch is thus merely demonstrating that a change in the *form* of national sales tax did not have a dramatic effect on the rate of growth of tax collections, compared with experience in countries with no VAT. That finding is hardly surprising and sheds virtually

[23]Treasury Department, *Tax Reform for Fairness*, p. 23.

[24]Aaron, *Value-Added Tax*, p. 15.

[25]Patrick L. Anderson, *The Single Business Tax Burden on Michigan Industries* (Midland, Mich.: Mackinac Center for Public Policy, 1987), pp. 28–29.

[26]J. A. Stockfisch, "Value-Added Taxes and the Size of Government: Some Evidence," *National Tax Journal* 38 (December 1985): 547–52.

Table 3.4

THE VALUE-ADDED TAX AND TOTAL TAXES AS PERCENTAGES OF GDP IN 12 COUNTRIES

Country	VAT as Percentage of GDP Year after Intro.	1985	Total Taxes as Percentage of GDP Year after Intro.	1985
Austria	7.3	8.9	38.4	42.5
Belgium	7.1	7.4	36.5	46.9
Denmark	6.8	9.9	36.1	49.2
France	9.7	9.0	36.3	45.6
Ireland	5.1	8.1	31.5	39.1
Italy	4.9	5.0	28.3	34.7
Luxembourg	4.1	5.5	34.3	42.8
Netherlands	5.8	7.3	39.9	45.0
Norway	9.6	8.7	42.4	47.8
Sweden	4.2	7.0	41.0	50.5
United Kingdom	3.1	6.0	35.5	38.1
West Germany	5.6	6.0	33.9	37.8

SOURCE: Henry Aaron, ed., *The Value-Added Tax: Lessons from Europe* (Washington: Brookings Institution, 1981), p. 14; and Organization for Economic Cooperation and Development, *Revenue Statistics of OECD Member Countries, 1965–1986* (Paris, 1987), pp. 82, 96.

no light on whether introducing a VAT in a country with no national sales tax would cause the growth of spending to accelerate.[27]

In the absence of empirical proof to the contrary, therefore, it would be best to rely on the theoretical proposition that any increase in a government's ability to tax will almost certainly lead to an increase in taxation.[28]

Of course, a VAT is not the only method by which the U.S. government could raise large revenues without increasing marginal tax rates or increasing the tax burden on capital. The federal budget contains a long list of so-called tax expenditures that could be

[27]Charles E. McLure, Jr., *The Value-Added Tax: Key to Deficit Reduction?* (Washington: American Enterprise Institute, 1987), p. 47.

[28]Brennan and Buchanan, *Power to Tax*, pp. 34–49.

Table 3.5

CHANGES IN THE VALUE-ADDED TAX AND GROWTH OF TAXATION IN 12 COUNTRIES

Country	Change in VAT (%)	Change in Total Taxes (%)	VAT Growth as Percentage of Growth in Total Taxes
Austria	+1.6	+ 4.1	39.0
Belgium	+0.3	+10.4	2.9
Denmark	+3.1	+13.1	23.7
France	−0.7	+ 9.3	—
Ireland	+3.0	+ 7.6	39.5
Italy	+0.1	+ 6.4	1.6
Luxembourg	+1.4	+ 8.5	16.5
Netherlands	+1.5	+ 5.1	29.4
Norway	−0.9	+ 5.4	—
Sweden	+2.8	+ 9.5	29.5
United Kingdom	+2.9	+ 2.6	111.5
West Germany	+0.4	+ 3.9	10.3

SOURCE: Table 3.5.

abolished or limited, and there is no lack of suggestions on other methods of raising taxes.[29]

Better and Worse Tax Proposals

Among other widely discussed methods of raising taxes are many better and worse proposals. Following is a discussion of some of these proposals.

Higher Taxes on the Rich

Raising taxes on the rich is always a politically attractive method of raising revenue. The problem is that the rich are not a fixed

[29]See, for example, U.S. Congress, Joint Committee on Taxation, *Description of Possible Options to Increase Revenues Prepared for the Committee on Ways and Means*, 100th Cong., 1st sess. (Washington: Government Printing Office, 1987); Congressional Budget Office, *Reducing the Deficit*, pp. 283–356; Yolanda K. Henderson, "Further Base Broadening: A Possible Source of Tax Revenues?" *New England Economic Review* (March/April 1988): 33–45; and Susan Dentzer and Gloria Borger, "The Inevitable Tax Hike," *U.S. News and World Report*, July 11, 1988, pp. 17–19.

supply. Experience and common sense show that if tax rates on the rich are raised too high, revenues from the rich decline.[30] More importantly, however, higher taxes on the rich invariably lead to higher levels of taxation on everyone. As F. A. Hayek put it,

> The illusion that by means of progressive taxation the burden can be shifted substantially onto the shoulders of the wealthy has been the chief reason why taxation has increased as fast as it has done and that, under the influence of this illusion, the masses have come to accept a much heavier load than they would have done otherwise.[31]

Raising the top tax rate would also be a betrayal of the principles of the Tax Reform Act of 1986, in which many deductions and tax preferences were given up in return for lower rates.

Oil Import Fee

Because imports are the marginal supply, higher prices for imported oil would lead to higher prices for domestic oil. (This is the reason why domestic producers favor an oil import fee.) Thus, an oil import fee would increase the price of all oil, which would tend to also raise prices for other fuels, such as natural gas, and put upward pressure on the general price level. The Department of Energy estimates that a $10-per-barrel oil import fee would raise gasoline prices by 16 cents per gallon and raise the consumer price index by 2 to 3 percent. Such higher prices would reduce real incomes, reduce the international competitiveness of U.S. industry, reduce growth and employment, and lead to international tensions with nations,

---

[30]See James Gwartney and James Long, *Income Tax Avoidance and an Empirical Estimation of the Laffer Curve* (Washington: Treasury Department, Office of the Assistant Secretary for Economic Policy, 1984); Charles Clotfelter, "Tax Evasion and Tax Rates: An Analysis of Individual Returns," *Review of Economics and Statistics* 65 (August 1983): 363–73; James Long, "Tax Rates and Tax Losses: A Preliminary Analysis Using Aggregate Data," *Public Finance Quarterly* 12 (October 1984): 457–72; and Roger Waud, "Tax Aversion and the Laffer Curve," *Scottish Journal of Political Economy* 33 (August 1986): 213–27.

[31]F. A. Hayek, *The Constitution of Liberty* (Chicago: University of Chicago Press, 1960), p. 311.

such as Canada and Mexico, from which the United States imports large amounts of oil.[32]

Tax Amnesty and Revenue Enforcement

Some people, including Massachusetts governor Michael Dukakis, have contended that tax amnesty coupled with increased IRS enforcement could raise as much as $105 billion in new federal revenue over five years.[33] Their estimates are based on the perceived success of tax amnesties in various states and on IRS data indicating that some $85 billion per year of federal revenue goes uncollected.[34] Such estimates, though, are far higher than anything that could reasonably be expected, would require a vast expansion of IRS resources, and could well undermine tax compliance at the same time.

One reason that tax amnesty would not be very productive is that at the federal level it is not comparable to amnesty experiences at the state level because federal tax enforcement is already far stricter than state enforcement. Thus federal officials estimate that federal tax amnesty is unlikely to raise more than $1 billion.[35] More importantly, amnesty could undermine compliance with the tax law as people wait for the next amnesty to pay up, and that would be unfair to those who pay their taxes honestly.

As to increased IRS enforcement, there is a point beyond which

[32]See Department of Energy, *Energy Security: A Report to the President of the United States* (Washington, March 1987), appendix D; Department of Energy, Energy Information Administration, *The Impact of Lower World Oil Prices and Alternative Energy Tax Proposals on the U.S. Economy* (Washington, April 1986); Robert Bradley, Jr., "Oil Protectionism: The New Threat," *Cato Policy Report* 7 (September/October 1985), pp. 1, 12–13, 15; and Roger Brinner and Christopher Caton, "Energy Tax: An Inferior Cure for the Federal Deficit," *Data Resources U.S. Review* (September 1983): 16–23.

[33]Jim Luther, "Task Force Suggests Ways to Close Tax Gap," *Washington Post*, May 5, 1987; Rose Gutfeld, "Like Pulling Teeth, Dukakis Tax Collection Plan Is Seen as Probably Helpful but Hardly Painless," *Wall Street Journal*, May 5, 1988, p. 62; and *Revenue Enforcement, Tax Amnesty and the Federal Deficit* (Washington: Center for National Policy, 1986).

[34]Internal Revenue Service, *Income Tax Compliance Research: Gross Tax Gap Estimates and Projections for 1973–1992*, IRS Publication no. 7285 (Washington, March 1988).

[35]Allen Lerman, "Tax Amnesty: The Federal Perspective," *National Tax Journal* 39 (September 1986): 325–32. A somewhat higher estimate of potential revenue is given in Herman B. Leonard and Richard Zeckhauser, "Amnesty, Enforcement, and Tax Policy," in Lawrence H. Summers, ed., *Tax Policy and the Economy*, vol. 1 (Cambridge, Mass.: MIT Press, 1987): 55–85.

higher enforcement would become self-defeating—when the cost of obtaining the revenue exceeds the revenue. Indeed, Governor Dukakis admits that his proposal would require virtually doubling the IRS budget. Furthermore, greatly increased enforcement would increase the intrusiveness of the government in our private lives and very likely reduce voluntary compliance with the tax law, as people adopt a more adversarial attitude toward the IRS.[36]

Higher Excise Taxes

From an efficiency point of view, higher excise taxes on tobacco, alcohol, and gasoline are among the least bad ways of raising revenue. Indeed, raising alcohol and tobacco taxes could have important social benefits by reducing consumption of such products, thereby reducing illness, accidents, productivity losses, and insurance and other health costs associated with them.[37] Although opponents of higher excise taxes tend to dwell on their regressivity, a more serious problem involves the effect of such taxes on the spending side. Most excise taxes flow into budgetary trust funds such as the Highway Trust Fund and the Airport and Airway Trust Fund. Thus, although such taxes could be raised for the purpose of funding general government expenditures, they show up in the budget as increases in such trust funds.[38] This encourages the supporters

[36]As it is, the cost to the taxpayers of tax compliance for individual income taxes is as much as $27 billion per year. See Joel Slemrod and Nikki Sorum, "The Compliance Cost of the U.S. Individual Income Tax System," *National Tax Journal* 37 (December 1984): 461–74. It is also worth noting that although many taxpayers underpay their tax, some overpay because the cost of itemizing deductions exceeds the tax saving. See Mark M. Pitt and Joel Slemrod, *The Compliance Cost of Itemizing Deductions: Evidence from Individual Tax Returns*, NBER Working Paper no. 2526 (Cambridge, Mass.: National Bureau of Economic Research, March 1988). On the civil liberties cost of IRS enforcement, see Ronald Hamowy, "The IRS and Civil Liberties: Powers of Search and Seizure," *Cato Journal* 1 (Spring 1981): 225–75. Lastly, it should be noted that tax evasion is very much a function of marginal tax rates and there is a trade-off between tax evasion and tax avoidance. Taxpayers may respond to increased enforcement by taking greater advantage of legal tax preferences. See James Alm, "Compliance Costs and the Tax Avoidance–Tax Evasion Decision," *Public Finance Quarterly* 16 (January 1988): 31–66.

[37]See Charles Phelps, "A Happy Hour for Higher Alcohol Taxes," *Wall Street Journal*, November 17, 1987; and Lawrence Summers, "A Few Good Taxes," *New Republic*, November 30, 1987, pp. 14–16.

[38]See Office of Management and Budget, *Special Analyses: Budget of the United States Government, Fiscal Year 1989*, Special Analysis C.

of higher expenditures for highways or airports to demand that such money be spent on their projects because the money is legally dedicated to this purpose. Consequently, higher excise taxes are likely to end up being spent on higher expenditures.

Lower Capital Gains Tax

As noted earlier, increases in the capital gains tax have led to declines in capital gains tax revenues. Conversely, cuts in the capital gains tax, as happened in 1978 and 1981, have led to increased revenues. Consequently, some analysts argue that the increase in the maximum tax rate on long-term capital gains from 20 percent to 33 percent, embodied in the Tax Reform Act of 1986, will lead to a reduction in capital gains tax revenues. Although there is disagreement about what the revenue-maximizing capital gains tax rate is, virtually all evidence indicates that it is well below 33 percent. Thus, a cut in the capital gains tax would increase revenues.[39]

User Fees

User fees are direct charges for federal services, the benefits of which accrue only to the users. Examples of federal user fees are postage fees, rents and royalties for the use of federal property, and Medicare premiums. However, many federal services are provided without charge or at less than cost. Proposals for federal user fees have been made for such services as deep-draft ports and harbors, inland waterways, Coast Guard services, and irrigation water. A 1983 CBO report estimated that charging full price for such services would raise federal revenues by more than $6 billion.[40] The benefits of imposing such fees include fairness, reduction of waste, reduced subsidies and the need for taxes, and discouragement of rent-seeking. It has also been argued that user fees could promote

[39]Lawrence B. Lindsey, "Capital Gains Taxes under the Tax Reform Act of 1986: Revenue Estimates under Various Assumptions," *National Tax Journal* 40 (September 1987): 489–504; idem, "Capital Gains Rates, Realizations, and Revenues," in Martin Feldstein, ed., *The Effects of Taxation on Capital Accumulation* (Chicago: University of Chicago Press, 1987), pp. 69–100; and Michael R. Darby, Robert Gillingham, and John Greenlees, "The Direct Revenue Effects of Capital Gains Taxation: A Reconsideration of the Time-Series Evidence," *Treasury Bulletin* (June 1988): 2–8.

[40]Congressional Budget Office, *Charging for Federal Services* (Washington, December 1983), p. 4.

privatization by assigning specific revenue flows to specific enterprises, thereby making it easier to sell them off.[41]

Privatization

The federal government engages in many activities and owns many assets that rightfully belong in the private sector. The sale of such assets would not only raise federal revenues but would also improve the delivery of services and economic efficiency. Among federal assets that could be sold for substantial sums are the U.S. Postal Service, Amtrak, the naval petroleum reserves, and the power marketing administrations.[42]

Stock Transfer Tax

This proposal, a favorite of Speaker of the House Jim Wright, would impose a tax of 0.5 percent on the value of stock and bond sales. Presumably, such a tax would have an impact only on the wealthy and would discourage "speculative" trading. In fact, much of the burden of the tax would fall on lower- and middle-income individuals in that most of the trading on the New York Stock Exchange is done by or on behalf of pension funds. Such a tax would raise the cost of capital, especially for new companies. And it would undoubtedly not raise anything close to the $10 billion per year forecast because institutions would simply shift their trading to London or Tokyo, where they can escape the tax. Furthermore, it should be noted that a similar tax proposal that was under consideration by the House of Representatives in early October 1987 is widely blamed for at least contributing to, if not causing, the stock market crash.[43]

[41]E. S. Savas, *Privatization: The Key to Better Government* (Chatham, N.J.: Chatham House Publishers, 1987), pp. 248–50.

[42]See *Privatization: Toward More Effective Government: Report of the President's Commission on Privatization* (Washington: Government Printing Office, 1988); Stephen Moore and Stuart Butler, eds., *Privatization: A Strategy for Taming the Federal Budget* (Washington: Heritage Foundation, 1987); and Stuart Butler, *Privatizing Federal Spending: A Strategy to Eliminate the Deficit* (New York: Universe Books, 1985).

[43]See Bryan Burrough and Thomas Ricks, "Wall Street Fears of Proposed Tax Bill, Interest Rates Spark Takeover Caution," *Wall Street Journal*, October 16, 1987; Eric N. Berg, "Plan for Takeover Taxes Stirs Fears in Markets," *New York Times*, October 19, 1987; Edward Yardeni, "That M&A Tax Scare Rattling the Markets," *Wall Street Journal*, October 28, 1987; Alan Reynolds, "What Scared the Markets?" *National Review*, November 20, 1987, pp. 47–52; and Steve Coll and David A. Vise, "What Killed Stock Boom? Some Point at Tax Idea," *Washington Post*, December 13, 1987, pp. H1, H6.

49

Increased Minimum Tax

Another idea that is perennially popular because it appeals to the widespread but incorrect notion that many wealthy corporations are not paying any taxes at all is to increase the minimum tax. When one examines specific instances where this occurs, however, it turns out that such corporations are paying substantial foreign and state and local taxes, carrying forward large losses from previous years, or making legitimate use of tax preferences put in the tax code precisely to encourage capital investment, charitable contributions, or other socially desirable activities. The minimum-tax advocates, however, seek to avoid addressing the desirability or legitimacy of existing provisions of the tax code and simply to cut them across the board by subjecting tax preferences to an additional, minimum tax. There has been a form of minimum tax in the code since 1969, but it was greatly expanded in the Tax Reform Act of 1986. Nevertheless, many people continue to push for still higher and broader minimum taxes, despite the negative effects of existing minimum taxes on investment and fairness.[44]

Restrict Deduction for State and Local Taxes

The federal government allows full deductibility against gross income for all income and property taxes imposed by state and local governments. The effect is to lower the effective burden of state and local taxes, thus encouraging such taxes (and spending) to be considerably higher than they would be without deductibility. Various studies estimate that state and local spending is between 10 and 20 percent higher than it would be without federal deductibility.[45] Federal deductibility has also been found to be a significant

[44]See Bruce Bartlett, "Minimum Tax Push Could Impale Investment," *Wall Street Journal*, May 21, 1985; Paul Craig Roberts, "Warning: 'Tax Equity' Hasn't Worked That Way," *Business Week*, May 6, 1985, p. 26; Byrle M. Abbin, "The Minimum Tax: 'Fair Share' or Penalty?" *IRET Economic Report* (November 13, 1985); and Gerard M. Brannon, "The Corporate Minimum Tax," *Tax Notes* (January 20, 1986): 269–70.

[45]Edward M. Gramlich, "The Deductibility of State and Local Taxes," *National Tax Journal* 38 (December 1985): 447–65; Roger H. Gordon and Joel Slemrod, "A General Equilibrium Simulation Study of Subsidies to Municipal Expenditures," *Journal of Finance* 38 (May 1983): 585–94; Helen F. Ladd, "Federal Aid to State and Local Governments," in Gregory B. Mills and John L. Palmer, eds., *Federal Budget Policy in the 1980s* (Washington: Urban Institute, 1984): 165–202; and Dennis Zimmerman, "Resource Misallocation from Interstate Tax Exportation: Estimates of Excess Spending and Welfare Loss in a Median Voter Framework," *National Tax Journal* 36 (June 1983): 183–201.

barrier to state and local tax cut efforts and to privatization.[46] For these reasons, deductibility would have a positive impact on reducing state and local taxes and spending. Although complete elimination of deductibility would constitute a major tax increase of some $25 billion per year, it could be coupled with a tax cut, such as raising the personal exemption, to minimize the impact.[47]

Conclusion

The foregoing discussion has only touched upon some of the most widely discussed methods for raising revenue. Some, such as a cut in the capital gains tax, would have positive benefits, whereas others could have a disastrous effect on the economy. The discussion has been limited to revenue-raising proposals because of the likelihood that efforts to raise revenues to reduce the deficit and fund new spending will dominate political debate in the 101st Congress, regardless of who is president.

Although tax increases will dominate the debate, there may be opportunities to press for specified tax cuts in this context to buy support for a tax increase. In this event two options should receive priority.

Expand the deduction for Individual Retirement Accounts

The 1986 tax bill restricted the deductibility of IRAs to people below certain incomes and not covered by a regular pension plan. This restriction has eliminated the availability of IRAs for the vast majority of people who previously used them, thereby making it more difficult for people to save in the future and increasing their later dependence on unreliable government pensions. Despite assertions to the contrary, there is considerable evidence that IRAs

[46]"Deductibility Hurts Local Tax Cut Efforts," *Dollars & Sense* (July-August 1985), p. 7; E. S. Savas, "Tax Plan's Boost to Privatizing Services," *Wall Street Journal,* July 10, 1985, p. 28; and Harry Hatry, *A Review of Private Approaches for Delivery of Public Services* (Washington: Urban Institute, 1983), p. 90.

[47]Peter Ferrara, "Tax Reform's Next Step: End State and Local Tax Deductions and Boost the Personal Exemption," Heritage Foundation Backgrounder No. 629 (Washington, February 5, 1988).

were a major stimulus to saving.[48] Given the need for national saving to finance investment, as well as growing concerns among those under 40 years of age that the social security system will remain solvent, the highest priority should be given to providing alternative retirement saving opportunities by expanding IRAs to at least their pre–1986 tax treatment.

Cut the social security tax

Recent press reports have drawn attention to the fact that the social security system is currently raising far more revenue than needed to pay current benefits. This is mistakenly called a surplus. In fact, the only meaningful calculation of the surplus or deficit of the system is on an actuarial basis; that is, the extent to which the system is capable of paying all promised benefits. On this basis the system is still in deficit. Nevertheless, the current cash surplus has the undesirable effect of in effect subsidizing federal expenditures.[49] For this reason it would be desirable to cut the social security tax to put more discipline on non–social security spending. Also, it should be noted that the social security tax rate has grown to a level far higher than ever contemplated and constitutes a significant tax on labor.[50] Therefore, priority should be given to at least deferring future social security tax increases already programmed into current

[48]Stephen F. Venti and David A. Wise, "The Evidence on IRAs," *Tax Notes* (January 25, 1988): 411–16; idem, "IRAs and Saving," in Martin Feldstein, ed., *The Effects of Taxation on Capital Accumulation* (Chicago: University of Chicago Press, 1987): 7–51; idem, "Tax-Deferred Accounts, Constrained Choice and Estimation of Individual Saving," *Review of Economic Studies* 53 (August 1986): 579–601; R. Glenn Hubbard, "Do IRAs and Keoghs Increase Saving?" *National Tax Journal* 37 (March 1984): 43–54; and Lawrence H. Summers, "I.R.A.'s Really Do Spark New Savings," *New York Times*, May 25, 1986, p. 43.

[49]See, for example, Paul Blustein, "Social Security Surpluses Said to Mask Size of Deficit," *Washington Post*, March 5, 1988; Peter Kilborn, "New Issue on Budget Horizon: What to Do About Surpluses," *New York Times*, April 2, 1988; and Paul Magnusson, "We Are Plundering the Social Security Till," *Business Week*, July 18, 1988, p. 92.

[50]For discussions of the growing social security tax burden and its economic effects, see Robert Barro and Chaipat Sahasakul, *Average Marginal Tax Rates from Social Security and the Individual Income Tax*, NBER Working Paper no. 1214 (Cambridge, Mass.: National Bureau of Economic Research, October 1983); Edgar Browning, "The Marginal Social Security Tax on Labor," *Public Finance Quarterly* 13 (July 1985): 227–51; and Aldona Robbins and Gary Robbins, "Effects of the 1988 and 1990 Social Security Tax Increases," *IRET Economic Report* (February 3, 1988).

law and to cutting the rate if possible. One option currently under discussion would allow workers a credit against income taxes for contributions to an IRA or other qualified savings plan.[51]

In conclusion it should be reiterated that no justification exists for higher taxes. To the extent that deficits are a problem, they should be dealt with entirely on the spending side. Higher taxes will only have the effect of reducing the pressure to cut spending and will lead to higher spending. Thus, higher taxes should be resisted most strenuously.

Nevertheless, it is likely that regardless of who is the new president, the pressure to raise taxes may prove overwhelming. It is important that those opposed to any additional taxes do not remove themselves entirely from the debate over the size and shape of a tax increase. As noted, some taxes are clearly worse than others, and some revenue-raising measures, such as a cut in the capital gains tax, could actually have benefits. Also, the debate on a big tax bill may provide opportunities for specific tax cuts as part of the package.

[51]See "U.S. Social Security Surpluses: Pitfall or Opportunity?" Morgan Guaranty Trust Co. *World Financial Markets* (July 1988); and Peter Ferrara, "The Great Social Security Surplus Hoax," Heritage Foundation Backgrounder No. 662 (July 11, 1988).

4. U.S. Trade Policy: Problems and Prospects

William A. Niskanen

U.S. trade policy turned sharply protectionist during the Reagan years. Moreover, all of the new trade restraints were initiated or approved by the administration, despite a general endorsement of free trade in its public rhetoric. Although the administration's trade policy was partly a response to strong congressional pressure, no major new trade legislation was approved until the Omnibus Trade Act of 1988—the effects of which are yet to be realized. This chapter addresses three questions: What happened to U.S. trade policy? What explains the change in trade policy? Where do we go from here?

The Reagan Trade Record

The facts are clear. Trade protection cost American consumers about $65 billion in 1986, an increase of nearly 100 percent since 1980.[1] About one-quarter of the products imported by the United States are now subject to trade restraints, up from about one-eighth in 1980.[2] And this major change in U.S. trade policy was implemented before any major change in trade legislation. The Reagan administration must bear the primary responsibility for this record.

Administration Measures

Only a brief summary of the major trade cases is sufficient to convey the scope and nature of the administration's import policies:

Automobiles. Following a 1980 Reagan campaign pledge that "one way or another . . . that deluge of [Japanese] cars must be slowed

---

[1]This estimate is attributed to Gary Hufbauer of Georgetown University and was cited in Carolyn Lochhead, "Consumer Groups Draw Fire for Ignoring Regulation Costs," *Insight*, February 16, 1988, p. 44.

[2]This estimate was cited in Michael Kinsley, "Talking Tough," *Washington Post*, March 25, 1987.

while our industry gets back on its feet" and the early 1981 introduction of a Senate bill that would sharply limit the import of
Japanese cars, the administration pressured the government of
Japan to impose a voluntary restraint agreement on car exports to
the United States. This VRA first limited car exports to 1.68 million
units through March 1982, plus small additional quotas on utility
vehicles and exports to Puerto Rico. To counter congressional pressure for a "domestic content" bill, the Japanese maintained this
limit at 1.68 million cars a year for two more years and increased
the limit to 1.85 million cars in the fourth year.

Although the Reagan administration did not ask the Japanese to
renew the VRA in 1985, the government of Japan, for its own
reasons, has maintained a limit of 2.3 million cars a year since that
time. For Japan the effects of the agreement were to increase the
prices and profits of the automobile firms, increase their relative
sales of higher-value cars, increase their production in the United
States, and increase the control by the Ministry of International
Trade and Industry (MITI) over the Japanese auto industry.

For the U.S. auto industry the effects of the agreement were to
increase the industry's prices, profits, and employment. For American consumers the effects were to increase the cost of automobiles—by a total of about $5.8 billion (in 1984), or about $105,000
per job saved in the domestic industry.[3]

It should be noted that the agreement with Japan was entirely
extralegal in that it was not authorized under U.S. law or under the
General Agreement on Tariffs and Trade (GATT), and it set an
unfortunate precedent for the administration response to most of
the other major trade cases.

Textiles and Apparel. As a candidate, Ronald Reagan also pledged
to "relate" the growth of imports of textiles and apparel to the
growth of domestic sales. In response to this pledge the Reagan
administration decided in 1981 to renew the MultiFiber Arrangement in a form that would meet this goal. (The MFA, an outgrowth
of the "short-term" cotton agreement of 1961, is a complex system
of quotas by the industrial countries on imports of textiles and
apparel from the developing countries.) A rapid growth of imports

[3]Gary Hufbauer, Diane Berliner, and Kimberly Elliot, *Trade Protection in the United
States: 31 Case Studies* (Washington: Institute for International Economics, 1986), pp.
257–58.

led the administration to increase the number of products covered by these quotas in 1983 and to change the country-of-origin rules for these quotas in 1984.

For the exporting countries the effects of these measures were similar to that for the automobile quotas—increased prices, profits, and government control of their textile and apparel industries. For the U.S. industry the effects were increased prices and profits and a slower decline in employment in the domestic firms. For American consumers the total cost was about $27 billion, or about $42,000 per job saved in the domestic industry.[4]

For three decades the United States has been the prime mover in establishing a worldwide cartel for textiles and apparel sales, one of the two commodity groups (along with agriculture) that are exempt from the normal GATT rules; the primary effect of the Reagan measures has been to increase the scope and cost of this cartel.

Steel. In response to a 1982 petition by the U.S. steel industry for antidumping and countervailing duties against imports of carbon steel from European firms, the Reagan administration arranged for VRAs to limit steel imports from Europe to 5.5 percent of the U.S. market. It also imposed a similar limit on pipe and tube imports from Europe and initiated negotiations to achieve similar limits on other countries.

The U.S. quotas available to individual European countries and steel firms were independent of the amount by which their products were determined to have been dumped or subsidized. Accordingly, the protectionist measure transformed an unfair trade case into a general limit on European steel exports to the United States, irrespective of the extent to which individual firms had been charged with unfair trade practices.

In response to a 1983 "escape clause" petition (based only on injury to the domestic industry, not some unfair trade practice by foreign firms or governments) from the U.S. specialty steel industry, the administration imposed a set of tariffs and quotas on imports of selective specialty steel products. Total steel imports, however, continued to increase, primarily from countries not included in these agreements.

[4]Ibid., pp. 148–49.

In response to a 1984 "escape clause" petition by the steel industry and the introduction of a bill that would limit all steel imports, the administration determined to seek VRAs with all major steel-exporting countries to limit total imports of finished steel to 18.5 percent of the U.S. market and to also place a small quantitative limit on semifinished steel. Strong U.S. demand and a delay in negotiating and implementing the VRAs, however, reduced the short-term effects of these agreements; total steel imports declined from a peak 26.4 percent of the U.S. market in 1984 to 23 percent in 1986.

Together, the administration's various measures to protect the domestic steel industry had the effect of creating a worldwide cartel of steel exporters to the United States, of increasing the prices and profits of the firms receiving the available quotas, and of increasing the government control of these firms. For the U.S. industry, the effects were increased prices and profits and a slower decline in employment in the steel industry. For American consumers the annual cost was about $6.5 billion, about $750,000 per job saved in the domestic industry.[5] Since steel is a major input to other products, these protectionist measures also reduced the international competitiveness of other U.S. industries.

Semiconductors. In 1986 the U.S. semiconductor industry petitioned to impose antidumping duties on imports of general-purpose memory chips from Japan. An examination revealed that the price of Japanese chips in the United States was higher than in Japan but was lower than a Department of Commerce estimate of the cost of Japanese production. As in the 1982 steel case, the administration chose to make a broader agreement with the exporting country rather than impose the duties authorized by law. In response to U.S. pressure, the government of Japan agreed to set a floor price on the sale of memory chips in the United States equal to the "fair market value" (as determined by the Department of Commerce), set a similar floor price on sales in third countries, and promote an increase in the sales of U.S. chips in Japan. Without this agreement,

[5]This estimate is specific to the effects of the actual reduction in the import share of the U.S. steel market in 1985 and 1986 and does not include the effects of prior import restraints implemented through 1984. I prepared the estimate on the basis of the analysis of the prior restraints in Hufbauer, Berliner, and Elliot, pp. 178–79.

the United States would have had no authority to impose the latter two provisions (third-country sales and U.S. sales in Japan).

In 1987 the Reagan administration determined that Japan had not met these two provisions (although it would not reveal the data on which it based this determination) and imposed 100 percent tariffs on imports of $300 million worth of other Japanese products. In fact, though, the government of Japan had already ordered a substantial reduction of chip production to reduce the large chip inventory being sold in third countries and had implemented several measures to promote the sale of foreign chips in Japan. The administration later determined that Japan has ceased dumping in third countries but maintained the punitive tariffs on a reduced set of products to induce Japan to increase the U.S. chip share of the Japanese market.

In effect the semiconductor agreement created a two-country memory chip cartel. This agreement, combined with a continued increase in demand, led to a sharp increase in the price of memory chips in both markets, rising from $2.50 per chip in early 1986 to $5.50 in March 1988.[6] In addition, because these chips are a major input in the production of computers, this agreement will reduce the international competitiveness of the much larger computer industries in both countries. What wondrous webs we weave . . .[7]

Other Cases. There was no consistent pattern in the other trade cases. In 1981 the Reagan administration established a system of quotas on sugar imports to maintain the domestic sugar price; these quotas were progressively tightened and later extended to the import of food products containing even minimum amounts of sugar. As of 1984 the domestic sugar price was about four times the world price, the highest effective tariff on any legal product, at an annual cost to American consumers of about $1 billion.[8]

In 1983 the administration set a high temporary tariff on large motorcycles to protect about 2,000 jobs in one company. In 1986 the administration decided to request VRAs on the imports of machine

[6]Kenneth Flamm, "U.S. Memory Chip Makers: In a Fix," *Washington Post*, March 1, 1988.

[7]For a summary of semiconductor trade issues, see Eugene Volokh, "The Semiconductor Industry and Foreign Competition, Cato Institute Policy Analysis no. 99 (Washington: Cato Institute, 1988).

[8]Hufbauer, Berliner, and Elliot, p. 295.

tools from four countries, after rejecting two prior petitions for restraints under different sections of U.S. law. Also in 1986, during the sensitive early negotiations on the U.S.-Canada free-trade agreement, the administration imposed substantial tariffs on imports of cedar shingles and softwood lumber from Canada.

On the other hand the administration rejected or removed trade restraints on three other products. In 1981 and 1985 it rejected petitions to continue or reimpose quotas on footwear. In 1984 it also rejected a petition to limit copper imports because of the adverse effects on the much larger copper products industry. And in 1986 the administration finally convinced Congress to delete the "manufacturing clause" in copyright law (a provision that dates from 1891) that required most books and magazines to be printed and bound in the United States to be eligible for copyright protection. The footwear and printing industries are the only industries for which trade restraints are now substantially lower than in 1980.

The administration's export policies are best described as inconsistent.[9] In 1981 the administration removed the embargo on grain sales to the Soviet Union but imposed an embargo on the sale of U.S. equipment and U.S.-licensed equipment made in Europe for the natural gas pipeline from the Soviet Union to Europe; after a protest from European governments, this embargo was removed in 1982. For foreign policy purposes the administration imposed selective embargoes on trade with Poland, Libya, Nicaragua, Syria, and, in response to strong congressional pressure, South Africa. At several times the administration proposed to reduce funding for the Export-Import Bank of the United States but agreed to increase subsidies on agricultural exports. The administration did not ask Congress to remove the bans on the sales of logs and Alaskan oil or the requirement that 50 percent of all government-financed agriculture exports be carried on U.S. ships. American firms still lack clear guidelines on the export of defense-related technology that are consistent with the rules affecting sales by other Western nations. For many years the federal government has promoted the export of some products and restricted the exports of other products, with little apparent rationale. For the most part, that is still the case.

[9]For a summary of the Reagan trade record, see Sheldon Richman, "The Reagan Record on Trade: Rhetoric vs. Reality," Cato Institute Policy Analysis no. 107 (Washington: Cato Institute, 1988).

On the other hand, the administration strongly increased pressure on other governments to open their markets to U.S. goods. The general tactic was to threaten limits on the countries' exports to the United States to induce them to reduce their limits on U.S. sales in their markets. The administration initiated 10 such cases during the first term and 22 such cases after the marked change in trade policy in September 1985. These measures had some success. Japan reduced or eliminated tariffs on aluminum products, cigarettes, and leather products, and it substituted high tariffs for the very restrictive quotas on beef and citrus. South Korea reduced its barriers on U.S. movies and television. Taiwan opened its market to beer, wine, and cigarettes. Europe reduced restraints on imports of corn and citrus goods. And so on.

But this process, by its nature, also risks substantial costs to the United States, both in terms of higher U.S. trade barriers and the erosion of U.S. bargaining leverage on more important issues. For example, in response to a loss of corn sales to Spain and Portugal that resulted from their joining the European Economic Community (Common Market), the Reagan administration threatened to impose a 200 percent tariff on imports of selected alcoholic beverages and agricultural products from Europe, an action that was only narrowly averted. The nature of this process is best described by the following example:

> In the Great Pasta War, the administration imposed 40 percent duties on European spaghetti and fancy pasta sold in gourmet groceries. The European Community retaliated against U.S. walnuts and lemons; the U.S. delayed a promised concession on semi-finished steel. Europe slapped duties on U.S. fertilizer, paper products, and beef tallow, in a complicated tit-for-tat that finally involved several industries. It wound down only when the Europeans reduced their disputed pasta export subsidies.[10]

One might hope that America's limited leverage on its major allies would be focused on more important issues, such as the shared defense burden. This process, by which we threaten to impose costs on both U.S. consumers and foreign producers to increase the

[10]Monica Langley, "Protectionist Attitudes Grow Stronger in Spite of Healthy Economy," Wall Street Journal, May 16, 1988.

benefits to U.S. producers—for the most part over trivial issues—may turn out to be a game of Russian roulette.

Congressional Measures

Congress bears a substantial responsibility for the change in U.S. trade policy during the Reagan years, although little trade legislation was approved until 1988. A large number of trade bills were introduced, but only a few bills were passed by one or both houses. An attempt to head off these bills, however, became the primary internal rationale for the administration's own protectionist actions.

Both congressional pressure and the administration's response increased over this period. In 1982 Congress overrode a veto to extend the manufacturing clause of the copyright law but allowed the provision to expire in 1986. In both 1982 and 1983 the House approved a bill that would have required domestic production of up to 90 percent of the value of all cars sold in the United States, but both of these bills expired in the Senate. A more general trade and tariff act was approved in 1984, after an extraordinary effort by William Brock (the U.S. trade representative in the first term) to delete most of the small protectionist provisions. This act strengthened the authority to retaliate against unfair trade practices, broadened the definition of injury in escape clause cases, and included a small number of minor protectionist provisions. On the other hand this act reduced tariffs on about 100 products, extended the generalized system of preferences on imports from the developing nations, and provided authority for bilateral negotiations for free-trade agreements with specific nations.

Trade policy turned more aggressive in the second term. In 1985 the House passed a bill to tighten the quotas on textile and apparel imports, and the Senate passed a similar bill, adding protection for the copper and footwear industries that had been denied relief by the president. This bill, however, was vetoed, and the veto was sustained by a narrow margin in 1986. Also in 1986, both houses began to develop much more comprehensive trade bills, focusing on trade authority and rules rather than on specific products. The general thrust of these bills was to broaden the conditions that would be defined as unfair trade practices, restrict the presidential authority to deny trade relief, and (for a few goods and services) to require "reciprocal treatment" of U.S. sales in foreign markets and foreign sales in the U.S. market. After two years of deliberations, negotiations with the administration, and the addition of a large number of extraneous provisions, the 1,000-page Omnibus Trade Act of 1988 was finally passed by large margins in each house.

The final stage of this legislative process was almost a farce. The president first vetoed this act, objecting primarily to a provision requiring early notice of plant closing and substantial layoffs, and he encouraged Congress to report promptly a second bill without this provision. Congress responded by passing a separate plant closing bill that the president did not veto and a trade bill representing a major change in U.S. trade policy that the president did endorse.

The primary problem of the Omnibus Trade Act is that it represents a unilateral U.S. declaration of the rules of trade, reversing 40 years of U.S. leadership toward a set of trade rules to which all parties agree. In effect the United States has now told the rest of the world, "Play by our rules or we will not buy your products"; in the name of reducing unfair trade by other countries, the United States has changed the rules of trade by an unfair process. One should not be surprised by the strong foreign opposition to this act or the prospect that other countries may apply such unilateral rules to the United States. Only a few provisions of the Omnibus Trade Act are likely to expand trade: the president is granted special authority to negotiate the new GATT round, the rules affecting U.S. business practices in other countries are more realistic, tariffs are reduced or eliminated on many products for which there is no U.S. source, and an extraneous provision eliminates the windfall profits tax on U.S. oil. The major trade provisions of this act, however, are a very high price to pay for these few desirable provisions.

International Agreements

One creative instrument of trade policy during the Reagan years was the initiation of bilateral free-trade agreements with selective countries. A free-trade agreement with Israel was approved in 1985. A broad free-trade agreement with Canada, our largest trading partner, was approved by Congress in 1988. A "framework agreement" with Mexico, our third largest trading partner, will provide guidance for future trade negotiations. Free-trade agreements also have been considered with other countries. These agreements promise to increase the benefits of trade to each participating country.

Moreover, this U.S. strategy of expanding a dollar-bloc free-trade area may be our only substantial leverage to achieve a desirable outcome from the new GATT round initiated in 1986. The United States entered these negotiations with an ambitious agenda to broaden the GATT rules to cover agriculture, services, and investment. The prospects for this round, however, are not encouraging. The Europeans have strongly resisted the elimination of trade-related agricultural subsidies and are more concerned about completing the integration of the European Economic Community in 1992. And most countries have been provoked by the more aggressive U.S. trade policy and the Omnibus Trade Act of 1988. In the absence of creative leadership, the world trading system may well devolve into regional trading blocs with higher barriers to trade among these blocs, a sad outcome for an administration that was once committed to "improvements and extensions of international trade rules."

The Political Economy of Trade Policy

What are the principal reasons for the substantial change in U.S. trade policy during the Reagan years?

First, the Reagan administration did not have strong, consistent convictions on trade policy. Specifically, the president and other key officials never resolved the tension between their public pro-market rhetoric and their private pro-business sympathies. The initial statement of the Reagan economic program barely acknowledged the international dimensions of economic policy. One paragraph described how the proposed policies were expected to improve international conditions, but there was no mention of the principles that would guide our economic relations with other nations. The initial program did state that the major objectives included increased spending for defense and business investment, but there was no recognition that these measures would have a substantial effect on the real exchange rate and the trade balance.

In mid-1981, however, the administration developed a more comprehensive "Statement on U.S. Trade Policy." The primary theme of this statement was "free trade, consistent with mutually accepted trading relations," and the statement committed the administration to five specific trade policy objectives consistent with this theme.

For the conditions anticipated in 1981, these five objectives would have been a satisfactory and sufficient statement of trade policy.

Second, unexpected changes in economic conditions—the most important of which were the long recession of 1981–82 and the rapid increase in the exchange-rate and trade deficit—led to strong pressure from business, unions, and Congress for selective trade restraints. This pressure, in combination with some 1980 campaign commitments and controversy within the administration, led to numerous breaches in the announced trade policy.

Third, the increasing disparity between the announced trade policy and the developing trade record was resolved by changing the official trade policy, rather than by correcting the record, even though the economy had recovered sharply and the dollar had declined. In September 1985 Donald Regan's aides revised a speech prepared for the president that would have renewed his commitment to free trade to conclude that "if trade is not fair for all, then trade is 'free' in name only." The major element of Reagan's new Trade Policy Action Plan was the initiation of a series of actions against "unfair" trade practices by other governments, including practices not covered by existing GATT rules. This unilateral definition of fair trade was a major change from the announced trade policy of the first term and set the stage for the broader U.S. definition of fair trade in the trade bills being developed by Congress. This change in policy was roughly coincident with the appointment of Clayton Yeutter as the new U.S. trade representative and Treasury Secretary James Baker's Plaza Agreement for coordinated action to devalue the dollar, signaling a more interventionist policy on a range of international economic issues.

Finally, trade policy became a major focus of the special-interest demands for government benefits. There may be a roughly constant total demand for such benefits. Several other major changes in economic policy during the Reagan years, however, reduced the amount of special benefits distributed by other means—specifically the substantial reduction in real spending for discretionary programs, continued economic deregulation, and broadening of the tax base in the Tax Reform Act of 1986. The large budget deficit will continue to constrain the potential to distribute special benefits through the budget and the tax code. For that reason the continuing demands for special benefits are likely to focus on trade policy and, probably, on new types of economic regulation, such as mandated benefits.

The administration's internal rationale for its major protectionist actions and, ultimately, for the change in its announced trade policy was to head off even more aggressive measures by Congress. In that sense the administration's developing trade policy was a strategic retreat, but the outcome was not satisfactory. For the first time since World War II the United States added more trade restraints than it removed. Although U.S. pressure led to some reduction in foreign trade-distorting practices, this pressure has consumed political capital that is important in the GATT and other international forums. And the Omnibus Trade Act of 1988 ended a half-century of U.S. leadership toward a more open world trading system based on mutually accepted rules of trade.

The Prospects for U.S. Trade Policy

Where do we go from here?

For the next several years, unfortunately, U.S. trade policy is likely to be increasingly aggressive—despite a sustained recovery, a declining trade deficit, and a sharply lower foreign-exchange value of the dollar. Although George Bush and Michael Dukakis generally support free trade, both endorsed the Omnibus Trade Act of 1986. Congress is in an ugly mood, both about foreign trade practices and foreign investment in the United States. The Omnibus Trade Act is best described as "procedural protectionism," inviting an increasing number of petitions for trade restraint and requiring more administration investigations of foreign trade practices. However, the act still allows the president and the U.S. trade representative some discretion about implementing trade measures, so the effective U.S. trade policy will continue to be dependent on how the new administration uses this discretion. My own judgment is that the prospects for the new GATT round are not encouraging, unless the United States develops an effective strategy to break the logjam on agricultural issues.

We now need to develop a longer-term strategy to preserve and extend free trade.[11] Supporters of free trade have been too defensive

[11]The following section was earlier presented as a speech to Consumers for World Trade in Washington on April 20, 1988, and to a conference of the National Association of Business Economists held in San Francisco on June 9, 1988.

66

for too long—opposing new trade restraints under existing law and incremental expansion of trade legislation. This is a no-win strategy. When we win, it is a draw; when we lose, the scope and level of trade restraints are increased. We now need to develop an offensive strategy to reduce trade restraints, both in the United States and abroad, with the hope of shaping the perceptions that will affect U.S. trade policy—not in the next few months, but well into the next century.

What could be the elements of such a strategy? The following five general approaches should be considered:

1. Regain the Moral and Economic High Ground for Free Trade

The fundamental moral case for free trade, both within nations and between nations, is based on the principle of consent. The most important role of government is to secure the rights of individuals to make consensual arrangements of any kind that do not affect the rights of others, including across national borders. The economic case for free trade is that it increases the combined income of the affected nations and, except in rare conditions, also increases the income of each nation.

This perspective on international trade, unfortunately, is now more threatened than at any time in the postwar years. Many of us, unfortunately, became too involved in the narrow politics of current issues to recognize the power of ideas in shaping legislation. During the past decade, however, three of the more important changes in U.S. economic policy have been the result of a convergence of elite opinion across party lines and without any significant popular pressure. These changes were the substantial reduction of domestic economic regulation, the Gramm-Rudman-Hollings deficit-reduction process, and the Tax Reform Act of 1986. We need to reassert the moral and economic case for free trade so that, at some point, free trade will be similarly recognized as an idea whose time has come.

2. Reduce the U.S. Trade Deficit

A trade deficit is of no particular concern when domestic investment is unusually high. The current U.S. trade deficit, however, is the result of conditions that are neither sustainable nor desirable—specifically, the unusually low level of U.S. saving net of government borrowing. In effect the current U.S. trade deficit is providing the net inflow of goods and services to permit an unsustainable level of private consumption and government spending. There is no prospect for changing the direction of U.S. trade policy until these conditions are changed.

The primary responsibility for reducing the U.S. trade deficit, of course, must rest with the United States. The several types of measures that should be considered include reducing the remaining biases in the tax system against private saving, reducing the growth of government spending for both services and transfer payments, and, only if politically necessary, increasing taxes to reduce the growth of private consumption. An increased tax on business investment would be a very effective way to reduce the trade deficit but should be vigorously opposed as counterproductive to the broader objective of increasing economic growth.

It is also important to recognize that measures by other governments to increase their private consumption, defense spending, or domestic investment would also reduce the U.S. trade deficit. As a rule, and unlike many U.S. government officials, I am most reluctant to pressure other governments to change their domestic policies. In the case of defense spending, however, the current U.S. share of our common defense is disproportionate. The United States now spends about 6.5 percent of gross national product for defense, about twice the proportion spent by our NATO allies and about six times that spent by Japan. Our disproportionate share of the burden of providing the common defense, in effect, is one of our largest exports but one for which we are not compensated.

For various reasons the United States is likely to reduce its overseas military forces during the next decade, forcing the governments of Europe and Japan to reassess their own contribution to the regional defense against the continuing Soviet threat. An increase in defense spending by Europe and Japan that matches the reduction of U.S. defense spending would reduce the U.S. trade deficit by more than the amount of the shift in the defense burden. This is a complex issue, but it cannot be avoided by pretending that it does not exist.

3. Avoid Extralegal Trade Restraints

Many of the U.S. trade restraints implemented since 1980, unfortunately, have been extralegal "voluntary" export restraints to which foreign governments have acquiesced to avoid a formal action under U.S. trade law. Such agreements, for example, have been the basis for the automobile, steel, machine tool, and semiconductor restraints. My own judgment is that the acquiescence of foreign governments, particularly that of Japan, to impose these extralegal restraints has been most shortsighted. In some of these cases, imposition has led to trade restraints that would not have been authorized under U.S. law. Agreement to impose such restraints has also weakened the influence of the supporters of free trade within the U.S. government. In effect I would advise foreign governments to resist U.S. pressure for such extralegal trade restraints. If they had already done so, it would have led—in some cases—to some restraints under existing law, or maybe a change in U.S. law, but I believe that the scope of U.S. trade restraints would have been less than did occur.

4. Broaden the Use of Bilateral Free-Trade Agreements

Half a dozen bilateral free-trade agreements have already been implemented, negotiated, or proposed: Israel: agreement approved in 1985; Canada: agreement approved by Congress in 1988; Mexico: framework agreement has been negotiated; ASEAN: negotiations were considered in 1983; Taiwan: agreement proposed by Taiwan; and Japan: agreement proposed by U.S. ambassador Mike Mansfield.

Such bilateral agreements serve two objectives. First, they broaden the dollar bloc of free-trade agreements, in the absence of a more general agreement under the GATT. Second, they put substantial pressure on the Europeans (who have expressed considerable concern about being left out of such agreements) to broaden and strengthen the GATT in the current negotiations.

My views on this issue were reinforced by hearing a presentation by the French agriculture minister on his proposal for a cartel of the world's major cereal exporters. The current European position on agricultural trade threatens to undermine any prospect for success of the Uruguay Round unless the United States presents a credible threat of walking out of these negotiations. The GATT may increasingly become an instrument of managed trade unless the United States presents a credible alternative framework for world trade, even if the alternative framework would be less desirable than some conceivable multilateral arrangement. The U.S. bilateral initiatives should not be regarded as a threat to the GATT but as part of a strategy to achieve a successful negotiation of a broader multilateral arrangement.

5. Reduce the Scope of U.S. Trade Law

My own suggestions are as follows:

- Exclude dumping, on either a price or cost basis, as a basis for duties. The dumping code now penalizes foreign firms for practices that are regularly used by domestic firms and is especially vulnerable to abuse under flexible exchange rates. And the accountants at the Department of Commerce have proved to be sufficiently creative to identify dumping in a wide range of conditions.

- Restrict countervailing duties to the amount of the net subsidy by foreign governments (subsidy minus the incremental cost of meeting specific domestic regulations). Two examples illustrate this issue. First, a small West German subsidy to steel mills offsets the requirement to use West German coal. This is effectively a subsidy to West German coal, not to steel, and should not be a basis for a countervailing duty against West German steel. Second, many governments subsidize firms to locate in specific regions. Such regional development subsidies typically offset the higher costs of operating in these regions, do not reduce the net cost of production, and should not be a basis for a countervailing duty. A net subsidy criterion, therefore, would apply a countervailing duty only when the subsidy reduces the price at which the good or service could be sold on the world market.

- Restrict or eliminate the Section 301 authority for trade restraints. This section of U.S. trade law has been used to authorize retaliation on the basis of foreign practices that are wholly consistent with the GATT, and it has been subject to considerable abuse.

Such changes would force the continuing pressure for trade restraints primarily through two existing sections of U.S. trade law. One is Section 201, which authorizes trade restraints when an increase in imports has been the major cause of injury to a domestic industry, does not require proof of unfair trade practices, permits the president to consider the interests of consumers and other industries in determining whether to approve or modify the recommended trade restraints, and requires compensation of the exporting country. The other is Section 232, which authorizes trade restraints when an increase in imports would threaten the industrial base necessary for national security. Even Adam Smith acknowledged that "defense is more important than opulence." The criteria and process for approving trade restraints under these two sections of U.S. trade law are wholly consistent with the GATT, and these sections have not been subject to substantial abuse.

In summary, a long-term strategy to preserve and extend free trade will require intelligence, a sense of realism, a commitment to principle, and considerable patience. In the absence of such an offensive strategy, however, we will spend much of our time responding to political pressure for new trade restraints, and the world trading system will continue to deteriorate. The future of U.S. trade policy and of the world trading system will depend on this choice.

5. Getting Deregulation Back on Track

Fred L. Smith, Jr.

> The social philosophy of the Enlightenment failed to see the dangers that the prevalence of unsound ideas could engender. . . . [The] classical economists and the utilitarian thinkers . . . blithely assumed that what is reasonable will carry on merely on account of its reasonableness. They never gave a thought to the possibility that public opinion could favor spurious ideologies whose realization would harm welfare and well-being and disintegrate social cooperation.
>
> —Ludwig von Mises

Thanks to the Reagan administration's neglect, many Americans have come to view deregulation as a mistake. The gains—lower prices, better service, and greater efficiency—have come to be taken for granted, whereas the consequences of implementation difficulties—such as flight delays, labor disputes, hostile mergers and bankruptcies, and vague but troublesome safety and monopoly concerns—are viewed as grounds for reregulation. The change in popular opinion encouraged the 100th Congress to spend much of its time debating new health, safety, environmental, and mandated-benefit regulations, as well as proposals for airline and railroad reregulation. Almost all the gains of deregulation will be at risk during the next Congress.

The new administration should learn from past mistakes and devote the necessary resources to ensure that existing deregulation gains are preserved and future deregulation efforts are better implemented. Deregulation has become even more important over the last eight years, as mounting deficits have led Congress to rely more heavily on off-budget spending and regulation. The result is an increased regulatory burden on our economy. The magnitude of these costs is unclear; however, the burden of regulation has

73

certainly grown over the last decade.[1] Moreover, the fact that regulatory costs fall outside current budget-control procedures ensures that this policy option will become increasingly popular.

This chapter provides a summary of the regulation/deregulation issue. It offers suggestions for the new administration in light of the Reagan administration's admitted failures and examines new initiatives and the tactics needed to ensure their implementation.

How to Succeed in Deregulation

Presidents Ford and Carter (and President Reagan in his first few years in office) succeeded in deregulating key sectors of the economy, including the trucking industry, the airlines, the railroads, energy, telecommunications, and financial services. In each sector, regulations were eased or—less commonly—eliminated. Even the antitrust regulatory laws were eased. In these instances, there were several reasons for success in deregulation. First, extensive analysis supported a reduction in political constraints. Clearly, most economic regulations failed to enhance public welfare. Second, for various reasons, political support for economic regulation had declined. Finally, economic deregulation was perceived as antibusiness and thus aroused the ideological support of left/liberal groups. The new administration should learn from these experiences in developing support for deregulation.

Build Intellectual Support for Deregulation

Academic work often undermines the intellectual and moral cases for economic regulation. It has worked in the past: Deregulation efforts in the late 1970s, for example, were preceded by studies finding no valid rationale for most economic regulations. Such studies showed that rather than stabilizing and promoting healthy

---

[1]The last major effort to estimate the costs of regulation was conducted by Murray Weidenbaum, former head of the Council of Economic Advisers, in the early 1980s. He estimated that annual regulatory costs at that time were $100 billion. Since then, Congress has enacted numerous new regulations and the various regulatory agencies have promulgated or tightened existing regulations—a process that is still going on. The annual cost of the several mandated-benefit regulatory programs introduced in the 100th Congress alone would have totaled tens of billions of dollars. These proposed programs included an increase in the minimum wage, provisions for parental leave and daycare, and other programs to do "good things" with other people's money.

74

industries, economic regulations stifle technological change and productivity, increase costs, and reduce service quality. These analytical findings suggested the elimination or major curtailment of transportation, financial, and telecommunication regulations and even argued for the reform of social regulations. More recently, academic studies have led to the successful defeat of minimum-wage legislation.

The academic approach can also work in the future. Case studies of different regulatory policies at the state level would be instructive. For example, intrastate airline service in California and Texas was not regulated. These states' "natural experiments" demonstrated that lower transportation costs would likely follow deregulation. Such results can be extrapolated to the national situation to quantify the potential gains of deregulation. As in the past, when informed of these possible cost savings, interested parties will begin to lobby for federal deregulation. Professionals within the various regulatory agencies can be encouraged by such efforts and can begin to act as reform forces within the bureaucracy.

Build Political Support for Deregulation

Economic regulations are always supported by effective coalitions of well-organized ideological and economic interest groups, bureaucrats, and politicians. Deregulation requires dismantling pro-regulation coalitions. Ideological support for regulation often weakens as the public realizes who benefits from regulations—that is, business people rather than consumers. In the past, such evidence led liberals such as Ralph Nader and Sen. Edward M. Kennedy to champion the deregulation of the trucking industry and the airlines.[2]

Business support for regulation can be neutralized. In many cases, technological or institutional changes undercut the special

---

[2]Fortunately, such empirical analysis was limited in large part to the price impacts of deregulation. Now that the American people have experienced deregulation, they know that the higher prices paid under regulation were largely absorbed by organized labor. That fact was not fully appreciated by the unions. Had the Teamsters and the Air Line Pilots Association realized just how vulnerable their wage structures were to competition, they might have resisted deregulation far more vigorously. Moreover, had it been more widely realized that the primary beneficiary of regulation was labor, not the corporate shareholder, it is possible that left/liberal groups might never have supported deregulation.

75

protection from competition that regulation once provided. In the financial services area, for example, advances in the use of computers and telecommunications systems have made it possible for unregulated firms to offer deposit-like accounts. When inflation rose during the Carter years, these deregulated firms were able to offer more attractive interest rates. The result was a massive outflow of funds ("disintermediation") from the regulated financial services sector. Regulation became more a hindrance than a benefit to regulated firms and led some of them to support the elimination of the regulation holding down interest rates (Regulation Q). In effect, here and elsewhere, de facto deregulation has come before de jure regulation.[3] Technological change, fortunately, has not disappeared, and the new administration should take advantage of this fact to further liberate the economy.

Deregulation Slows Down

Introducing market forces into a government-controlled sector of the economy is akin to occupying hostile territory. Existing arrangements and loyalties are disrupted and new arrangements and new loyalties must swiftly be reestablished. Special interests disadvantaged by deregulation are swift to regroup and can be expected to fight for reregulation or its equivalent. Deregulation is always partial and tensions are inevitable between the freed and still-captive areas of the economy. If these tensions are not resolved—by further deregulation, privatization, or government reform—problems will emerge. Some of the gains made possible by deregulation will not be realized, and the adjustment costs will be excessive. More importantly, these problems will weaken the prospects for further deregulation.

Deregulation means change, and change is always disturbing. Some interest groups inevitably find themselves harmed by deregulation. The mechanics and pilots unions, for example, have found

[3]The interesting question is why such loopholes in the system of political control have not been swiftly closed by new legislation. The answer seems to be that enacting new regulations is not always easy. Once a new service has been offered, politicians must consider both the producers and the users. Regulation rarely serves both parties. Moreover, the agencies and congressional committees involved with the unregulated firms or the new technology may differ from those overseeing the original regulatory program. Maintaining political control is also difficult given the fact that technology changes more rapidly than politics.

their wage scales and work rules highly unrealistic in today's deregulated environment. Moreover, deregulation has freed the airline industry to experiment with new work rules and new institutional arrangements. Since such changes had been suppressed for decades, deregulation has resulted in major changes that would have evolved far more slowly and smoothly had the industry not been regulated. Firms experimented with new price/service options but quickly withdrew them if they proved unprofitable. All this appeared chaotic to those not familiar with markets. The Reagan administration failed to keep the public informed about these changes and the reasons behind them. The new administration can and should improve upon this performance.

One illustration of the problem in the Reagan administration was its handling of airline deregulation. The air travel system consists of three elements: the airlines, the airports, and the air traffic control system. Only the first of these three was deregulated. The latter two systems remained under political control. The result is an air travel industry that remains two-thirds regulated.

Airlines have become far more user-friendly, but the industry has suffered from the irrevocable rigidities associated with government mismanagement of the infrastructure. The problems that have emerged in airline deregulation, for example, stem largely from the failure of the federally controlled air traffic control system and the locally controlled airports to respond to the larger, more volatile traffic flows induced by deregulation.[4]

Bottlenecks have developed and delays are mounting. Such delays and crowding triggered further concerns about air travel safety and possible monopolies, but the resulting backlash could have been avoided had the Reagan administration moved rapidly to identify

---

[4]To achieve lower costs, the airlines moved to the hub-and-spoke system that now dominates air travel. The hub concept ("invented" by Frederick W. Smith of Federal Express) is a simple but profoundly important innovation that minimizes the number of aircraft and crews required to link various city-pairs. For example, to connect 10 city-pairs with nonstop direct flights requires 45 aircraft and crews, whereas to do so using the hub-and-spoke system requires only 9. As the hub-and-spoke system was implemented, load factors increased significantly and prices dropped, but delays also mounted as the federally controlled air traffic control system failed to adapt its operations to this new system. Deregulation must be accompanied by corresponding changes in infrastructure management if the benefits of a more user-friendly air travel system are to be achieved.

77

and resolve this problem. A new administration should complete the job of deregulation by ensuring that the infrastructure system is capable of responding to the demands of a deregulated industry.

The history of airline deregulation also illustrates the safety-enhancing value of deregulation. The new administration should note that airline deregulation has left intact all existing safety regulations, and that deregulation promotes safety. Airlines lose heavily when they experience an accident or even appear to be likely to have one. Airline travel has always been very safe; however, by making it possible for a careless or even unfortunate airline to go bankrupt (almost an impossibility under regulation), deregulation has created a new economic safety incentive.

Moreover, there is an excellent statistical case to be made that shows that air travel has indeed become safer since deregulation. Although the Reagan administration did make that point, it did so defensively and tentatively, as though it was surprised that the system had become safer. It should have done much more.

The new administration should point out that rational safety policies should not ground airlines or force fares to all-time highs. Higher costs translate into higher fares and thus reduce demand for air travel. Since air travel is far safer than land travel, we run the risk that overall safety may decline.[5] The debate is not between safety and costs but rather between safety and safety, in that higher costs may translate directly into lower safety. The risks associated with political safety regulation deserve far more consideration, and the new administration should begin immediately to force this topic onto the discussion agenda.

The administration should anticipate that those enjoying special privileges under regulation will shop around for some other government agency to champion their cause. Railroad deregulation, for example, eliminated the broker role of the Interstate Commerce Commission. Rates became a private matter between the individual shipper and railroad. Those having special political clout naturally

---

[5]Richard McKenzie of Clemson University argues that this modal-transfer impact has been extremely important in improving the overall safety of travel in the United States. Safety regulations that increase costs unduly may threaten these gains and make travel less safe. See Richard B. McKenzie and John T. Warner, "The Impact of Airline Deregulation on Highway Safety" (St. Louis: Washington University, Center for the Study of American Business, December 1987).

found this shift upsetting and sought some new champion. To a distressing degree, the Antitrust Division of the Department of Justice has rushed to accept that role. The Antitrust Division has long sought to expand its power over transportation and other regulated industries, and transportation deregulation has given it a great opportunity to do so. Since antitrust regulations retain considerable support, special interests can be expected to cloak their reregulation requests in antitrust colors.

Keys to Successful Strategy

Considerable effort will be required to get deregulation back on track. The Reagan administration's efforts to reform social regulations failed in part because the administration had sought major changes without first demonstrating that existing programs were performing poorly or that superior alternatives existed. If the deregulation effort is to advance beyond the economic area, the American public must gain a more realistic understanding of how government programs often fail and how markets frequently succeed. There is a need for a major expansion of research examining the actual performance of regulatory programs. The model for this work is the extensive research done on the Food and Drug Administration (the "drug lag" literature) by Sam Peltzman, Louis Lasagna, and others over the last several decades.[6]

Markets must not be viewed as rigid, frozen arrangements unable to address emerging concerns. The challenge is to flesh out the approach suggested by Ludwig von Mises in his response to "market-failure" concerns. Von Mises noted that although markets do fail, this fact is "not the outcome of alleged deficiencies inherent in the system of private ownership . . . [but rather] . . . a

---

[6]See Sam Peltzman, *Regulation of Pharmaceutical Innovation: The 1962 Amendments* (Washington: American Enterprise Institute, 1974); William Wardell and Louis Lasagna, *Regulation and New Drug Development* (Washington: American Enterprise Institute, 1974); Rita Ricardo-Campbell, "Drug Lag: Federal Government Decision Making," Hoover Institution Studies no. 55 (Stanford, 1976); General Accounting Office, *FDA Drug Approval: A Lengthy Process that Delays the Availability of Important New Drugs* (a report to the Subcommittee on Science, Research and Technology of the House Committee on Science and Technology, May 28, 1980); and Dale H. Gieringer, "Compassion vs. Control: FDA Investigational-Drug Regulation," Cato Institute Policy Analysis no. 72, May 20, 1986.

consequence of loopholes left in the system."[7] He went on to argue that such failures were best addressed "by a reform of the laws concerning liability for damages inflicted and by rescinding the institutional barriers preventing the full operation of private ownership."[8] Again, pro-choice economists should advance the "failure to allow markets" paradigm as an alternative to the now dominant market-failure model for public policy. That advance will not be easy, and the new administration must devote resources to that task. Moreover, case studies are needed of situations in which such property rights extensions have been effective.

The new administration should also avoid semantic traps that prejudge regulatory issues. Freedom from political control is not a special privilege granted to industries and activities that can prove their innocence. For example, firms free from antitrust regulations should not be viewed as having received a special "exemption." In a free society, political control should never become the accepted norm.

Aggressive Educational Campaign

The new administration should use the "bully pulpit" of the White House and the various federal agencies to free up the U.S. economy. In instances in which this approach has been used aggressively (for example, Secretary Drew Lewis speaking on gasoline taxes), it has had a major impact on public policy. The administration should also conduct an effective public education campaign to reduce the tensions created by deregulation. Unfortunately, the Reagan administration did little, creating an information void that was soon filled with misinformation from those hostile to deregulation. Deregulation, we were told, increased profits excessively, lowered service quality, compromised safety, and permitted monopolies everywhere. Numerous studies counter these myths, and the new administration should bring these studies to the public's attention.

Develop Deregulation Support

The new administration should also realize that deregulation is a political act. Success requires that political support for regulation

[7]Ludwig von Mises, *Human Action: A Treatise on Economics*, 3d ed. (Chicago: Henry Regnery Co., 1966), p. 657.

[8]Ibid, p. 658.

80

be reduced. Whenever a deregulation breakthrough occurs, the administration should identify and mobilize those people likely to benefit from it. For example, airline deregulation has made air travel possible for younger people, the elderly, and the less affluent; business also has gained as more frequent flights between cities and lower fares reduced transportation and logistics costs. Little effort, however, has been made to mobilize these interests, and thus there has developed little effective political support for deregulation. In contrast, groups losing out under deregulation—in particular, unions and expense-account travelers—have been very articulate and outspoken. When only one side is heard, we should not be surprised at the result. In the future, the administration should place high priority on mobilizing support for deregulation.

Whenever possible, of course, the new administration should seek to moderate or reduce the losses accompanying deregulation. Much of the opposition of business travelers stems from their inability to purchase priority flights. All air travel work is done on a first-come, first-served basis, making it impossible for those travelers having higher time values to improve their situation. The administration should encourage the time resource to be recognized by encouraging airports and the air traffic control system to price landing and air transit services accordingly. Deregulation need not imply inexpensive but lower-quality service; a free market can and should provide a range of service/price options.

Resources and Timing

The difficulties faced by the Office of Management and Budgets' Office of Information and Regulatory Affairs in its efforts to gain control over the regulatory burden in the past decade are similar to those OMB has faced in the effort to gain control over spending.[9] Regulations present an even more complex process; not only are the benefits of regulation difficult to determine, but so are its costs. We have few tools to estimate the costs of restricting or handicapping any specific economic activity and even less under-

---

[9]Cabinet agencies once submitted their budgets independently and protested vigorously when they were required to gain prior approval from a centralized budget office. That fight to coordinate and control the spending of the federal government continues today, but most analysts accept the need for such a role. A similar agreement has not yet been reached in the areas of regulation and loan guarantees.

81

standing of how such handicaps divert research and investment into less-productive avenues. Efforts to construct a regulatory budget are necessary but present great intellectual and practical difficulties.

The new administration must grant the regulatory policy area adequate priority and resources. It should appoint a new regulatory review task force headed by a top-level official (possibly the vice president). The task force should receive additional resources, specifically in the analytical area so as to improve its abilities to better account for the impact of regulations on the economy. The task force should examine the implementation problems arising in each deregulated area and propose solutions—such as privatization, additional deregulation, or public education—to resolve them. The new administration should begin as soon as possible to lay the groundwork for an eventual effort to restructure our approach in the social regulatory area. To that end, the task force should commission research papers addressing both the performance of current regulatory programs and the potential value of market alternatives.

Specific Deregulation Recommendations

The new Administration should secure and extend the deregulation gains and move to reform social regulations (mandated benefits, health, safety, and environmental regulations).

Air Travel

In the airline area, the defense of deregulation requires that the infrastructure problem be solved. That is best achieved by shifting operational control of the airports and air traffic control system first to the localities and ultimately to the users themselves. Free-market groups have worked out in some detail how best to achieve this reform, and the administration should work with the industry and Congress to craft a proposal that would meet the test of political feasibility. The administration should encourage local communities to adapt more market-oriented infrastructure management schemes and to monitor and document their experiences.[10] Concerns over airline safety and airline competitiveness should be addressed directly (see the discussion of safety and antitrust regulations below).

[10]See Robert W. Poole, Jr., "Privatizing the Air Traffic Control System" (Santa Monica, Calif.: Reason Foundation, November 19, 1986).

Trucking Industry

Trucking deregulation faces two problems: first, continued aggressive efforts by the Antitrust Division to extend antitrust regulations over this industry and, second, continued and even expanded state rate and entry regulation. The administration should treat the limited freedom from antitrust regulations that the trucking industry now enjoys as a natural experiment. The experiment could provide the data to reassure Congress and others that antitrust regulations are not necessary for such competitive industries as trucking.

The state regulation problem is complex. An argument can be made that the federal government should not preempt those regulations that impact only the citizens of a given state; however, most transportation regulations affect overall shipment costs and thus extend to citizens outside the state. At a minimum, the new administration should mount a major education campaign pointing out the costs of regulation to the citizens of heavily regulated states. Also, the Federal Trade Commission should target state transportation regulations under its consumer-intervention program.

Railroads

Railroad deregulation is also under serious attack. Several aggressive reregulation campaigns have been mounted and Congress came very close to enacting such legislation in 1987. The Reagan administration vigorously defended railroad deregulation, but it also allowed the Antitrust Division to critique the results of that deregulation. Consequently, there has been growing support for the view that the rail industry enjoys major monopoly power and that some form of government oversight remains essential over much, if not most, of the industry.

Rail deregulation is not yet 10 years old, and it is not surprising that many would still seek its reversal. However, the new administration should resist these pressures. An increasing fraction of freight rates are now handled through the use of contracts; moreover, shippers and the railroads are becoming increasingly sophisticated in negotiating mutually advantageous arrangements. If the political door remains closed, the industry will soon prefer market-determined rates and the clamor for political intervention will decline.

Telecommunications

There has been very little formal deregulation in the telecommunications industry. The regulators have gradually legitimized changes that technology has already ensured. Technological forces are still driving the process, and the new administration should take advantage of that fact to promote further deregulation. The current system is an uneasy blend of deregulated companies (AT&T and the other long-distance firms) competing with a range of partially regulated regional ("Baby Bell") companies. Both sides seek greater operating flexibility while resisting greater operating freedom for their competitors. The Baby Bells argue that they should be allowed to compete in all markets, while potential competitors argue that their regional "natural monopoly" status provides them with an unfair advantage.

The new administration should cut through this Gordian knot by encouraging local telephone deregulation. Technology now permits substantial competition in telecommunications even at the local level. Cellular telephones provide one option, as do satellite-dish or fiber-wired "smart" buildings. Simultaneously, the administration should authorize the widest possible telecommunications freedom for all companies.[11]

Financial Services

Financial services deregulation received considerable attention during the Reagan years. Because technology and institutional changes had transformed the industry in many ways, Congress and the regulators sought to reestablish control. Earlier outflows of funds from banks and savings and loan associations (S&Ls) into more lucrative money market accounts mandated the phaseout of deposit rate ceilings (Regulation Q) and the expansion of allowable activities for banks and S&Ls. However, Congress did little to loosen

---

[11]Some people who would normally favor free-market approaches argue that we cannot permit the regional telephone companies to compete in the deregulated area. Their argument seems to be that the regional companies would use their monopoly profits to dominate the competitive sector. I disagree. The chance that a local utility board would allow a Baby Bell to charge higher rates to permit subsidized service in the nonregulated sector seems small. Indeed, one can argue that local regulators might request rate reductions (thus imposing an economic penalty) on any Baby Bell seeking to enter the competitive market based on the premise that any additional profits should be shared with telephone users.

84

the restrictions on ownership, product lines, and location that have so fragmented the U.S. financial services industry. Nevertheless, economics and the reality of world competitive pressures are gradually forcing financial services firms into larger groupings, and institutional innovations are weakening many of the current regulatory restrictions.

However, financial deregulation will likely take a back seat in the next few years while the administration decides how best to handle the S&L crisis that has bankrupted the Federal Savings and Loan Insurance Corporation. The root of the problem is the federal deposit insurance system, which permits banks and S&Ls to attract deposits regardless of their economic condition. That creates a major moral hazard for the thrift industry, a hazard that has already resulted in losses approaching $100 billion.

The most likely scenario is for the S&L bailout to be accompanied by tightened regulatory controls over the entire financial services industry. Indeed, the minor S&L bailout during the 100th Congress included provisions restricting the growth and allowable activities of "nonbank" banks owned by diversified firms. Those regulatory pressures are still very much present today. The new administration therefore, faces a major challenge. It should develop and propose a package deal that would permit the industry to select continued deposit insurance and tightened government regulation or reduced deposit insurance and increased operating flexibility. The administration should propose such a plan as soon as feasible, and hearings should be held to obtain early comment and criticism. A revised plan should be available for consideration and passage during 1989.

Antitrust Reform

Congress has been considering a range of new antitrust laws that would roll back recent pro-consumer court decisions, which have provided more operating flexibility for U.S. firms. Bashing business remains politically popular, thereby encouraging further antitrust regulation. The new administration should form an antitrust reform working group headed by an official favorable to reform, possibly the new secretary of commerce. It should charge the group to commission research on the impact of antitrust policy on the ability of the United States to compete in world markets and to improve productivity at home. Similar questions should be asked about the impact of antitrust policies on cooperative research and development, on voluntary standard setting and professional self-regulation efforts, and on voluntary economic stabilization moves. The academic research on the efficiency costs of antitrust regulation should be summarized and disseminated by means of conferences and government publications. The goal should be an informed debate on the wisdom of expanding regulations predicated on the inefficiency of business and the wisdom of government.

Environmental Policy

Conservatives and liberals have shared a common belief that environmental concerns can be addressed only by political means. Yet, environmental regulations are now the most pervasive and costly of all regulations. There has been some criticism of environmental regulatory programs but almost always by groups seeking solutions outside the voluntary private sector. There is little awareness that as Ludwig von Mises noted, environmental problems result from the failures, first, to extend private property to such resources and, second, to enforce the "polluter-pays" principle.[12]

Risk Regulation

One of the dominant modern rationales for the expansion of government control over the economy has been the belief that government is a more effective means of managing risk. The risk-management rationale for government regulation accounts for most recent environmental regulations, most controls over new technologies, and many financial services regulations. The argument is made that an innovation may be risky (true) and therefore that someone must choose whether that innovation should or should not be introduced (true)—and therefore that a government agent must be selected to make that decision (false).

The new administration should point out the weakness of allowing any political agency to act as a gatekeeper for technological change. Political risk managers have every reason to treat new ideas as inherently more risky than the status quo. The risks of techno-

---

[12]For a more in-depth analysis of the complex issue of environmental deregulation, see Fred Smith, "What Environmental Policy?" in *Assessing the Reagan Years*, ed. David Boaz (Cato Institute, 1988), pp. 333–49. See also Fred Smith, *Law, Economics, and Civil Justice: A Reform Agenda for the '90s* (Free Congress Foundation, forthcoming).

logical innovation are weighed heavily, whereas the risks of technology stagnation receive little attention. Our current emphasis on addressing safety concerns through the delegation of ever more power to political regulatory agencies is a potential threat to the safety of our population. The administration should begin to tell this story.

This safety bias becomes increasingly serious as we create more and more product- and service-specific safety programs. A world in which a few politically salient products and services are made very safe (and very expensive) is likely to be a far more dangerous world for the average consumer. This problem should receive more attention. The wealthy already have access to safe transportation. Regulations that price safer alternatives beyond the reach of the poor are wrong.

Past administrations have failed to grasp the basic problem of political risk regulation: the inevitable bias of such a process against innovation and change. Consider a very simple situation in which an agency must decide to approve or disapprove of a new product (say, a novel pesticide or a new type of nuclear reactor). The agency can err in two ways: it can approve the product and find later that it was dangerous, or the agency can deny and never know.

Both types of error can have serious safety consequences. If the product is approved and subsequently found to be dangerous, the agency can expect to be called to Congress to explain its error. The agency and the professionals involved are likely to be castigated for incompetence. In contrast, if the agency disapproves of the product—or, as happens more commonly, delays any decision pending further data—it is likely to avoid most criticism. The only organized party harmed directly by the delay is the product's promoter, who thus has little credibility in the political environment of regulation. Those who are harmed by the disapproval of, say, a new drug to dissolve blood clots are not easily identifiable, even to themselves. Political regulatory bodies have a strong bias against approving any new or novel product or process. Yet, since most direct safety gains and most wealth increases (also a health-enhancing process) have been the result of such innovations, political regulation may be very risky to society.

The AIDS tragedy brings forward an informed and highly motivated group of individuals who desire greater freedom from the

87

restrictions imposed on the sick by the Food and Drug Administration (FDA). The AIDS crisis changes the framing of the traditional regulatory process in which profit-making firms petition their regulatory agency, and it has created the first pressures on the FDA to rethink its traditional bias against innovation.

One approach would be to require the FDA to conduct a post-regulatory approval audit. The FDA would track the improved effectiveness (improved health effects and lower costs) of those drugs surviving the regulatory process. As estimates of the improved marginal effectiveness of the products become available, the agency would apply those factors to the population that remains at risk during the regulatory approval process. The losses (higher fatality rates and increased morbidity) would then be calculated and reported in an annual report. This statistic would provide one estimate of the costs of delay and would encourage the FDA to take a more balanced view of the risks of innovation and delay.

The second reform that must take place is to restore the right of voluntary contract. Under a host of theories viewing the individual as incapable of rational choice, the right of contract has largely been destroyed in the United States. In many areas, no recourse has been left except to expand the role of government to reduce the inevitable problems that exist when individuals are not allowed to make their own arrangements. How best to restore that right remains unclear. Nevertheless, it should be a major goal of the new administration. The tort-reform effort is a less effective approach to that same goal and yet has received far more attention. Moreover, tort reform appears negative—the objective is to reduce compensation, limit standing, and eliminate pain-and-suffering payments. Such reforms can be defended but they are unlikely ever to attract popular support.

"Consumer-Protection" Legislation

One major growth area for government control of the economy arises from the belief that consumers need government help in an increasingly complex world. Consumers don't know everything and thus the government must require that information be provided and must assist consumers in obtaining that information. In fact, information is an attribute of a good that, like any other attribute, can be made available in greater or smaller quantities at various quality levels. Economists rarely believe that they are best equipped to determine the color of a product, its durability, its price, or even its function, but they are eager to discuss the need for "full disclosure" of information about the product and its attributes. These requirements, of course, have costs that are rarely considered by the regulators.

Consumers are confronted with lengthy information disclosures in almost every product they purchase, which present many facts that may or may not interest them. Information that consumers might desire is drowned out by the noise created by government-mandated disclosures. Some of the worst aspects of this policy are at the state level (for example, Proposition 65 in California). Merchants are required to scare their customers with low-probability possibilities. Eventually, we can imagine that prior to buying garden tools, every homeowner will be required to sit through the movie *The Texas Chainsaw Massacre*.

Conclusion

Efforts to bring about regulatory reform are in trouble. Congress is now considering not only a wide array of new and expanded social regulations but also reregulation proposals in the transportation area. Regulations already impose major costs on the U.S. economy, handicap entrepreneurial activities, make it harder for small businesses to succeed, and reduce U.S. competitiveness in world markets. Moreover, regulations reduce the rate of innovation, slowing our ability to compete in the future.

The new administration should move swiftly to address these threats. In doing so, it should realize that the current situation reflects the failure of the Reagan administration to respond adequately to the deregulation challenge. Partial deregulation inevitably creates tensions between the freed and the still politically controlled portions of the economy. Deregulation, like any complex task, must be actively implemented, and that requires resources. Lacking any coherent implementation plan, deregulation has encountered unnecessary problems. These have reduced the potential benefits and weakened support for deregulation. Moreover, the Reagan administration failed to make the intellectual investment necessary to ensure consideration of voluntary market alternatives in the social regulatory area.

The new administration should assign to regulatory policy the priority and staff it warrants. The goal should be to ensure that every proposed new regulation receives at least the scrutiny received by a direct spending proposal. Such scrutiny will become increasingly essential, as tighter budgets make regulations more popular with the political entrepreneurs. The challenge is to make the costs of regulation more politically visible and thus to use these costs to mobilize more effective political opposition. The post-regulatory approval audit is one reform directed to that end.

The next administration must also insist on a comparative analysis of the relative value of market versus political approaches in areas in which new regulations are proposed. Placing a "government-failure" spotlight on existing regulatory regimes would help ensure a more balanced policy debate. For too long, antitrust, health, safety, consumer protection, and environmental regulations have enjoyed immunity from criticism.

Most importantly, the new administration must counter the view that sees markets as static and rigid but idealizes regulatory agencies as dynamic and flexible. Where analysis has been conducted, regulatory agencies have been found wanting. Unfortunately, there has been too little work in these areas. A twofold approach is dictated: first, the administration should require all agencies to consider market approaches prior to moving forward with their legislative agenda; second, the administration should periodically assess the actual achievements of existing regulatory programs. This effort to ensure a more balanced review of the pros and cons of political versus private approaches is essential to any broad-scale reassessment of regulatory policy.

6. "Black Monday" and Reforming the Capital Markets

S. David Young

On August 25, 1987, the Dow-Jones industrial average closed at its all-time high of 2722, the culmination of an extraordinary five-year bull market. Stock prices drifted lower for the next two months and then collapsed on "Black Monday," October 19. On that day the market lost nearly one-quarter of its capitalized value. Predictably, newspaper and television commentators evoked memories of the 1929 market crash and the devastating depression that followed. A presidential task force was appointed, chaired by Nicholas Brady of the Dillon, Read investment banking firm, to investigate the causes of the crash and recommend reforms. Meanwhile, Congress began conducting its own hearings, with several of its members calling for a larger government role in regulating financial markets.

In the deliberations of the Brady commission and other investigative panels, suspicion fell on two highly publicized financial innovations that became popular during the bull market: portfolio insurance and program trading. The commission concluded that the market dive was caused largely by a small number of institutions using these strategic tools, both of which rely on the use of stock index futures. This chapter discusses the controversy and assesses several of the proposals for reform.

The Accused

Stock index futures enable investors to place bets on where the stock market is going without buying or selling stocks. First introduced in 1982, index futures give portfolio managers a chance to hedge their stock portfolios. In so doing, index futures work much like the agricultural futures that have been traded in Chicago for over a century. But instead of corn, wheat, or soybeans serving as the deliverable commodity, these new financial futures use "bas-

91

kets" of stocks. Hence, a short, or selling, position in stock index futures requires the holder to "deliver" a basket of stocks if the position is held to the expiration date of the contract. A long, or buying, position requires acceptance of delivery of the stocks if held to expiration. Of course, delivering an index of stocks is not really possible; index futures use a delivery procedure known as cash settlement, in which traders' accounts are adjusted with bookkeeping entries instead of there being delivery of a physical commodity such as stock certificates.

Before the crash there was a popular hedging strategy using index futures. At first it was known by its formal, academic title, "dynamic hedging," but later it came to be known by the unfortunate term "portfolio insurance," which was adopted because it sounded better. (Why this term is unfortunate will soon become apparent.)

In this strategy, money managers sell stocks as the market goes down, with the proceeds invested in risk-free securities such as U.S. Treasury bills. As the market rebounds, funds are taken from the risk-free side of the portfolio and reinvested in stocks. The idea is to provide a floor return for the portfolio in the event of a serious market decline, while also allowing the portfolio to participate in favorable market movements.

To understand how this strategy works, one must recognize that dynamic hedging is essentially equivalent to purchasing a put option on a stock portfolio or index. A put option on a stock index gives the option holder the right, but not the obligation, to sell a basket of stocks at a prearranged "strike" or "exercise" price. In effect the purchase of a put option locks in a floor price for the stock portfolio and therefore is the closest thing to real insurance in the stock market.

For some portfolio managers, however, put options with the desired strike price and maturity (that is, time to expiration) may not be available on the options exchanges. For instance, managers may wish to insure their portfolios for a year or more, but the most popular index option—the Chicago Board Options Exchange's S&P 100 or OEX option—is available only with maturities of four months or less. By carefully buying and selling stocks in the manner just described, however, portfolio strategists can create a "synthetic" option possessing the desired strike price and maturity.

At first, money managers implemented these strategies by purchasing and selling stocks directly on the floor of the New York Stock Exchange (NYSE). But strategists soon realized that the same effect could be achieved in less time and at much lower transaction costs by taking positions in future contracts. Because the contracts represent baskets of stocks traded on the exchanges, a short position in futures is essentially the same as selling a portfolio of stocks outright, just as a long position is the same as buying a portfolio of stocks. Thus, as markets fall, portfolio insurers sell futures contracts; as stock prices recover, insurers buy back the futures.

Among the many charges leveled against portfolio insurance is that it contributed to inflated precrash prices by lulling money managers into a false sense of security. As more managers thought they were protected by their portfolio-insurance programs, the less restrained their buying became, which boosted high stock prices even higher. Put another way, the big institutional investors kept on buying stocks long after prices had reached levels that were unsupportable by economic fundamentals. When a downturn began and everyone sought protection at the same time, this supposedly fail-safe system broke down. Portfolio insurance became, as one observer described it, like trying to buy collision insurance for your automobile as it careens toward a fire hydrant.[1]

Of course, any system that causes managers of large funds to think they have protection against a bear market is likely to make them less cautious. Yet, even at the height of its popularity, portfolio insurance never covered more than $80 billion of assets—in a market with a capitalized value of well over $2 trillion. A sizable portion of these funds would certainly have been invested in the stock market anyway. Therefore, the incremental funds remaining in the stock market because of portfolio insurance are unlikely to have been responsible for the inflated stock prices of the precrash period. In fact, a recent study shows that portfolio insurance contributed to less than 5 percent of the increase in the value of American stocks between January 1987 and the crash.[2] It should also be noted that the firms that adopted insurance programs were generally more averse to risk than firms that did not obtain such insurance. Hence,

[1]Joel A. Bleeke, "Portfolio Insurance: When, Not What," *Wall Street Journal*, December 11, 1987.

[2]Committee of Inquiry Appointed by the Chicago Mercantile Exchange to Examine the Events Surrounding October 19, 1987, Draft of Final Report, June 13, 1988, p. 7.

many of them would likely have been heavy sellers during the crash even without a formal insurance program.[3]

In the days immediately preceding Black Monday, stock prices dropped because of fears of renewed inflation and higher interest rates, a persistent trade deficit, and the threat of a new corporate tax on mergers and acquisitions. Sharply lowered stock prices in New York triggered portfolio-insurance activity in Chicago. As prices declined, the insurers' computer programs instructed them to sell heavily in the futures markets, which they did mostly in the S&P 500 pit at the Chicago Mercantile Exchange. The short, or selling, end of futures trading was so heavy that the futures were selling at sizable discounts to their theoretical (that is, arbitrage-free) values. This pricing discrepancy attracted another group of participants in the futures markets—the index arbitrageurs.

These traders—"index arbs" for short—who were also targeted for blame by the Brady Commission, try to earn quick arbitrage profits from the temporary pricing discrepancies that sometimes arise between markets by launching simultaneous, computer-driven program trades of huge blocks of stocks in New York and index futures in Chicago. Hence, index arbs are sometimes called program traders (although program trading also encompasses activities other than index arbitrage).

As portfolio-insurance activity drove the price of index futures below their theoretical levels on the days leading up to and including October 19, program traders stepped in to buy the relatively cheap futures in Chicago while selling baskets of stocks in New York. Not surprisingly, this activity drove stock prices even lower. In effect, program trading transmitted the selling pressure in the futures pits, initiated by the portfolio insurers, to the floor of the NYSE. As prices in New York dropped still further, insurance programs triggered another round of selling in the futures pits, and the process just described started all over again. This type of market activity—a seemingly endless cycle of portfolio insurance and index arbitrage ratcheting stock prices lower and lower—is the focus for so much of the resentment against the futures pits and computer-driven trading strategies.

---

[3]Mark Rubinstein, "Portfolio Insurance and the Market Crash," *Financial Analysts Journal* (January-February 1988): 38.

Before blaming these strategies for the crash, however, we should first acknowledge the limits to this "cascade" phenomenon.[4] When futures are selling at huge discounts in terms of their theoretical values, there is a decline in the attractiveness of futures as a hedging vehicle. It should be remembered that insurers *sell* futures in declining markets; hence, discounts on index futures reduce the proceeds to sellers and thereby effectively increase the cost of the insurance. Indeed, by late afternoon on Black Monday, the markets were in such disarray and index futures were selling at such discounts that practically all insurance activity ceased. This fact suggests that the role of portfolio insurance in the market crash was overstated by the financial news media and by the numerous panels charged with investigating the crash.

Moreover, some of the concerns expressed by the Brady Commission and others regarding portfolio insurance may already have dissipated, simply because the product did not work as advertised. Before the crash the success of portfolio insurance depended on two preconditions: low transaction costs and more or less price-continuous markets. Both of these conditions were seriously violated during the crash.[5]

The transaction costs of portfolio-insurance strategies include more than just brokers' commissions. Large differences between futures prices and prices in the cash market (as described earlier) can also impose heavy costs. During the crash, some insurers were able to avoid this problem because they could implement an insurance program directly by selling stocks, just as all insurers did before the advent of stock index futures. Most money managers using the strategy were not so lucky, however.

Discontinuous markets were also a problem. The last 200-point drop in the Dow-Jones average occurred so quickly that many futures sales called for by insurance programs simply could not be executed. The designers of the strategy were unprepared for such a rapid and staggering market decline.

In response to problems with portfolio insurance that arose during the crash, investment firms have since devised option-replica-

[4]Paula A. Tosini, "Stock Index Futures and Stock Market Activity in October 1987," *Financial Analysts Journal* (January-February 1988): 31.

[5]For an extended discussion of this issue, see Rubinstein, pp. 38–41.

tion strategies that provide much the same protection as the old portfolio-insurance approach but without relying on futures markets. In one such program the desired long-term put option is synthetically created with a portfolio of short-term, exchange-traded options. The portfolio of options is structured in such a way that once the hedge is established, portfolio managers can leave it alone for several weeks. Under the old approach, frequent trading of futures was required to create the synthetic option. Under the new approach, if prices decline sharply in New York, trading in the futures or options pits is unnecessary because the desired hedge is already in place.

Program trading has also come under intense criticism. Despite overwhelming evidence that index arbitrage affects only the route by which buy and sell orders reach the NYSE,[6] the activity has come under attack from many legislators and market professionals. The NYSE has even banned the use of its computerized order-routing system by program traders on days when the Dow-Jones average swings up or down by more than 50 points.

A recent study suggests several reasons for this hostility, including a fear on the part of some institutional investors that brokerage firms are "front running"—trading index futures to profit on the knowledge of their customer's impending order in the stock market.[7] Stock traders in New York resent program trading because of the strains that it sometimes imposes on the order-processing capabilities of the NYSE. Finally, some market professionals believe—albeit without supporting evidence—that program trading contributes to both excessive market volatility and a loss of investor confidence in the financial markets. Yet, as the same study points out, even the Brady commission's own report notes that the markets

---

[6]To illustrate this point, if declining stock prices trigger heavy futures selling by insurers, price discounts on the futures attract a round of program trading. The program traders, who then buy the futures and sell stocks, transmit the initial selling pressure from futures to the NYSE. Of course, insurers may choose to forgo the futures markets and sell stocks directly. Either way, however, heavy selling by insurers, whether of stock indexes or of stocks themselves, exerts selling pressure in New York. The only difference is that in the first case, program traders serve as an intermediary between the futures exchange and the stock market. The same general argument applies when insurers exert buying pressure on the markets.

[7]Committee of Inquiry, p. 9.

were most chaotic precisely when the arbitrage link between Chicago and New York was broken.

The Real Villains

The case against portfolio insurance and program trading is further weakened by the fact that, although the two strategies never really caught on in foreign markets, the crash was international in scope.[8] Even in countries without index futures markets or portfolio insurance, prices fell just as much and market conditions were just as chaotic as in the United States. Moreover, prolonged periods of high volatility in U.S. markets in the weeks and months after the crash and after portfolio insurance had been largely abandoned suggest that other, more important factors were at work.

Portfolio insurance and program trading can hardly be blamed for the widespread panic that ensued on the afternoon of October 19. By that time, the market was in a free fall, rendering useless any computer-driven strategies. For the most part the portfolio insurers and program traders were on the sidelines in the final hour of trading, waiting for the markets to settle. And it was in this final hour that much of the day's loss was incurred. Critics of portfolio insurance and program trading, including the Brady commission, appear to have overstated the role of large institutional investors and underestimated the role of small investors in causing the market to plummet as dramatically as it did.

On Black Monday the NYSE's computerized trading system broke under the sheer weight of the unprecedented trading volume. At over 600 million shares, the trading volume doubled the previous daily record. With a trading system unable to handle the volume, price quotes were delayed. Financial markets run on information, and when vital information is delayed, investors panic. Instead of having firm and up-to-the-minute price quotes and then being able to execute an order in the usual one minute, traders had no idea how far prices for a given stock had fallen. To make matters worse, when an order was entered, confirmation was delayed. A trader did not know at what price a trade had been executed or even whether the trade had actually been executed.

Although block-trading activity—trades of 5,000 shares or more—

[8]Rubinstein, p. 42.

was high on Black Monday and the day after, it represented only about 50 percent of total business, a situation that has been normal since the mid-1980s. The volume of nonblock trades, which were made mostly by individual investors and not by the large institutions, far exceeded the previous high. The panic caused by the mechanical breakdown in the system came from frantic selling by a large number of small investors and not, as alleged by some commentators, from a small number of large investors. It hardly seems fair, then, to place so much responsibility for the market collapse on large institutional investors and their trading strategies.

Since October 1987 the NYSE's trading structure has come under intense scrutiny, especially because of its specialist system. Each stock on the exchange is assigned to one of several specialist firms, which are then given a monopoly right to make a market in that stock. In exchange for this lucrative monopoly, specialists are expected to maintain an orderly market, matching buy and sell orders from the investing public so that each trade is as close as possible in price to the previous trade. To carry out this function, specialists must sometimes commit their own money to buy stocks when there are no other buyers or sell when there are no other sellers. When sell orders flooded the market on Black Monday, however, many specialists were simply unable to cope. The Brady commission found that nearly a third of the NYSE's specialists sold more shares on October 19 than they bought, "effectively pouring gasoline on an already raging fire."[9]

Another major culprit was an outdated rule requiring specialists to maintain capital equal only to the value of 1,250 shares of each stock assigned to them. No attempt was made to adjust the capital requirements for a particular stock's trading volume or for its price volatility. Not surprisingly, specialists' capital had failed to keep pace with the rapid growth of trading volume in the 1980s. (Despite the considerable problems with the specialist system, no other mechanism did better in maintaining market liquidity, and many did far worse. The market-making system in the over-the-counter market, for example, was a near total failure, as many market makers simply declined to answer their phones.)

[9]Steve Swartz, "Study Raises Serious Questions About Performance of Specialists," *Wall Street Journal*, January 11, 1988.

The Prescriptions

The NYSE is taking steps to shore up the chronic undercapitalization of specialists. For example, large brokerage firms are now allowed to buy specialist firms, which will certainly deepen the specialists' pockets. Also, to ease the strain on its specialists, the NYSE is planning improvements to its order-processing system so that trading volumes comparable to Black Monday's may be easily accommodated.

The NYSE has also reached an agreement with the Chicago Mercantile Exchange on a series of coordinated trading halts. The program is aimed at boosting investor confidence by preventing another market free-fall. The idea draws on a Brady commission recommendation to install "circuit breakers" to slow or temporarily halt trading in a market crisis. Whenever the S&P 500 futures contract drops by the equivalent of 100 points in the Dow-Jones average, the Chicago exchange would suspend trading for 30 minutes. Should the Dow drop by 250 points, the NYSE would close for 60 minutes—and double that if a subsequent drop of 150 points occurs.

This unprecedented cooperation between New York and Chicago, each of which had been blaming the other for the crash, is certainly an encouraging sign. Still, serious doubts remain about whether such moves would suppress volatility in a crisis or promote orderly markets. Price limits on agricultural commodities have been around for years, but there is little evidence that they reduce price volatility. And should the market fall far enough to trigger the price limits, portfolio managers who are unable to short index futures to protect their holdings will almost certainly try to dump stocks, which would only worsen a weakening market.

Circuit breakers such as price limits might spread a major market move over a few days instead of a few hours, but it should be noted that countries with daily price limits did no better during the 1987 crash than other countries. Price limits may be able to compress volatility and restore order when trading imbalances are temporary in nature, but when more fundamental changes in market value occur, investors will feel a great urgency to sell before the limits can block them. In other words, limits can become self-fulfilling as traders scramble to get out of markets approaching the limits. In essence, then, limits would act as price magnets.

No price-limit rule can distinguish between panic and fundamentally justified price changes. Price limits did little to ease the silver crisis a few years ago; there were 17 successive days when the price dropped to its limit.[10] If fundamental changes in market value are under way, price limits could trap investors into positions that increase their risks. Investors could be in such a hurry to exit that the market could go "limit-down" as soon as it opened the next day. Days might pass before everyone who wanted to sell would be able to.

Another popular suggestion for reform, and an idea widely supported in New York and Washington, is that the futures exchanges should be required to raise their margins on index futures to the same 50 percent level used in the stock market. Lower margin requirements make futures easier to buy. Funds that would otherwise be invested in stocks or other "worthy" securities, so the theory goes, are instead devoted to speculative activities in the futures pits. However, institutional investors account for most of the open interest (that is, outstanding contracts) in index futures. These investors use futures to hedge, not speculate; many are even prohibited by fund bylaws or policies from speculating in index futures. This fact challenges the notion that low futures margins lever up the market and increase volatility. In fact, the performance of stock markets outside the United States indicates no association between severity of the crash and margin requirements.

There are also important differences between margin on stocks and margin on futures. Under the current margin requirement for stocks, set by the Federal Reserve Board, investors can buy stocks for half the purchase price and borrow the rest from their brokers. Stock margins, therefore, are down payments: the buyer receives a loan for the remaining cost of the stock, which he or she will then own and control. In contrast, a futures contract on a stock index does not establish a claim on stock certificates. A futures margin, which is set by the exchange that trades the contract, is not an extension of credit but a performance bond paid by both the buyer and seller to ensure that they will honor their obligations. There is no loan.

Futures exchanges base margins on the need to protect their

---

[10]Fischer Black, quoted in Robert E. Norton, "The Battle Over Market Reform," *Fortune*, February 2, 1988, p. 24.

financial integrity. In so doing they strive to maintain a balance between the need to insure against the risk of customer defaults, on the one hand, and the need to avoid margins that are so high as to inhibit trading, on the other. A logical reason for lower margins in futures is that futures markets post gains and losses to traders' accounts each trading day, in a process called "marking-to-market." Any shortfalls result in margin calls, in which traders either put up more money within a day or see their positions liquidated. Because the futures exchanges settle traders' accounts daily, their margins have usually approximated the maximum price move likely in a single day, with a built-in safety factor. When price volatility increases, so do margin requirements. In contrast, stock traders have several days to come up with the money, so their margin requirements must ensure that they pay enough to cover price moves lasting more than one day. In effect, stockbrokers substitute larger cash deposits (that is, higher margins) for the quicker collection procedures used by the futures exchanges.

Finally, margin requirements in the stock market apply only to individual stocks, whereas index futures relate to portfolios of stocks. A well-accepted principle of finance is that the price volatility of a portfolio of stocks is less than that of the stocks that compose it. It is true because the price volatility of some individual stocks in the portfolio partially offsets the price volatility of other stocks in the portfolio. Hence, if the function of margins is to protect the financial integrity of the exchanges, margins on baskets of stocks should be lower than on individual stocks.[11]

Conclusion

Much of the concern over the events of October 1987 reflects confusion and misunderstanding about the extraordinary changes that have taken place in financial markets in the 1980s. Investors now face a bewildering array of financial instruments, some of which rival common stocks in importance. For example, the critical economic function of price discovery occurs in the futures markets, not in New York. Some market analysts now argue that futures-based trading strategies—namely, portfolio insurance and program

[11]Committee of Inquiry, p. 20.

trading—far from worsening the crash, kept it from lasting longer.[12] These strategies merely accelerated a process of price adjustment that sooner or later would have been triggered anyway. Legislators and regulatory authorities should think carefully before trying to resist these developments. As a recent editorial in *The Economist* says, "Their efforts would prove as futile as every Luddite urge in history."[13]

In many ways, American capital markets still enjoy a comparative advantage over foreign competitors. Our markets are more liquid, information is more plentiful, and American investment professionals tend to be better trained than their foreign counterparts. Moreover, recent scandals notwithstanding, ethical standards on Wall Street compare favorably with those in practically every major capital market in the world. However, as markets become increasingly internationalized, as communications systems improve, and as foreign markets become better capitalized, American dominance will be seriously challenged. The capitalized value of stocks on the Tokyo Stock Exchange already exceeds the value of stocks on the NYSE. Heavy-handed regulation of our capital markets—for example, restrictions on portfolio insurance and program trading, price limits, or government control of futures margins—would be an open invitation to both American and foreign investors to take their business elsewhere. Such a threat could not have been taken seriously a few years ago, when investment opportunities outside the United States were relatively sparse. But that is no longer the case.

If there is one market phenomenon that nearly all observers can agree on, it is that today's institutions respond to changes in investor psychology with more speed and power than ever before. The introduction of stock index futures and options has made it possible for large institutions to buy and sell large blocks of stock practically in an instant. This trend has been enhanced by rapid advances in computer technology. These developments point out the critical importance of the two steps toward reform that have true merit: expanding capital requirements for specialists and improving the order-processing capabilities of the NYSE. These reforms are essen-

[12]Avner Arbel, Steven Carvel, and Erik Postnieks, "The Smart Crash of October 19," *Harvard Business Review* (May-June 1988): 124.

[13]"Stopping Another Crash," *The Economist*, March 19, 1988, p. 14.

tial if stock-market professionals are to maintain liquid and orderly markets when deluged with large orders.

In conclusion, the following is a summary of the policy recommendations made in this chapter:

- Margins on stock index futures should continue to be set by the futures exchanges and not mandated by regulatory authorities.
- Price limits should be resisted. At the very least, limits should be wide enough to allow substantial corrections in stock prices without the limits being triggered.
- The NYSE's trading system requires substantial reform. Computer capacity for its order-routing system must be improved, and capital requirements for specialists should be increased.
- The problems associated with portfolio insurance have largely self-corrected. Efforts to regulate insurance activities, therefore, should be opposed.
- The role of program trading in correcting pricing discrepancies across markets should be acknowledged. Because the principal effect of restrictions on program trading, including the rule recently adopted by the NYSE, will be to reduce market efficiency, any further restrictions should be opposed.

7. A Market Approach to the Savings and Loan Crisis

Catherine England

The financial services sector facilitates the operation of the rest of the economy by performing two basic functions. One is that financial firms move money to the highest valued use by gathering information and acting as intermediaries between savers and borrowers. The other is that financial institutions help individuals spread risk by pooling their resources.

To be able to perform these functions, and thereby help promote broadly based economic growth, the financial services sector needs to be both stable and efficient. Unfortunately, though, current government policies make it difficult to achieve these objectives. Federal laws and regulations applied to banks, savings and loan associations, insurance companies, securities firms, and the real estate markets introduce instability, and many government practices encourage excessive risk taking. Financial institutions are limited in their ability to diversify their portfolios, are kept from adapting to changing market conditions, and are constrained in their ability to efficiently serve consumer and business markets.

These are serious charges. They are meant to be. To correct existing problems, it is necessary to understand how current policies are counterproductive vis-a-vis their stated goals.[1]

Government Failures

It is widely accepted that the banking industry is inherently unstable. Because bankers hold only a portion of their deposits as liquid reserves and use those deposits to fund illiquid loans, it is

[1]This chapter is intended to consider the future of the broadly defined financial services industry. But the most serious problems are found among depository institutions, and the regulatory responses to these strains lie at the center of debates about the future of the broader financial sector. Consequently, much of what follows focuses on the regulation of depository institutions.

argued that an unregulated banking system would be exposed to periodic panics and collapses that could disrupt the broader economy.

This line of reasoning is disturbing for those who believe that markets generally behave rationally. In the several centuries that bankers have offered their services, why has no superior system developed? It is difficult to believe that an economic function as important as banking can be carried out only through inherently unstable institutions.

An alternative to the generally accepted market failure view deserves further attention. Although many scholars have described how specific government policies have undermined the stability of the banking system, few have asked more basic questions. For example, has a history of government intervention in monetary and banking arrangements prevented the market from developing a superior financial system? And has the observed instability been caused by government policies rather than by an inherent flaw in the market? A strong case can be made that the widely identified problems in the banking industry can be more accurately attributed to policy failures rather than to market failures.

To explore this case, three government failures are discussed here: (1) the problems with federal deposit insurance, (2) the government's misdirected failure resolution policies, and (3) the problems introduced by an inflexible regulatory apparatus.

Instability through Federal Deposit Insurance

Federal deposit insurance was introduced to add stability to the banking system. Because depositors are presumed to be unable to differentiate healthy banks from unsound ones, federal guarantees were designed to protect banks from unfounded panic-driven withdrawals by depositors and to give banking regulators an opportunity to close insolvent banks or thrift institutions in an orderly manner. Given the economic chaos of the 1930s, the arguments made by proponents of federal deposit insurance carried considerable weight, especially as the program offered a means of doing something tangible to address the depression-era banking crisis.

Not everyone in the early 1930s was enthusiastic about introducing federal deposit insurance, however. In fact, the banking industry, in the form of the American Bankers Association and several state banking organizations, registered its strong opposition to the introduction of federal guarantees of deposits.[2]

Critics argued that federal deposit insurance would lead depositors to become indifferent about the relative stability of insured banks. In a brief filed with the House Committee on Banking and Currency, the American Bankers Association described the consequences of introducing federal guarantees: "[The deposit guaranty plan] proposes to place the reckless and speculative banks on the same level with the best managed and the most conservative, which will lead to competition calculated to drag all of them down to the least meritorious."[3] Thus, it was recognized as early as 1932 that removing depositors as a source of market discipline would free more aggressive bank managers to pursue additional risks in a search for higher profits, a phenomenon we now call moral hazard.[4]

These early criticisms of federal deposit guarantees were prescient. It has become increasingly apparent that few federally insured depositors care how bank and thrift managers invest their funds. Indeed, depositor apathy has progressed to the point of so-called rate chasing. Frequently, individuals holding accounts in failed S&Ls have taken their federal deposit insurance checks and deposited them with whatever institution is then paying the highest rate on deposits—without asking any questions about the financial health of their new thrift, and confident in the knowledge that the government guarantees not only principal but also accrued interest. And although federal regulation is supposed to replace depositor oversight, it is apparent that federal examiners who visit a bank twice a year are no match for innovative depository managers searching for new ways to enhance the profitability of their institutions.

[2]For a more extensive discussion of the debate over federal deposit insurance, see Helen M. Burns, *The American Banking Community and New Deal Banking Reforms, 1933–1935* (Westport, Conn.: Greenwood Press, 1974).

[3]Thomas B. Paton, "Federal Guaranty Fund for Bank Depositors," brief in behalf of the American Bankers Association filed with the House Committee on Banking and Commerce, April 9, 1932.

[4]The term "moral hazard" comes from the insurance industry. It refers to the tendency of individuals, once they have obtained insurance, to take less care to avoid the insured-against event. Unless the insurer takes steps to encourage more prudent behavior among clients, the insurance company will face a greater risk than the uninsured individual would have encountered.

To make matters worse, the government has expanded the range of its deposit guarantees considerably during the 55-year experiment with federal deposit insurance. Not only has the minimum size of fully protected deposits increased, but the Federal Deposit Insurance Corporation (FDIC) and other federal banking authorities have also developed closure policies that generally protect all depositors, regardless of the size of their account. In some cases, federal protection has been extended beyond depositors to the general creditors of the bank and bank holding company. Thus, even the discipline expected from larger, presumably more sophisticated depositors and general creditors has been muted by federal policies.

The presence of federal deposit insurance has reduced the stability of the banking industry by alleviating depository managers of the need to compete for customers on the basis of sound banking practices and financial health. The system designed to eliminate unfounded panics has created an environment in which individuals knowingly place large sums of money in insolvent institutions to earn a slightly higher return on their deposits. Depositors are no longer running from unsound institutions; in many cases they are running to them. This places the entire supervisory burden on federal examiners. By its nature, however, centralized supervision is inadequate to replace depositor discipline.

Instability through Eliminating Failures

This situation would be dangerous enough if federally insured institutions were closed promptly when stockholder equity was exhausted. Depositors and the insurance fund would be largely protected, incompetent or overly aggressive managers would be out of a job, and stockholders who had failed to insist on prudent management behavior would lose their investments. But current regulatory policies delay or prevent the exit of uneconomic depository institutions, and by doing so, they compound rather than alleviate government-sponsored risk. Moral hazard is made more pronounced, healthy institutions are penalized, and an industry marked by overcapacity is prevented from restructuring itself.

The moral hazard introduced by federal deposit insurance has been compounded by the realization among depository managers that there may be long delays between the insolvency of an institution and its closure. Such policies further weaken the incentive to pursue a stable course. Why behave cautiously when managers of insolvent institutions often are given years to attempt to correct their mistakes? Why pursue a prudent path when large numbers of depositors decide where to place their funds solely on the basis of the interest rates paid?

By failing to deal promptly with insolvent depositories or by providing financial assistance to failing institutions, regulators reinforce depositors' lack of concern about the financial health of their banks and S&Ls, and federal authorities send depository managers a message that undermines the impact of threats of regulatory action directed at inappropriate behavior. Rather than taking steps, as private insurers do, to alleviate the moral hazard problem, the federal guarantors have pursued actions that compound the problem.

The failure on the part of federal regulators to allow the financial market to rid itself of dead wood also penalizes healthy institutions. Several hundred insolvent S&Ls continue to gather deposits and make loans. Many other uneconomic banks and thrifts have received regulators' attention only to be supported through government-sponsored bailouts and below-market loans. These practices have skewed the competitive environment in a way that has encouraged even conservatively managed banks and thrifts to move toward portfolios embodying more risk.

The managers and owners of insolvent or near-insolvent depository institutions focus on short-term survival. They bid up interest rates paid on deposits and force down interest rates charged for loans as they seek to cover near-term cash commitments and pursue riskier investments in the hope of a quick killing that will recapitalize their ailing institutions. Healthier depositories, forced to compete with these zombies, must often match, or at least approach, the uneconomic rates set by the riskiest portion of the industry.[5]

[5]Higher interest rates on deposits and lower rates on loans are among the important benefits that have accrued to consumers as a result of relaxing the geographic protections long enjoyed by so many banks. But the government's decision to allow hundreds of insolvent S&Ls to continue operating has unloosed on the financial markets competitors who have nothing more to lose by attracting funds through promises to depositors of ever-higher rates. In addition, these institutions often need new sources of cash just to meet current operating expenses. Indeed, these operations have been compared to Ponzi schemes. For a recent discussion of the

The long-term survival of the solvent banks and thrifts is made even more difficult when bailout and merger deals give troubled depositories a cost advantage over their healthier counterparts. To minimize short-term cash outlays and avoid politically undesirable failures, the federal authorities often agree to strip problem institutions of their bad loans, guarantee the income from the remainder of their portfolio, and throw in tax concessions for good measure. Thus, a depository that should have been closed is rebuilt with federal assistance into an institution that has advantages over competitors that have not required assistance.

Finally, increasingly integrated domestic and international financial markets, coupled with legal and regulatory changes, have created a need for industry restructuring, a need that is being thwarted by government efforts to prevent failures.

Rapid advances in communications technology have allowed high-quality corporate borrowers to gain direct access to the credit markets, while depositors have expanded their search for institutions in which to place their money. Nationwide competition has been further increased by legislative changes that have removed interest-rate ceilings on most deposits and have expanded the powers of thrift institutions. New interpretations of existing statutes by regulators and the courts have allowed securities and insurance firms more freedom to offer banklike services to their customers. These forces have eroded the legal walls that protected geographic and product markets. Increasingly, banks, S&Ls, insurance companies, and securities firms find themselves competing in nationwide, even worldwide (rather than local or regional), markets for financial services (rather than banking or insurance).

As competition has become more intense, overcapacity has developed in the traditional banking functions—particularly in making commercial and consumer loans.[6]

We no longer need 30,000 separately capitalized and managed depository institutions, if we ever did. Weaker firms should be leaving the industry, and the survivors should be consolidating and reorganizing their operations to reduce costs and more effectively

---

impact on healthy competitors, see "A Report from the Front," *ABA Banking Journal* (May 1988):31.

[6]See, for example, Lowell L. Bryan, *Breaking Up the Bank: Rethinking an Industry Under Siege* (Homewood, Ill.: Dow Jones–Irwin, 1988), chap. 3.

serve customers. Unfortunately, regulatory practices are slowing this process by keeping insolvent depositories in operation and imposing legal barriers on institutions attempting to restructure their operations.[7] Relief for the overcrowded banking industry has been delayed, and profit margins for the industry have been reduced.

The federal government's deposit insurance and closure policies are rapidly creating a system where indiscriminate risk taking is rewarded while prudence is discouraged. Furthermore, market forces attempting to rid the industry of unneeded capacity are being counteracted by federal policies. For financial institutions, this is a recipe for disaster. If these policies are not corrected, a taxpayer bailout is certain, and eventual nationalization cannot be ruled out.

Instability through Regulatory Policies

Although the deposit insurance and closure systems of the federal government are the most important sources of government failure, they are only part of the problem. The entire regulatory apparatus, anchored as it is in a 1930s view of banking and financial markets, has contributed to the difficulties facing the U.S. financial system.

The most egregious example of regulatory restrictions introducing risk is the long-standing prohibition against nationwide branching. U.S. banking law has made it difficult for banks to diversify either the sources of their deposits or their loan portfolios, and consequently, these constraints have created a history of recurring local and regional banking crises.[8] The regional difficulties apparent today among "energy" banks and "farm" banks stem from the concentrated nature of their loan portfolios and are only the most recent example of this self-inflicted wound.

Similarly, the beginnings of the thrift industry crisis can be found

---

[7] The legal barriers that constrain depositories' reorganization efforts are discussed more fully below.

[8] In fact, recent reexaminations of the banking collapse of the 1930s have made it clear that the widespread failures were caused in large part by the fractured nature of our banking system. See, for example, Bert Ely, "The Big Bust: The 1930–1933 Banking Collapse—Its Causes, Its Lessons," in *The Financial Services Revolution: Policy Directions for the Future*, ed. Catherine England and Thomas F. Huertas (Boston: Kluwer Academic Publishers, 1988), pp. 41–67. The Canadian experience during that period offers an enlightening contrast. Canada also suffered a reduced money supply and falling prices during the depression, but its banks, which were able to branch nationwide, survived without a single failure.

in regulations closely defining the economic role of thrifts and restricting their activities to fit that part. S&Ls historically have been required to invest the lion's share of their portfolios in long-term, locally generated, fixed-rate home mortgages, and these loans have been funded by collecting short-term savings deposits. When interest rates began to rise rapidly during the early 1980s, thrift managers found their cost of funds rising while the returns on their loan portfolios remained flat.[9] Equity capital was rapidly absorbed, and an increasing number of savings and loans became insolvent.

The federal regulators either would not or could not close the growing number of insolvent savings and loans in a timely manner. Attempting to hide this regulatory failure, federal authorities lowered the minimum acceptable amount of capital and redefined the accounting rules to allow S&Ls to artificially inflate their reported capital accounts. Federal deposit insurance protected these decapitalized institutions from runs by their depositors. Owners and managers of insolvent thrifts rightly concluded they had little to lose in pursuing greater risks that promised large returns. Success could mean a newly recapitalized institution—and failure would only mean a bigger bill for the Federal Savings and Loan Insurance Corporation (FSLIC).

While not as important to date, regulations restricting the range of activities in which commercial banks may engage also have become increasingly binding. The restrictions that prevent commercial banks from offering investment banking services have been of particular concern. The best credit risks have been lost to the commercial paper and noninvestment-grade bond markets, while margins between interest rates charged and the costs of banks' funds have been reduced, even for less-creditworthy customers.[10] Many bankers have responded by taking on more credit risk and by pursuing

[9]Obviously, few new mortgages were being generated at the time, precisely because they carried such high interest rates.

[10]Again, this is not to argue that consumers have not benefited from increased competition, but when public policy provides government support for bankers who price loans below their expected costs—for example, by ignoring expected losses on the loan portfolio—the stituation is unsustainable and must lead to future problems for the financial system.

new fee-for-service and off–balance-sheet activities in their attempt to replace lost revenue.[11]

The current regulatory system was written using a strictly defined view of the proper business of banks, thrifts, securities firms, and insurance companies.[12] This model might have been appropriate to the mid-1930s, but it is not as suitable today. Just as the communications and transportation industries have evolved with an array of products and services unforeseen 50 years ago, the financial services industry must also be allowed to progress. The current regulatory structure, with its built-in definitions and expectations about the economic role that different financial firms can and should play, cannot accommodate widespread change in financial products and services. The fact that banks of the 1930s funded illiquid loans with potentially volatile deposits does not mean banks would necessarily operate in the same way today. If banks were liberated from the mold established by long-standing regulatory practices, new methods for providing secure liquid-deposit instruments and meeting the credit needs of individuals, as well as small and mid-sized companies, would be more likely to develop. That brings us to the final criticism.

Even allowing for the possibility of banking-law revisions, extensive regulation is destabilizing because it is inflexible. Regardless of how well-intentioned or well-thought-out the original regulatory system, and despite the appointment of intelligent, diligent administrators, government-sponsored regulatory structures simply cannot keep pace with a changing marketplace.

It is difficult if not impossible for regulatory systems to anticipate and accommodate change. They are based on the world as we know it, not as it may become. Furthermore, political decisionmakers balancing the claims of competing interest groups often are rewarded for resisting the emergence of new technologies and new compet-

[11]Robert E. Litan, "Taking the Dangers Out of Bank Deregulation," *The Brookings Review* (Fall 1986): 6, or Bryan, chap. 4. As I argue below, securities powers are not necessarily the most important for the majority of banks, but they are the most widely discussed. And as of this writing (summer 1988), expanding banks' ability to compete more directly in the securities market is the most likely subject of the next banking-law revision.

[12]Some would argue this view was intended to establish the criteria for dividing the financial markets in a cartel-like fashion. See William F. Shughart, II, "A Public Choice Perspective of the 1933 Banking Act," in England and Huertas, pp. 87–105.

itors. When politicians do act, cost-effective service to consumers and long-term stability frequently take a back seat to protecting the profits of a well-identified producers' group and delaying problems until after the next election. Thus, as market-driven events unfold, regulatory constraints (even those originally designed to increase the industry's profitability) can become binding restrictions that encumber the ability of financial institutions to compete effectively and survive.

Recommendations

No one disputes that there are extensive problems facing the nation's financial institutions, particularly the depositories. But there is considerable disagreement about what should be done.

Many observers argue that federal examiners have not been diligent enough or had the necessary legal or financial resources to deal with existing problems. They suggest more restrictive laws and regulations, more legal sanctions against unacceptable behavior, and more manpower for the federal banking authorities.

Although a short-term increase in government involvement might be necessary to resolve the savings and loan crisis, this is the wrong approach overall. Telling the nation's depositors that they should rely even more heavily on the regulatory activities of the federal government will not enhance the stability of banks and thrift institutions.

No matter how dedicated or well-intentioned federal bank examiners are, the government cannot adequately monitor thousands of depositories on a continuous basis. The incentive structure built into a civil service system neither encourages nor allows federal employees to be as innovative in identifying infractions or enforcing rules as bank employees are in avoiding even the most detailed regulations. Even more importantly, the government cannot place an examiner in every bank on a day-to-day basis. Nor would we want it to. Thus, the federal authorities do not have the human resources to monitor depositories as closely as depositors can.

If government policies have failed, if government examiners cannot be relied on to oversee the operations of banks, how does the country return to a stable financial system that will help promote economic growth? How does it develop a regulatory apparatus that will adapt to changing market and technological conditions without requiring future political gamesmanship like that involved in the current debates over funding the FSLIC and restructuring the financial regulatory system? In the long-term, we must deemphasize the government's regulatory role and strengthen the supervisory capacity of the market. In the short-term, however, it will take concerted action to extricate us from the quicksand that is the savings and loan industry.

Reform the Federal Deposit Insurance System

The very first financial issue with which the incoming president will have to deal is the savings and loan industry crisis. There are more than 500 insolvent S&Ls operating. Almost as many are technically solvent but losing money. Analysts estimate that the FSLIC needs $60 to $70 billion to close currently insolvent institutions and pay insured depositors. The longer Congress delays, the worse the problem becomes. In 1987 the $13.4 billion in reported losses suffered by the thrift industry's troubled institutions swamped the $6.6 billion in profits reported by healthy savings and loans. Industrywide losses in the first quarter of 1988 were reported at $3.3 billion and indicate no ebbing in the tide of red ink.[13] Observers place the daily losses of insolvent institutions at $1 billion per month or more than $30 million per day. Finally, these losses are taking place during a period of relative economic prosperity, and it would be difficult to even speculate about the wave of red ink that would build in the face of substantially higher interest rates or a recession.

It is vitally important that insolvent thrifts be closed as quickly as possible. The resources of the FSLIC, including the capital of the healthy portion of the thrift industry, are clearly inadequate for the cleanup job. Nor can the banking industry or the FDIC absorb the shortfall. If we are to stop the financial hemorrhage represented by these institutions, taxpayer funds must be used, but their use must have at least four conditions.

First, a time limit, say two to three years, should be set for closing all insolvent thrifts. An elite task force of examiners and closure

---

[13]It should be noted that although these estimates are based on the best available information, the accounting rules peculiar to depository institutions generally and thrift institutions in particular may cause an underreporting of the extent of industry losses.

experts, gathered from among the state and federal banking agencies, should be established to do nothing but close ailing S&Ls.

Second, in closing these institutions, examiners should emphasize speed. Past attempts to conserve cash in the short term have proved counterproductive. Further delays while searching for suitable merger partners will only allow greater losses to accumulate, and the out-year liabilities the FSLIC is assuming to consummate some of these mergers could create another set of equally serious problems down the road.[14] Therefore, liquidations should be the preferred form of failure resolution where decapitalized savings and loans are involved.

Third, ownership restrictions on undercapitalized savings and loan institutions should be eliminated. Anyone willing to assume a thrift institution and recapitalize it should be allowed to do so, and there should be no limit on the number of adequately capitalized S&Ls an individual or corporation can own. But in attempting to attract new capital, the federal authorities should make no more guarantees about future returns on existing portfolios.

Fourth, deposit insurance should be limited to $100,000 per depositor every 12 months. The losses incurred by insolvent institutions awaiting closure must be slowed, and depositors must be discouraged from playing the rate-chasing game. Once a depositor with an account in a failed institution is paid, he should be eligible for a similar reimbursement only to a total of $100,000 if he is then found to hold an account in another failed institution within a specified time period.[15] For the consumers who are truly ignorant of the condition of their depository, safe investment alternatives exist—mutual funds backed by Treasury bills, for example—and those depositors who are abusing the federal deposit insurance system would be discouraged from doing so.

This policy could be further strengthened by changing the federal

[14]In an attempt to make some of the sicker S&Ls appear more attractive to potential merger partners, the FSLIC is guaranteeing returns on many loan portfolios. Should there be a severe recession that undermines what now appear to be good loans, the FSLIC, or whatever government entity assumes its obligations, may find itself making payments to remaining depository institutions far into the future.

[15]Thus, individual protection still would extend to a total of $100,000. If a depositor received a federal insurance fund check for his $65,000 account in one S&L, he would still be covered for up to $35,000 in another bank or thrift.

deposit insurance contract to insure principal, not interest rates. Thus, an individual's initial investment would be protected, but those people who blithely searched out the highest rates without regard for financial stability would not profit from their irresponsible behavior in the event of a failure.

The situation in the savings and loan industry has deteriorated to the point that the only solution is a taxpayer bailout of depositors. Allowing the problem to fester places healthy institutions at risk, adds to the eventual cleanup costs, and could lead to the nationalization of a large portion of the industry. Given the weakened state of both the thrift and banking industries, reneging on the promises to insured depositors would cause widespread panic. For the sake of the nation's future economic health, the incoming president and congressional leaders must be called upon to behave responsibly and address the savings and loan crisis early in 1989.

The drastic surgery needed will be politically more palatable for a new administration (regardless of party) and a new Congress, as the actors can resolve to address a problem "not of their own making." Delay will force the new president and the 101st Congress to accept an increasing share of the responsibility.

Dealing with the thrift industry's problems should be only the first step in reforming the federal deposit insurance system, however. The problems encountered by the FSLIC are endemic to the federal deposit guarantee system as it has operated over the past half-century. The banking industry is exhibiting the early symptoms of a similar crisis, especially among the smaller institutions. Bank failures numbered 187 in 1987, compared with an annual average of six failures from 1945 to 1980, and there are disturbing signs of more trouble ahead. In 1986 and 1987, the commercial banking industry wrote off $32 billion in bad debt, not including the additions to loan loss reserves for questionable loans to less-developed countries (LDCs). To place that number in perspective, in the 30-year period from 1951 to 1980, the banking industry wrote off a total of $28 billion in uncollected loans.

It is vitally important, therefore, that as Congress moves to resolve the savings and loan crisis, it also institute reforms for the entire federal deposit insurance system. To avoid future repetitions of the FSLIC crisis, we must begin to decrease our dependence on the narcotic of federal deposit insurance.

117

First and most important, a strict closure policy should be applied to all federally insured institutions. Capital standards should be strengthened, and henceforward, strict penalties should be established for all federally insured banks, credit unions, and thrift institutions with capital below federal standards. Financial penalties or higher insurance premiums are one means of punishing undercapitalized institutions, but depending on the circumstances of the problem depository, they may not be the most effective way to force recapitalization.[16] Thus, federal regulators also should have the authority to prohibit institutions with insufficient capital from paying dividends to shareholders. Public notices alerting stockholders and depositors to the situation would be another way to encourage bank managers to turn their full attention to recapitalizing their institutions. Federal insurance authorities also should be empowered to enforce stoplending orders for institutions with deteriorating capital positions, as a means of controlling eventual losses.

As a last resort, federally insured depository institutions with capital measured at some predetermined positive amount—say 2 percent—should be given 60 days to raise new equity capital so that they meet the regulatory minimum; if they fail to do so, they should then be liquidated or merged.[17]

Second, in measuring capital, gimmicks should be eschewed, and regulators should move the system toward market-based accounting. Currently accepted accounting procedures for depos-

[16]Suggesting higher premiums for undercapitalized institutions is as close as I come to recommending federally administered risk-based insurance premiums. For a discussion of the difficulties with such a proposal, see Catherine England, "A Proposal for Introducing Private Deposit Insurance," in *Proceedings of a Conference on Bank Structure and Competition* (Chicago: Federal Reserve Bank of Chicago, 1985), pp. 319–21.

[17]It is important that liquidation/merger proceedings begin while bank capital is still measured at some positive amount for several reasons. First, currently accepted accounting procedures allow depository institutions to carry assets at book, or acquisition, value. Especially in the case of a troubled bank, this policy is likely to overstate the value of the loan portfolio. Thus, the appearance of remaining equity capital may well prove an illusion. Second, closing undercapitalized institutions sooner rather than later would protect the resources of the insurance fund and hence the remaining depository institutions. Third, such a policy would protect all depositors more fully, reducing the chance of an unexpectedly large cash withdrawal by the bank's most important depositors and providing a more stable environment in which to find a merger partner or liquidate the institution.

118

itory institutions frequently allow banks and their auditors to hide an institution's true financial condition from stockholders, depositors, and general creditors. For example, loans can be carried at full face value on a bank's books as long as interest payments are current, even if new loans have been necessary to allow the borrower to make his interest payments. The attitude toward the public that is expressed by bankers and regulators who support these accounting rules is patronizing and should lead to creditor skepticism about the honest intent of depository managers and owners. It is doubtful that loan officers would accept at face value income statements and balance sheets incorporating similar techniques from other firms seeking to borrow money. Nor are these practices in keeping with the widely accepted view that capital markets operate most efficiently when investors and creditors have accurate and timely information about the firms with which they deal.

Bankers frequently respond that there exists no "market value" for many of the assets in their portfolios. It is true that many loans to individuals and businesses are based on unique circumstances and are difficult to evaluate quickly. But regulations that encourage and reward, rather than discourage, more honest accounting procedures would offer several advantages to banks and their customers.

One such advantage would be that progress toward market-based accounting would diminish the basis of the "inherent instability" problem that supposedly plagues depository institutions. Undertaking the analysis necessary to periodically mark their assets to market would make it easier to raise funds using these assets as collateral in the event of unexpectedly large deposit withdrawals. Not only would an illiquid bank have better documentation concerning the current value of its loans, but the more liquid institutions that might serve as a source of cash would also have experience with valuing bank loans and a better basis for deciding the market value of another depository's assets.

There are also other advantages. Many loans have no readily recognized market value because there has been little incentive for depository institutions to develop secondary markets for these assets. Indeed, such an innovation is largely prohibited by the laws that restrict bank entry into the securities markets. However, an increasingly wide range of loan types are being packaged and offered on secondary markets. Home mortgages are the best known example, but there are now also "securitized" credit card loans, automobile loans, and agricultural loans, to name a few. Developing deeper secondary markets for many of these assets would provide banks with better information for internal management decisions and would enable smaller, more locally oriented insitutions to better diversify their earnings portfolios.[18]

Regardless of the preferences of bankers and their regulators, as more market discipline is introduced depositors whose funds are at risk will demand more honest accounting from depository managers and their auditors. The move to market-based accounting cannot occur overnight, but in attempting to set the industry on a more stable course, regulators should rewrite guidelines in ways that reward those institutions that are more forthcoming in their public financial reports. For example, lower minimum capital standards can be justified for institutions using market-based accounting; similarly, closure rules could be made more liberal for banks that regularly mark their portfolios to their market value.

Third, current deposit insurance should be enforced and depositors, not deposits, should be insured. Successful implementation of the preceding policy recommendation—that is, responding to undercapitalized banks in a timely manner—will fully protect depositors in most failure situations. When a bank's losses do exceed its equity capital (owing to undiscovered fraud, for example), uninsured bank creditors should bear a part of the loss whether the solution is an arranged merger or liquidation and regardless of the size of the bank. In addition, as mentioned earlier, deposit insurance should be attached to depositors, not to individual accounts. This would place some depositors at risk for a limited period of time, but very small depositors would continue to be protected up to a total of $100,000, and others could protect themselves by placing their accounts in a variety of institutions or by investing in risk-free assets.

[18]In his book, Lowell Bryan argues that securitized lending eventually will prove to be a more efficient system for delivering credit services to large segments of the population. He predicts that if banks do not find ways to move into this market and take advantage of rapidly improving technology and securitization techniques, other firms offering financial services will replace banks as primary lenders to all but the very smallest borrowers and the poorest credit risks.

Placing depositors at risk would aid regulators in determining which institutions deserve more attention. Business and individual depositors have better ongoing information about the stability of local bank managers' business practices than do visiting examiners.[19] If local customers were encouraged to act on this information, federal authorities would gain important allies in monitoring the condition of banks and thrifts. By observing deposit outflows and relative interest rates paid to attract deposits, regulators could quickly determine which institutions warranted closer scrutiny. Further, a greater emphasis on market discipline would reward better-managed banks in that their relative stability would be reflected in lower funding costs.

Fourth, to provide the political backbone necessary to limit federal deposit insurance along the lines suggested, the FDIC and the Federal Reserve Board should develop a plan of action for handling large bank failures. The federal banking authorities' lack of nerve during the 1984 failure of Continental Illinois caused them to overreact and undermine the positive steps toward deposit insurance reform that had been taken.[20] To avoid a similar response to the next crisis at a large bank, the incoming president should ask federal banking authorities to think carefully about how such an event should be handled and contained. The resulting plan should involve a procedure for conducting routine business through the failed depository, should merger or liquidation arrangements take some time. It should contain a stated policy for handling potential liquidity problems at solvent banks or thrifts that have correspondent or

[19]It came as no surprise to many residents of Oklahoma City, for example, when Penn Square was closed by federal authorities and the extent of the bank's questionable business deals became more widely known. Similarly, many businessmen in East Tennessee were aware of the unsound practices at the Butcher banks long before federal examiners reacted.

[20]William Isaac, chairman of the Federal Deposit Insurance Corporation during the first Reagan term, clearly understood the destabilizing tendencies accompanying federal deposit guarantees. In fact, he was one of the first public officials to talk widely about the existence of moral hazard and the need for reform. Isaac attempted to reinforce market discipline by developing a "modified payout" failure resolution program whereby even when mergers were arranged for insolvent banks, large depositors shared in the losses suffered by the failed institutions. This program was ended when all creditors of the Continental Illinois holding company were protected, and small bankers protested policies that placed their large depositors at risk while protecting similar accounts placed in larger institutions.

other business relationships with the troubled institution. The plan should be announced in advance and reiterated in the event of a large bank failure. Swift, predictable action by the federal authorities would alleviate any unfounded public unease.

Fifth, deposit insurance should be rolled back over a 10-year period. A new law should limit the extent of federal deposit insurance to $90,000 per individual beginning January 1, 1991, to $80,000 beginning January 1, 1992, to $70,000 beginning January 1, 1993, and so on. The federal government's assumption from depository owners and managers of the responsibility for retaining depositor confidence has proved a serious mistake. This policy has allowed the managers of insured institutions to turn their attention to empire building and the pursuit of additional profits instead of emphasizing policies that produce stable institutions. By forcing depository managers to compete in providing safe deposits, we would return the banking system to long-term stability and encourage the development of new methods for providing payment services that are not subject to runs.

Even under such a system, it would not be necessary for every depositor to become expert at evaluating bank balance sheets, however. With less dependence on federal guarantees, information about individual banks would become more widely available. More important, the behavior of a relatively few sophisticated depositors placing large sums of money would affect bankers' behavior, causing them to put increased emphasis on stability.[21]

Evidence from before the Great Depression indicates that depositors had access to a number of public sources of information about the relative stability of competing depositories. Nor were runs on healthy institutions a frequent event. Economist George Kaufman reports that from the end of the Civil War until 1919, failure rates among banks were below that for nondepository firms, and the average annual losses for the nation's depositors represented only 0.2 percent of total deposits.[22]

Unfortunately, depositors are not as prepared to protect them-

---

[21]For a more detailed discussion of mechanisms likely to develop among uninsured depositors, see Catherine England, "Agency Costs and Unregulated Banks: Could Depositors Protect Themselves?" in England and Huertas, pp. 317–43.

[22]George G. Kaufman, "The Truth About Bank Runs," in England and Huertas, p. 16.

selves today as they were in 1919. The FDIC has replaced most of the private-sector sources of information about the financial health of individual banks and thrift institutions, and ignorance about the operations of banks has replaced informed consumerism. It will be necessary, therefore, to provide some time for an educational process. In addition, the market will need time to build on existing sources and establish new outlets for information about relative bank stability. But given the advances in communications technology and the increasing financial sophistication among a significant segment of the population, depositors are more than capable of once again serving as the primary disciplinary force in the banking markets.

Finally, some transition time will be needed to allow bank managers, currently unaccustomed to emphasizing safety as a means of attracting and retaining depositors, to reposition their banks' balance sheets. A learning process among depository owners and managers will be required to determine what sorts of competitive strategies will allow them to maintain their depositors. But it is precisely this sort of renewed attention to stability that will return the banking industry to long-term health.

Sixth, depository institutions should be allowed to opt out of the federal deposit insurance system. Many of the preceding suggestions would give government officials extensive powers to intervene in the operations of privately owned banks. These powers can be justified as long as the government is guaranteeing payment of a significant portion of the liabilities of depository institutions. But banks and thrifts should not be forced to accept such intrusive measures. Those that are willing to give up their government insurance also should be freed from government supervision and closure procedures. Any institution that feels capable of going it alone should be allowed to do so. A bank that attempts to retain its depositors' confidence without federal guarantees (with or without private deposit insurance) faces the strictest regulators of all, in the form of uninsured creditors.

Deposit insurance reform is the most important step in reintroducing long-term stability into the financial services industry. Reducing the dependence on federal deposit guarantees will be more effective in returning the banking industry to a sound footing than any commitment by regulators to better supervise bank behavior

123

or any new laws describing in more detail what managers should and should not do. To produce a healthier banking system, we must first produce skeptical depositors. Then bankers will be forced to place safety first, and the industry will benefit with the economy as a whole.

The extensive problems faced by the savings and loan industry have focused recent attention on the urgent need to reform the federal deposit insurance system. But there are also other sources of instability that are contributing to the upheaval among depository institutions. In particular, regulations that limit the ability of financial firms to better diversify their earning assets and prevent these institutions from adapting to changing market conditions ought also to be removed.

Move to Full Interstate Branch Banking

Congress should pass a law overriding all existing state branching restrictions as of some specified date, say January 1, 1995. After that date a bank should be allowed to open or close a branch anywhere in the country, without prior permission from any local, state, or federal government authority, and bank holding companies should be permitted to convert their fully owned subsidiary banks to branches.

This law would move us beyond the current trend toward allowing interstate holding companies. Although interstate mergers and acquisitions have represented an improvement over the earlier, more restrictive system, the fully owned subsidiary of a bank holding company is more expensive to open, operate, and close than a branch is. Thus it is more expensive for bank holding companies to enter new markets than it is for branched banks, and competition in less populated markets is consequently reduced. Closing a subsidiary bank is also more disruptive and expensive for both the bank holding company and the bank's customers than is closing an uneconomic bank. Nor can the functions of banks within a holding company be as easily coordinated as can the branches of a larger bank.

A policy of interstate branching also would help stabilize the banking industry by removing one of the most important factors contributing to the 1930s fiasco.[23] Bank portfolios would be better

[23]Indeed, moving to interstate banking was viewed by Roosevelt's first comptroller

124

diversified, and a branch experiencing an unexpectedly heavy out-flow of deposits could turn first to sister branches for more cash. Interstate branching would also increase the ease with which information about the relative stability of banking institutions is evaluated and disseminated, in that individual branches would not need to be judged by outsiders on a stand-alone basis. Furthermore, nationwide branching would improve service to consumers by increasing the ease with which they would have access to their bank accounts, allowing for deposits, as well as withdrawals, from more locations and increasing the acceptability of checks nationwide.

Removing current restrictions against interstate branching does not imply, however, that the U.S. banking system would be dominated by a few large supermarket banks with nationwide offices.[24] One or two such institutions might develop, but most depository institutions would probably find it advantageous to remain within the local or regional market they know well. Nor would small and mid-sized businesses or local consumers find branches any less responsive to their credit needs than are subsidiary banks. Experience has shown that the most successful regional bank holding companies have been those that left in place managers with considerable expertise in local markets and with area customers. Finally, a branch manager able to draw on the greater resources provided by a larger banking organization would be in an even better position to serve customers whose businesses are growing.

Remove Ownership and Activities Restrictions Affecting Banks and Other Financial Firms

Finally, the artificial distinctions among financial services firms and between banking and commerce should be removed. Both the Glass-Steagall Act and the Bank Holding Company Act should be repealed. These restrictions only slow the development of new products and services and prevent banks and other institutions facing similar prohibitions from adapting to changing economic conditions. Given the existing federal deposit insurance system, however, there are legitimate concerns expressed about extending

---

of the currency as preferable to federal deposit insurance during the debates in early 1933. See Burns.

[24]Countries in which this pattern has developed also are marked by prohibitive government-imposed entry requirements for new banks.

the range of firms with which banks can be affiliated. Current guidelines and recent decisions make it unclear how far the federal safety net would be extended in the event of trouble at a bank subsidiary of a diversified holding company. In an effort to prop up a bank, it is certainly not desirable for the taxpayers to have to bail out, say, Sears, Roebuck. But there are several considerations that undermine this as a long-term argument against freeing bank owners and managers from current restrictions.

First, by strictly limiting the extent of federal guarantees and reducing our dependence on them, the deposit insurance reforms described above would resolve this conflict and allow regulatory reform to proceed.[25] Second, nonbank parent companies and affiliates have proved to be, so far, a source of strength for their depositories, rather than a drain. Clearly a different situation could arise someday, but given the insufficient capital in the industry as a whole, we should be searching for new sources of financial strength rather than eliminating potential providers out of hand. Third, and most important, the success or failure of limiting the extent of the federal safety net has less to do with the actual legal terminology than it does with the will of political decisionmakers. Federal authorities committed to limiting federal guarantees to the insured depository could do so today without any legal changes.[26] Similarly, even without explicit federal protection, politicians committed to providing assistance to any particular firm can commit taxpayer funds to that purpose.

Balanced against the concerns about insulating banks within diversified holding companies are the advantages to removing current activities and ownership restrictions. Allowing banks to offer new services (and other firms to offer banking services) would introduce new competition into many markets for financial services,

---

[25]It should be reemphasized that deposit insurance reform is vital to the long-term interests of the narrowly defined banking industry, even without the broader deregulatory efforts described here.

[26]The point that existing law is sufficient to limit deposit insurance to the bank within a holding company has been made by several analysts. Among the most influential is the study, *Mandate for Change*, produced by the Federal Deposit Insurance Corporation (1987).

thereby benefiting consumers.[27] In addition, permitting those institutions that so choose to provide a range of financial products would allow them to experiment with bundles of services that would offer increased convenience and better prices to consumers. Removing current ownership and affiliation restrictions also could increase the banking industry's stability by allowing each holding company to more adequately diversify its earnings, thus placing the holding company in a better position to support its depository institutions. Finally, freeing ourselves from narrow-minded and legally binding views of what a bank, securities firm, or insurance company is supposed to do could lead to the creation of financial institutions that avoid the problems caused by funding illiquid loans with volatile deposits.

Conclusions

The federal government's regulatory attitudes toward banks and other financial institutions have caused more problems than they have solved in the past half-century. Although federal deposit insurance is seen by some as the glue holding the thrift industry together, it is more accurately pictured as a sticky spider's web that has brought the nation's S&Ls (and many banks) to the precipice. Furthermore, the moral hazard that is the narcotic of federal deposit guarantees has been enhanced by closure policies that first delay dealing with inadequately capitalized institutions and then provide bailouts or below-market loans when forced to respond to an insolvent depository. Finally, the federal government's regulatory policies have failed because decisionmakers have responded to political considerations rather than economic and market concerns in debates over possible reform. The evolution of U.S. financial markets has thus been stifled by the weight of 50-year-old definitions and attitudes concerning the acceptable role for each financial institution.

It is time to move forward. It is time to establish government

---

[27]There is evidence, in particular, that underwriting fees in some securities markets would be reduced by the entry of banks as competitors. See Thomas A. Pugel and Lawrence J. White, "An Analysis of the Competitive Effects of Allowing Commercial Bank Affiliates to Underwrite Corporate Securities," in *Deregulating Wall Street*, ed. Ingo Walter (New York: John Wiley & Sons, 1985), pp. 93–139. It is also widely believed that introducing new competition into market for insurance would drive down brokerage fees.

policies that promote efficiency and stability among our financial institutions. Four broad policy initiatives are required:

1. Resolve the thrift industry crisis as quickly as possible, in order to minimize the expenditure of taxpayer funds.
2. Move to reduce dependence on federal deposit insurance and emphasize market discipline.
3. Remove existing barriers to interstate branching.
4. Remove existing ownership and affiliation restrictions applied to banks and other financial institutions.

PART II

FOREIGN AND DEFENSE POLICY

8. The Price of Defense
Earl C. Ravenal

The new administration faces the inevitability of economic troubles, including the persistent budget deficit and trade deficit, both financed by heavy capital inflows from the rest of the world, and the consequent mounting national debt. The political atmosphere is rife with suggestions on eliminating the abuses of fiscal management that precipitated the crisis. Almost universal among them is the proposal to cut the federal budget. But where to go for cuts? Surely, entitlement programs, farm subsidies, the expenses of running the federal government—and finally, defense.

Yet few commentators, in the "usual" places, seem to have a firm grasp of the magnitude and kind of defense cuts that must be made in order to be useful—even to be meaningful in this gargantuan context. For example, the *New York Times* ran an editorial entitled "Defense Cuts That Won't Hurt Defense"[1] (the headline itself being almost enough to describe, and indict, the thesis of the *Times*'s editorialist), that detailed miscellaneous military base closings that would add up to a mere $1 billion a year. Even *Fortune* (a fairly reliable source of economic analysis) comes up with this advice: "On the military front the U.S. could save billions by shopping smarter for supplies and spare parts and by cutting back expenditures. For example: slow down the rate of spending for the Strategic Defense Initiative; eliminate such flawed programs as the Bradley Fighting Vehicle. . . ."[2] There is little chance of achieving large savings with that meager list.

We need a reduction in our present $291 billion military budget of as much as 45 to 50 percent, but let's settle for about 10 percent in the first fiscal year of the incoming administration. Where are we

---

[1]*New York Times*, October 23, 1987.

[2]Ann Reilly Dowd, "Where Does the U.S. Go from Here?" *Fortune*, November 23, 1987.

going to cut costs of that magnitude? We have to dismantle parts of our force structure. Every army division we have costs us $5 billion a year. Every aircraft carrier we put in forward waters costs almost $12 billion a year.

Of course, cutting forces would be the beginning of the end of America's global empire. But if we are to keep from becoming an economic pygmy, we must stop trying to be a political-military leviathan. Since cutting defense budgets has inevitable consequences for foreign policy, and it is our foreign policy in the first place that has occasioned the high defense spending over the past four decades, the task now is to devise a defense budget that is both affordable and consonant with a fundamentally revised foreign policy and national strategy.

The Logic of Defense Policy

There is a need—not for more alternatives, in the sense of nuances, clever gimmicks, and ploys to rescue present policies from their disabilities—but rather for some logic. First, we must understand that there is a logic in defense policies—that to do some things requires that one does other things. Second, we must realize that we cannot do things as we have been accustomed to doing them. Third, we must accept that we must give up something to get something else: to get remedies, we must accept some penalties. There will be adjustments, and they will be cosmic, not cosmetic. Real adjustments cause pain. Perhaps there are no "good" alternatives. It is the peculiar myth of the liberals that all good things go together—peace and justice, economy and defense, helping congenial allies and yet staying out of trouble, saving the world and also saving ourselves.

I say no. Each of those pairs is a trade-off, a hard choice. In particular, we see the defense program as crushed between the upper and nether millstones of the global requirements of our foreign policy and the constraints—economic, social, and political—that arise from our domestic system. Familiar features of our geopolitical landscape, such as the encompassing doctrine of containment, must be reconsidered, weighed, and, I think, transcended.

The Paradigm of Containment

For the past four decades, since the beginning of the cold war in the late 1940s, U.S. national strategy has been devoted to the containment of the Soviet Union and Soviet-inspired communism. During that period, the paradigm of U.S. national strategy has consisted of two basic elements—deterrence and forward defense—that are both devoted to containing communist power and influence. Deterrence is roughly equated with strategic nuclear forces; we seek to maintain at least a balance of strategic nuclear arms with the Soviet Union and to provide a nuclear umbrella over our allies and various other countries. Forward defense, or alliance, involves our protection, mostly by means of general-purpose forces, of allies and other countries that occupy strategic positions or have sympathetic social and political values.

But containment must be arrayed against its costs, the expectations held of it, and the projected costs and expectations of alternative doctrines of national strategy. The problem with the strategy of containment has been the continuing high costs associated with the requisite military preparations, and the occasional egregious costs of heightened crises and regional wars; and the risk, under certain circumstances, of being plunged into nuclear war. The costs can be attributed mostly to the generation of conventional forces, primarily for the defense of Europe; the risks can be attributed to reliance on the earlier use of nuclear weapons, also particularly in a confrontation arising from a conventional war in Europe. To some extent, cost can be transmuted into additional risk, and risk can be transformed into mere cost. That is what is meant by "lowering" or "raising" the nuclear threshold. But the choice itself arises from the policy of containment of the Soviet Union. Accordingly, containment must be judged by its requisites, and by the capacity—political, social, and economic—of our system to sustain those requisites.

The Price of Defense

Perhaps present U.S. national strategy could be tolerated if it could be demonstrated that the cost could be trimmed without impairing the U.S. ability to implement the strategy, and if the nation found itself in comfortable fiscal circumstances. But neither is the case. In fact, even what the Reagan administration requested, let alone what Congress granted that administration, was insufficient to execute the tasks of containing Soviet communism around the world. To implement containment with high confidence—that is, so that our worldwide conventional defense would not be breached and so that we would not need to decide to escalate to the use of nuclear weapons—would mean a probable defense budget of as much as 10 percent of our gross national product, or something like $477 billion.

If anything, therefore, we are spending too little, not too much, to implement our present policy of containment. Some evidence of this is the fact that the Pentagon is double-counting divisions and other units in the active force structure so as to cover certain areas of U.S. defensive concern. The starkest statement of that appeared in the annual report of then-Secretary of Defense Caspar Weinberger for FY 1986:

> Our forward-defense strategy dictates that we be able to conduct concurrent deployments to widely separated areas of the globe. Our present goal is to achieve the capability to deploy forces to a remote theater such as Southwest Asia, while maintaining an acceptable capability to reinforce NATO and key areas of Northeast Asia.[3]

A further examination of the secretary's report indicates that in some cases the same units are assigned to "concurrent deployments." What this suggests is an imbalance of commitments and resources. The Reagan administration somewhat exacerbated the contradiction with its implication of a wider strategic scope of simultaneous responses to Soviet aggressions (the "maritime strategy" and "horizontal escalation") and with its more tangible implementation of the commitment—initiated by Jimmy Carter in 1980— to defend the Persian Gulf and Southwest Asia, without significantly increasing the overall force structure or overall military manpower. Of course, there is no law against creating such gaps and contradictions. Furthermore, they can be maintained, often for some time, in that such states of affairs are not always tested sharply or conclusively by events. But ultimately, events—or the foreshad-

---

[3]Caspar Weinberger, *FY 1986 Annual Report to the Congress* (Washington: Department of Defense, February 4, 1985).

owing of events by analysis—will challenge these relationships. And something will have to give.

The urgent question, then, is whether the United States can afford even its present scope of containment. What the United States faces, at the beginning of the new administration, is a crisis of solvency, in several pertinent senses of the word: not merely fiscal solvency but also a gross misalignment between the country's strategic objectives in the world and its manifest willingness to pay for them.

The major candidates for president in 1988 variously rebuffed or entertained the option of raising taxes to pay for defense and other governmental functions. But the fact that there are options does not make them desirable or even feasible. All of the fiscal options (taxes, inflation, more government borrowing) are destructive. Resources are not automatically granted; to be available to the state, they must be mobilized from society, which is the base and context of the state. Even if the government could balance its books by exacting more resources in the form of taxes (and possibly also conscription at low military wages) to support a large defense establishment and extensive foreign commitments, that would be just the end of one problem and the beginning of another. Solvency means that the external and internal stances of this country comport with each other. An extensive, engaged foreign policy and a large, active military posture require big, intrusive, and demanding government. If, as we were promised at the outset of the Reagan administration, we were to have a more reserved, less extensive government, then we must have a more detached, disengaged foreign policy.

Chimerical Solutions

In typical critiques of the U.S. defense program, containment of the Soviet Union is assumed; it is taken as indispensable, not challengeable in itself. True, various constraints—involving budgets, demographics, resources, and popular support—are often enumerated. But such exercises generally move abruptly, negligently, and optimistically to a proposed series of mild correctives. Some studies suggest "force-multipliers" or other gimmicks, such as "dual-missioning" of our forces—that is, treating as expeditionary forces, available for broader regional assignments, the units that the United States keeps in Europe and Northeast Asia. But such superficial

135

global flexibility can be achieved only by robbing the primary areas of some measure of U.S. protection.

Another kind of solution—"selectivity," or picking and choosing among our defensive commitments— is the most prevalent kind of argument used by liberal critics. Selectivity purports to mitigate the need for extensive armament and deployments in the implementation of containment. Virtually all proponents of selectivity would still contain our adversaries, in some sense; but they are selective in that they strive for some principle of limitation and impute to their more extreme opponents the scheme of "universality."

Most proposals of selective intervention—as diverse as those of George F. Kennan, Robert W. Tucker, Stanley Hoffmann, and Ernst B. Haas[4]—are subject to the same problems. In the last analysis, all such proposals lead back to, or are operationally indistinguishable from, the more comprehensive versions of containment. This is true in four major respects.

First, such proposals support virtually all the same objects of our defense—objects, as it turns out, that make up the major portion of our present and projected defense expenditures. To understand this criticism, we need to conduct a brief examination of the U.S. defense budget, attributing the full costs of all active forces to regions of the world that the United States undertakes to defend. The three main theaters (which virtually all proponents of supposed selectivity would retain) are Europe/NATO, which takes $124 billion a year; East Asia/Western Pacific, which takes $39 billion a year; and the Persian Gulf/Southwest Asia, which takes $46 billion a year. In contrast, other theaters and the strategic reserve take no more than $15 billion a year. All this constitutes the general-purpose force, or, roughly, the conventional component of our force structure, accounting for $224 billion a year. The strategic nuclear component accounts for $67 billion a year. Together, the two components account for the $291 billion defense budgetary authority

---

[4]George F. Kennan, *The Cloud of Danger* (Boston: Little, Brown/Atlantic Monthly Press, 1977); Robert W. Tucker, "The Purposes of American Power," *Foreign Affairs* (Winter 1980–81); Stanley Hoffmann, "The New Orthodoxy," *New York Review of Books*, April 16, 1981; idem, "Foreign Policy: What's to Be Done?" *New York Review of Books*, April 30, 1981; and Ernst B. Haas, "On Hedging Our Bets: Selective Engagement with the Soviet Union," in *Beyond Containment: Alternative American Policies Toward the Soviet Union*, ed. Aaron Wildavsky (San Francisco: ICS Press, 1983).

requested by the Reagan administration for FY 1989. Thus the peripheral areas—some parts of which most proponents of selectivity might dispense with—take only about 5 percent of the defense budget. There may be good and even sufficient reasons for not intervening in such peripheral areas, but they are not budgetary. In this respect at least, selective containment is hardly less demanding than supposed global universal containment.

Second, advocates of selectivity would implicitly support—in addition to the supposedly necessary prime objects—a host of minor, intrinsically dispensable objects "for the sake of" the major objectives.

Third, when these proposals of selectivity are costed out, they may turn out to be even more expensive than the supposedly universal schemes they would supplant. This is because, in emphasizing certain situations as "vital," advocates tend to add these to all the others, which they are wary of discontinuing.

Fourth, the logic of threat and response, coupled with the diagnosis of the nature or source of the threat, leads these supposedly limitationist arguments back to an espousal of any act or response that would constitute effective containment. Selectivity becomes universality, although the authors of these proposals sometimes disown or disfigure their intellectual offspring.

One should not be unduly impressed by modifying and mollifying adjectives such as "limited," "selective," or "moderate." Containment, of its essence, must remain contingently open-ended— indeed, triggered by contingencies determined by the adversary. The circumstances of Soviet aggressive or expansive behavior are not subject to American definition and delimitation. Implicit in the definition of "the Soviet threat" is that the Soviets exercise the initiative. Therefore, once committed to containment, how can we keep it limited?

In the end, selectivity is an artifact of the debate, not a real policy of state. The extremes of universal containment and consistent disengagement may be unpalatable, but that is just the point. The choice of extreme positions approximates the present predicament of the United States. In the face of this real and poignant choice, the formula of selective intervention or moderate containment is more an incantation than a proposal.

Another attempt to solve the problem of America's situation in the world is to displace it, to find a surrogate goal that is more congenial or putatively more amenable to solution than the unilateral pursuit of security. The classic solution is to posit "world-order norms," conditions of the international system that should be sought instead of the narrower and presumably more contentious security interests of the United States. An elaborate expression of this thesis is Stanley Hoffmann's book, which embodies in its title the choice he sees as meaningful and critical: *Primacy or World Order*.[5] As Hoffmann put it:

> We should strive for the advent of an international system that goes beyond the past forms of moderation characteristic of balance-of-power eras. The resort to force and the accumulation of weapons will have to be drastically curtailed by a combination of balances of force and cooperative schemes for arms control and the settlement of disputes. Interdependence will have to be made bearable and beneficial both by collective management and by the reduction of excesses of mutual dependence or of the dependence bred by inequality—so that the actors will be provided with greater autonomy and with a greater sense of security.

This, however, is an attempt to wish away the problem. The kind of world order we would recognize as congenial or livable would include a vast component of U.S. primacy. World order is not self-enforcing, and no one can hope for overarching impartial mechanisms or wish for the dominance of another great power. In the critical cases, therefore, it would even be hard to distinguish world order from effective U.S. primacy. More importantly for prescribing U.S. security policy, it would be hard to distinguish the amount of U.S. power needed for the more direct and comprehensible tasks of self-protection from the amount (presumably Hoffmann would say the lesser amount) sufficient to establish world order. Indeed, it might take a concentration and persistence of U.S. power far in excess of the more modest requirements of our own security to enforce world order.

Still another approach is to assert that military means are interchangeable with nonmilitary means, and that the substitution is a matter of choice or preference. But this proposition is not much

---

[5]*Primacy or World Order: American Foreign Policy since the Cold War* (New York: McGraw-Hill, 1978).

more than a placebo. To propose nonmilitary means, or any kind of means, one must have in mind certain interests that might be served or protected by them. In a crisis of conflicting interests, of course, everyone hopes that diplomacy, economic inducements, and sympathetic ties will help resolve the problem. But what if those nonmilitary instruments do not work? Or what if they work only because military instruments lurk in the background—that is, if they depend for their efficacy, in the last analysis, on the threat of force? Simply to ignore this problem is to be thrown back on a nonpolicy: hoping that nothing happens. Everyone favors nonmilitary instruments, where they are appropriate. But to defend, decisively and confidently, a nation's security, one needs force, at least residual force. If the object is to minimize the use of military force, the task is to devise a system and a foreign policy that do not occasion violent intervention. Nonmilitary means might have to be taken into the calculus, but they do not excuse us from the calculation.

An associated confusion arises when we ask whether our political leaders could enhance U.S. power in the world by mobilizing the national will. It had become fashionable to deplore the supposed absence of presidential leadership (at least until 1981, when America was dealt the semblance of presidential leadership in spades). The absence of this commodity was deplored precisely because it was felt that will was not only a necessary but also a sufficient condition for restoring U.S. influence in important international situations.

Pundit-journalists, professional strategists, and even many national security bureaucrats talk almost obsessively about will. Foreign challenges and probes are seen as tests of our resolve; Vietnam was a "trauma" that impaired our capability to respond to threats; we are paralyzed by a "failure of nerve." But we are not talking about "will" in some primal personal sense, and the responses referred to are not subjective psychological phenomena. Rather, we are talking about the operation of a complex political and social system—not even an organism except in a partially useful but mostly misleading metaphor. "Will" represents the ability of a president to generate and sustain the support of the rest of the political system for some specific purpose. What we are really describing, then, is the structure of a problem, and the structure of the system that deals with the problem.

139

An Alternative to Containment

The entailments and disabilities of the policy of containment suggest consideration of a major, coherent alternative. Such a policy would be one of strategic disengagement and nonintervention. In such a program, both of the cardinal elements of the present U.S. strategic paradigm would change. Instead of deterrence and alliance, we would pursue war avoidance and self-reliance. Our security would depend more on our abstention from regional conflicts and, in the strategic nuclear dimension, on finite essential deterrence.

These are not rhetorical terms. Although an extensive statement of their meaning and their implications for our forces is not possible here,[6] suffice it to say that our military program would be designed to defend the most restricted perimeter required to protect our core values. Those core values are our political integrity and the safety of our citizens and their domestic property—a much smaller perimeter than the one the United States is now committed to defend. We would defend against military threats directed against our homeland. However, this is not—and deliberately not—to be considered an overtly geographical criterion. We should not be fixated on drawing lines in the sand, although this is the simplest and most comprehensible exercise. Rather, we should characterize correctly the nature and import of other countries' actions, and appreciate the characteristics of foreign events that cause us to consider them "threats." Functional criteria may be less definitive than geographical ones, but they are more important.

In a program of nonintervention, the United States would defend against an umbra of direct threats to those values that are so basic that they are part of the definition of state and society. Because those values are inalienable, their defense must be credible. We would also defend against a penumbra of challenges that are indirectly threatening but are relevant because of their weight, momentum, direction, and ineluctability. We would be looking for a new set of criteria—decision rules—that condition and bound our responses to future events that could be considered challenges. This is an intensive, rather than extensive, definition.

---

[6]But see Earl C. Ravenal, *Defining Defense: The 1985 Military Budget* (Washington: Cato Institute, 1984).

The concomitant is that the United States would encourage other nations to become self-reliant, to hedge. In fact, some with foresight already discount U.S. protection in a wide range of possible cases, in spite of our formal obligations to come to their assistance. War avoidance invokes primarily, though not exclusively, the strategic nuclear component of our counterparadigm. We will always need a strategy that discourages direct nuclear attacks on our homeland or intolerable coercion of our national political choices by nuclear threats. But today, given the parity between the nuclear arsenals of the two superpowers, our safety depends on maintaining a condition that is called "crisis stability," wherein both sides have a strong incentive to avoid striking first with their nuclear weapons.

A design for nuclear stability would go like this: since an enemy's first strike must logically be a damage-limiting attack against our nuclear forces, we would eliminate our land-based systems as they become even theoretically vulnerable to a Soviet preemptive strike. Those systems are inevitably vulnerable, despite the efforts of a succession of administrations to put them in multiple or closely spaced shelters (as with the MX), or to acquire a redundant and dispersed force (as with the prospective Midgetman single-warhead missiles). Instead, we would move to a diad of strategic nuclear forces: submarines, and bombers armed with medium-range, air-launched cruise missiles. Then, in our targeting doctrine, to discourage further a Soviet first strike, we would not aim at Soviet missiles. (Nor does it make any strategic or moral sense to aim at Soviet cities.) Rather, we would develop a list of some 3,000 military targets, such as naval and air bases, concentrations of conventional forces, military logistical complexes, and arms industries that are relatively far from large civilian population centers.

Beyond that, a serious proposal of nonintervention must make some assumptions about the world: the global political-military balance—specifically, between the United States and the Soviet Union; the situation in important regions of the world; and particularly the fate of Western Europe. For the United States the most important region is Europe. What would be the probable status of Europe without U.S. protection? I would envisage a Europe that is politically and diplomatically independent, that is strategically autonomous, and that acts in greater military concert, although not

141

with political unity or strategic unanimity. Actually, Europe could go quite far toward defending itself without U.S. help, and it need not be "Finlandized," either in whole or in part. If the United States were to withdraw, the principal European countries would probably increase their defense spending gradually, perhaps to 5 or 6 percent of their gross national product. The countries of Western Europe, even if not formally united in a new military alliance, have the economic, demographic, and military resources, and the advantage of natural and man-made barriers, to defeat or crucially penalize a Soviet attack.[7]

Costing Out the Alternative

The alternative of strategic disengagement and nonintervention is objective, substantive, and consequential. This judgment is reinforced by a comparison of costs. We can make large cuts in our defense budget if—but only if—we severely limit our foreign policy objectives. We could defend our essential security and our central values with a much smaller force structure than we now have. Such a force structure would provide the following general-purpose forces: 8 land divisions (6 army and 2 Marine Corps), 20 tactical airwing equivalents (11 air force, 4 Marine Corps, and 5 navy), and 6 carrier battle groups. With the addition of a diad of nuclear forces, submarines and cruise-missile–armed bombers, this would mean manpower of 1,125,000 (330,000 army, 300,000 air force, 360,000 navy, and 135,000 Marine Corps). The total defense budget at the end of a decade of adjustment would be about $150 billion in 1989 dollars. In contrast the Reagan administration's original request for FY 1989 was 21 land divisions and 44 tactical airwing equivalents, with 14 carrier battle groups; this force requires 2,138,000 men and a budget authorization of $291 billion.

These differences will multiply considerably unless we change our course. The defense budget will be about $451 billion by 1998, and cumulative defense spending during that decade will be over $3.6 trillion. Under a noninterventionist policy the 1998 defense

[7]See the more ample treatment of this point in Earl C. Ravenal, *NATO: The Tides of Discontent* (Berkeley: University of California, Institute of International Studies, 1985).

budget would be 53 percent less, and the cumulative cost over a decade would be about $2.5 trillion.[8]

Adjusting to the World

The case for nonintervention is not a pure prescription of a state of affairs that is inherently and universally attractive. It is prescription mingled with prediction. Nonintervention is proposed as an adjustment to the world as it is shaping up and to the constraints of our polity, society, and economy. Our national orientation should not depend entirely on whether some objective, such as containment, is worthy of our commitment. Worthy causes are not free. As in all things, there is a price to be paid, and that price has been growing higher. The multidimensional costs of containment—the specific acts and the general stance of perpetual preparedness—should be weighed against the consequences of not containing and not preparing to contain. Part of the prediction is that our country, taken as a decisionmaking system, will not pay those costs.

The consistent pursuit of nonintervention by a nation would entail a fundamental change in its foreign policy and national strategy. We would have to test our foreign and military policies against the harder questions about national security. In the first instance, this means distinguishing sharply between the interests of our allies and dependents and the interests of our own country. We would also have to learn to differentiate even our own interests from our security. This is not to deny that our other interests (defined in terms of the objective goals of actual individuals and organizations) are real and mostly legitimate. Rather, it is to challenge the automatic notion that we must prepare to defend our panoply of interests by the use or threat of force, overt or covert, wholesale or piecemeal, through proxies or by ourselves. As in the case of the Persian Gulf, some national interests cost more to defend than they are worth.[9]

---

[8]These figures, based on official Pentagon estimates, assume 4 percent inflation plus 1 percent real annual increase. My alternative assumes 4 percent inflation only, with my prescribed cuts taken over a 10-year period.

[9]See the analysis in Earl C. Ravenal, "Defending Persian Gulf Oil," *Intervention* (Fall 1984); and idem, "The Strategic Cost of Oil," testimony before the Subcommittee on the Panama Canal and the Outer Continental Shelf, House Committee on Merchant Marine and Fisheries, June 27, 1984.

When put up against these more stringent criteria, most of our alleged and asserted interests are alienable, in the sense that we can choose not to defend them against all kinds of threats. We can draw back to a line that has two interacting and mutually reinforcing characteristics: credibility and feasibility—a line that we must hold, as part of the definition of our sovereignty, and that we *can* hold, as a defensive perimeter and a strategic force concept that can be maintained with advantage and within constraints over the long haul.

Admittedly, such a national strategy would not maximize gross U.S. interests in the world. But it would be designed to optimize the net interests of American society in the world, in terms of the value of these interests measured against the costs (and costs disguised as risks) of defending them. Ultimately, we may have to settle for less than we would like—even for less than we think we need.

The preceding analysis suggests the following policy prescriptions for a new administration.

Five Concrete Proposals

- Reduce our defense budget progressively, over a 10-year period, from $291 billion (the present requested budgetary authority for FY 1989) to $272 billion for FY 1990, $254 billion for FY 1991, and so forth, down to $150 billion for FY 1998 (all in 1989 dollars)—with concomitant reductions of our force structure.
- Annul, "operationally"—that is, in terms of our real predictable propensity to intervene in conflict—our alliance commitments to defend in Europe, Asia and the Pacific, the Persian Gulf and Southwest Asia, and such other regions as Africa and South America, giving proper diplomatic notice and allowing orderly logistical adjustments.
- Cancel our extended deterrence—that is, the nuclear umbrellas we hold over other countries—by understandings that eliminate the practical possibility of a U.S. nuclear response to an attack upon them.
- Terminate our present overall defense philosophy of containment of the Soviet Union, Soviet proxies, and revolutionary factions in the Third World, leaving the responsibility for balancing (or accommodating) such pressures to regional countries.

- Encourage self-reliant regional and national defense by independent individual countries—particularly in Western Europe, with defense pivoting on the existing British-French nuclear deterrent.

9. NATO and the Next Administration

Christopher Layne

The next administration will take office at a time when the political, economic, and military balance of world forces will continue to shift dramatically. The diffusion of global economic power, ideological pluralism, and the gradual transformation of international politics from the bipolar system of two superpowers to full-fledged political and military multipolarity signals the end of the post-1945 world order.

These ongoing changes in the international system reflect the end of the postwar era of U.S. hegemony. In the 1990s the world will be far different from that of the late 1940s or early 1950s. Consequently it will be necessary to rethink the tenets of post–World War II U.S. foreign policy. One of the key challenges facing the new administration will be to align the external policy of the United States with the new realities in world politics.

The impact of change will be felt most directly in U.S.–West European relations because changing geopolitical circumstances have called into question both the wisdom and affordability of the U.S. commitment to NATO. The Atlantic alliance once rested on two foundations that allowed the United States to defend Western Europe with a minimal risk and at a tolerable cost: the United States' strategic nuclear superiority and its global economic predominance. Today, the disappearance of the U.S. strategic nuclear advantage has lessened the convincingness of its nuclear commitment to NATO. At the same time, the decline of America's economic power relative to that of the rest of the world has made U.S. global military commitments more burdensome and has led, in fact, to dangerous strategic overextension.[1]

---

[1]See Christopher Layne, "Atlanticism Without NATO," *Foreign Policy* 67 (Summer 1987): 22–45; idem, "Ending the Alliance," *Journal of Contemporary Studies* 6 (Summer 1983): 5–31; David Calleo, *Beyond American Hegemony* (New York: Basic Books, 1987); and Paul Kennedy, *The Rise and Fall of Great Powers* (New York: Random House, 1987).

Moreover, even as the bases of America's postwar European policy have been undermined, the nature of the superpower competition in Europe has changed rather remarkably. The most serious Soviet threat to U.S.–West European cohesion is now political, not military, in nature. Soviet leader Mikhail Gorbachev is well placed to exploit intra-Alliance dissension, especially the widening U.S.–West German rift. Gorbachev is not driving a wedge between the United States and Western Europe; the fissures stem from NATO's internal contradictions, not Soviet machinations. What Gorbachev has done, however, is demonstrate an uncanny skill at taking maximum advantage of the tempting targets of opportunity that NATO's fault lines present.

At the same time, under Gorbachev's leadership, the Soviet Union has completely overhauled its diplomatic image. Thus Americans can only watch with amazement as the Soviet Union successfully projects itself as the leading force for peace and constructive change in Europe while simultaneously depicting Washington as the chief obstacle to the stabilization of East-West relations. The Gorbachev challenge has revealed the intellectual and policy sclerosis besetting America's traditional Atlanticist foreign policy establishment.

The Erosion of the Atlantic Alliance

Since 1979 NATO has been beset by a succession of crises—Afghanistan, Iran, Poland, the Siberian natural gas pipeline controversy, Grenada, the U.S. air strikes on Libya, the deployment of intermediate-range nuclear forces (INFs), the October 1986 Reykjavik superpower summit, and the recently ratified "double-zero" treaty eliminating U.S. and Soviet INFs. Superficially the alliance has weathered these storms intact. In reality, though, these multiple shocks have had a cumulative, corrosive effect. NATO is now dramatically weaker politically than it was 10 years ago. The events of the past decade have focused attention on the alliance's structural problems and the sharp divergence of U.S. and West European interests. The stresses fraying the transatlantic bonds between the United States and Western Europe are illustrated by differing U.S. and West European perceptions of the Soviet threat, and U.S. and West European differences about NATO strategy.

A major cause of NATO's erosion is that West Europeans—in contrast with the general outlook of the U.S. foreign policy community—view the Soviet Union as relatively unthreatening politically and ideologically. Although not unconcerned about Soviet military power in Europe, the West Europeans regard the Soviet Union as a troublesome but manageable neighbor with which they share important common interests. Moreover, the West Europeans view the Soviet Union as increasingly preoccupied with its internal reforms, which reinforces the perception of a reduced Soviet threat. Both the lingering fear of war and the positive benefits of cooperation impel Western Europe to follow accommodative policies toward Moscow. Aware of America's waning power and cognizant of its own postwar recovery, Western Europe is driven by both fear and confidence toward a more autonomous geopolitical role. In the process it is positioning itself between the superpowers—not morally, but politically. Although it is a sensible response of those in the middle of a conflict over which they have no control, this West European equidistancing understandably irritates many U.S. policymakers.

In the present, unbalanced NATO relationship, the United States, which believes it bears the brunt of NATO's risks and costs, expects compensation in the form of Western Europe's conformity to U.S. policies. The United States resents a transatlantic division of labor that gives it the unpleasant duty of defending Western interests while leaving Western Europe to enjoy détente's fruits. Americans ask why they should bear the burdens of what seems more like a one-sided protectorate than a true alliance based on reciprocal obligations. Because West European backing of U.S. initiatives is likely to become the sine qua non of continuing U.S. commitment to the alliance, Washington will come under severe domestic pressure to maintain NATO's cohesion by disciplining Western Europe. But such a coercive approach is bound to backfire, inflaming anti-American nationalist sentiments in Europe and further widening the transatlantic rift.

This illustrates NATO's fundamental problem: Western Europe's humiliating and anachronistic dependence on the United States lies at the root of the turmoil in transatlantic relations. An alliance based on U.S. supremacy and West European subordination is inherently vulnerable to reinforcing resentments on both sides of the Atlantic. These tensions will grow worse as U.S. and West European interests increasingly collide on a broad spectrum of political, military, and

149

economic issues. It is the clash of fundamental interests, not Western Europe's "Finlandization," wimpishness, or alleged welfare state addiction that accounts for transatlantic frictions. The intra-NATO debate about the linked issues of NATO strategy and burden sharing illustrates this point.

Burden Sharing and Risk Sharing in NATO

Propelled by the United States' fiscal and trade woes, and the timely publication of books by David Calleo and Paul Kennedy, "burden sharing" has emerged as an important issue in the U.S. public policy debate.[2] It is easy to see why attention has focused on the costs of America's NATO commitment. Washington's strategic obligations to Western Europe absorb somewhere between 42 and 60 percent of U.S. defense expenditures; that is, the United States spends approximately $150 billion a year just on NATO.[3] With tax increases economically unsound and politically infeasible, social security and national debt service untouchable, and domestic spending already cut, NATO is the obvious target to bring the budget deficit under control.

Moreover, U.S. overseas military commitments have serious hidden costs that place the United States at a disadvantage in the global economy and worsen the trade deficit. While U.S. capital and technology are diverted from the private sector to the military sector, Western Europe and Japan take advantage of U.S. security guarantees by enhancing their own economic competitiveness with resources they otherwise would have to spend on defense. Unsurprisingly, there is a negative correlation between high military spending and national productivity gains. For example, in 1983 Japan devoted a mere 1 percent of its GNP to defense; between 1973 and 1983 its national economic productivity improved 2.8 percent. The comparable figures for West Germany were 3.4 percent

---

[2]See Calleo and Kennedy. On the role of burden sharing in the 1988 campaign, see "The High Cost of NATO," *Newsweek*, March 7, 1988. See also U.S. House, Committee on Armed Services, *Report of the Defense Burdensharing Panel*, 100th Cong., 2d sess. (Washington: Government Printing Office, August 1988).

[3]See Leonard Sullivan, "A New Approach to Burden Sharing," *Foreign Policy* (Fall 1985): 91–110; Richard Halloran, "Two Studies Say Defense of Western Europe Is Biggest Military Cost," *New York Times*, July 20, 1984, p. A2; and Earl Ravenal, *NATO: The Tides of Discontent* (Berkeley: University of California, Institute of International Studies, 1985).

for defense and 2.3 percent in productivity and for France 4.3 percent for defense and 2.2 percent in productivity. The United States, which spent 6.9 percent of its GNP on defense, realized a minuscule 0.3 percent gain in national economic productivity.[4]

The present allocation of strategic burdens between the United States and Western Europe reflects the geopolitical realities of the late 1940s, not those of the late 1980s. By devolving to Western Europe full responsibility for its own defense, the United States could go a long way toward curing its fiscal and strategic overcommitment. Devolution and NATO's "Europeanization" would enable a prosperous, politically stable, and technologically advanced Western Europe to assume a strategic role consistent with its potential military strength.

Far from being a radical idea, devolution and Europeanization would mark a return to the original vision of the alliance's architects, who looked at NATO and the Marshall Plan as a means of bolstering war-weakened Western Europe's self-confidence. They expected that Western Europe would move toward political and military integration and ultimately reemerge as an independent force in world politics able to defend itself. The American architects never intended that the U.S. security commitment to Europe would be permanent. In 1951 NATO's first supreme commander, Dwight Eisenhower, stated that NATO would be a failure if American troops remained in Europe for more than 10 years.[5] It is a historical anomaly that, more than 40 years after World War II, the United States remains central Europe's leading power and the Continent remains artificially divided. Certainly the United States has no intrinsic interest in remaining in central Europe indefinitely. As then-senator Gary Hart (D-Colo.) said in an address at Georgetown University on June 12, 1986: "We are not the Romans. We do not intend to stay in Germany for 300 years or until we are driven out."

Although recent years have seen an upsurge of West European discussion about bolstering NATO's "second pillar," only a few symbolic steps have actually been taken to Europeanize NATO. West Europeans are reluctant to confront the knotty political and

[4]Fred Hiatt and Rick Atkinson, "The Hidden Costs of the Defense Buildup," *Washington Post* (national weekly edition), December 16, 1985, p. 10.

[5]Stephen E. Ambrose, *Eisenhower* (New York: Simon and Schuster, 1983), vol. 1, p. 506.

nuclear problems of West Germany's role in a Western European defense community. The West Europeans have also hesitated to increase their contributions to the alliance's conventional defenses.

Clearly, economic and demographic pressures partially explain West European reluctance to do more to build up NATO's conventional strength. However, the real reason the West Europeans do not do more for conventional defense is strategic, not economic: Any increase in NATO's conventional strength will raise the nuclear threshold—that is, make less certain NATO's prompt resort to nuclear weapons—and thus weaken the deterrent effect of nuclear weapons.[6] For Western Europe, any war—conventional or nuclear—would be disastrous. Hence the West Europeans hope to avoid war by maintaining a credible NATO deterrent strategy backed by U.S. strategic nuclear forces. This is why President Reagan's Reykjavik offer to move toward a nuclear-free world sent tremors throughout Western Europe's traditional Atlanticist circles.

On this side of the Atlantic, however, there is a growing realization that America's nuclear guarantee to Western Europe is a source of danger, not of security. Only now is the mainstream U.S. foreign policy community coming to grips with the fact that in a nuclear world, alliances are high-risk entanglements, not sources of enhanced national strength. If Washington ever honored its nuclear pledge to Western Europe, the American homeland would be destroyed by a Soviet retaliatory strike. Throughout the U.S. foreign policy community, there is a deepening awareness that NATO's extended-deterrence/flexible-response strategy is no longer a credible or rational strategy for the United States. Simply put, in a crunch the United States would not—and should not—deliberately sacrifice New York to defend Hamburg.

The U.S. response to the diminishing efficacy of extended deterrence is to encourage NATO to shift away from its reliance on nuclear weapons and adopt a conventional-defense strategy. Of course, this is unacceptable to the West Europeans. Risk sharing, not burden sharing, is at the heart of the alliance's strategic impasse: The risks of nuclear deterrence fall disproportionately on the United

---

[6]See Josef Joffe, *The Limited Partnership: Europe, the United States and the Burdens of Alliance* (Cambridge, Mass.: Ballinger Publishing, 1987); and Karl Kaiser, Georg Leber, Alois Mertes, and Franz Joseph Schulze, "Nuclear Weapons and the Preservation of Peace: A Response," *Foreign Affairs* 60 (Summer 1982): 1157–80.

States and those of conventional defense fall disproportionately on Western Europe. This strategic conundrum is probably insoluble and—as the transatlantic controversy over the INF treaty demonstrated—politically explosive as well.

The Post-INF Crisis

The conventional (and self-congratulatory) wisdom is that the INF treaty demonstrated NATO's ability to hold together in the face of severe Soviet political pressure. In fact the INF affair will force the next administration to come to terms with NATO's gradual unraveling. The treaty has forced into the open the divisive debate about future NATO strategy. In the process the divergent political and strategic interests of the United States and West Germany—the alliance's two key members—have been highlighted and the intractability of NATO's risk-sharing dilemma has been underlined. The INF treaty has focused attention on two intimately connected issues: the role of U.S. nuclear weapons in Western Europe's defense, and the nature of future European security arrangements—that is, the relationship of the United States to Western Europe and of both to the Soviet Union.

The INF affair revealed an important twist to NATO's risk-sharing dilemma.[7] West Germany's traditional security elites went along with the INF treaty because they had to, not because they wanted to. The reason for their tepid support of the treaty is simple. After removal of the INFs, the only U.S. nuclear weapons remaining in West Germany are tactical nuclear weapons. These weapons can only reach targets in Germany (including East Germany). West Germans have long feared that a NATO deterrent posture based on tactical nuclear weapons would tempt the superpowers to fight a limited nuclear war at Germany's expense. What the West Germans have long wanted is the coupling of U.S. strategic nuclear forces to their defense; if the worst happens they want the superpowers to fight the nuclear conflict over their heads, not on their soil.

The INFs were important to Bonn precisely because they linked West Germany's defense to the U.S. strategic nuclear arsenal—

[7]For an extended discussion of the strategic impasse in U.S.–West German relations, see Christopher Layne, "Continental Divide—Time to Disengage in Europe," *The National Interest* 13 (Fall 1988): 13–27.

thereby decreasing West Germany's nuclear risks while increasing the United States'. West Germans correctly perceive that with the INFs gone, the enhanced importance of battlefield nuclear weapons in NATO strategy will have the opposite effect. Bluntly put, in a war, tactical nuclear and conventional weapons would destroy West Germany; strategic nuclear weapons would destroy the United States. Understandably, Washington wants NATO strategy to emphasize tactical nuclear and conventional forces, and Bonn wants Europe's defense coupled to U.S. strategic nuclear forces. In the final analysis, U.S. and West German strategic interests are antithetical—a fact that goes a long way toward explaining why the alliance's prospects of surviving in its present form into the early 21st century are extremely problematical.

In the wake of the INF treaty, modernization of NATO's remaining in-theater nuclear forces and the East-West conventional balance will emerge as the top transatlantic items on the next administration's foreign policy agenda. Convinced that the Soviet threat remains unabated, American Atlanticists will press the new administration to bolster NATO by modernizing the alliance's battlefield nuclear weapons and building up the alliance's conventional capabilities. The next administration should reject this course of action because a militarized approach to European security is certain to prove counterproductive. Invariably, U.S. attempts to strengthen the alliance militarily backfire and weaken it politically—pushing the United States and Western Europe further apart rather than drawing them closer together.

The majority of the West German public does not share the stark view of the Soviet threat held by American Atlanticists. On the contrary, West Germans believe the Soviet Union's preoccupation with internal restructuring and Gorbachev's diplomatic "new thinking" offer an unparalleled opportunity to significantly ease East-West tensions and mitigate the effects of Europe's partition. Given this prevailing climate, U.S. pleas for a new NATO buildup are bound to receive a chilly reception (especially since fiscal constraints practically ensure that America's own NATO contribution will not increase).

Similarly, U.S. calls for modernization of tactical nuclear weapons will have an especially harmful impact on U.S.–West German relations. A showdown on this issue was postponed at the March 1988

154

NATO summit, but if Washington insists on modernization, it will alienate Bonn from its security partners, set the West German government against its public, and further undermine the United States' political standing in West Germany. American Atlanticists' approach to NATO's post-INF strategic policy suggests that U.S. policymakers learned nothing from the INF episode. Those who seem to have forgotten recent history (even though the ink is hardly dry) should remember that although West Germany's traditional security elites are addicted to U.S. nuclear weapons, the West German public is allergic to them. If the United States persists in trying to force Bonn to accept modernization of battlefield nuclear weapons, it will trigger a repetition of the domestic crisis that gripped West Germany during the early 1980s. With West Germany due for national elections in late 1990 or early 1991, the next administration cannot afford to blunder in formulating its European policy.

The New German Question

Although proclaimed by some Atlanticist Pollyannas as a "victory" for NATO, the INF episode has been a Pyrrhic victory at best. The INF deployments—which were supposed to recouple the United States and West Germany—have dramatized the political and military differences that separate Washington and Bonn. The postwar security consensus in West Germany has been shattered by the INF episode. Within the Social Democratic party, Helmut Schmidt's Atlanticist followers have been driven to cover. The emerging Social Democrat leaders, such as Saarland premier Oskar Lafontaine and party activist Andreas von Bulow, talk about taking West Germany out of NATO's integrated military command, demanding withdrawal of U.S. troops from Germany, and shifting to an avowedly neutralist foreign policy. The Social Democrats already are on record as favoring a "security partnership" between Western Europe and the Warsaw Pact and a central European nuclear-free zone.[8] On the right, conservative members of the Christian Democratic party reacted with bitterness to the October 1986 Reykjavik summit meeting and

[8]On the Social Democrats' current views on security issues and East-West relations, see Horst Ehmke, "A Second Phase of Detente," *World Policy Journal* 4, no. 3 (Summer 1987): 363–82; and Oskar Lafontaine, *European Security Policy* (Washington: Friedrich Ebert Stiftung, 1987).

the double-zero INF treaty.[9] Alfred Dregger, the Christian Democrats' Bundestag floor leader, accused the United States of "betraying" German interests and "abandoning" the federal republic. In a position paper, Dregger's colleague Bernhard Friedmann argued that because the United States inevitably is going to withdraw from Europe, Bonn should seek Soviet support for a united, neutral German state. On both the political right and left, German nationalism—and the question of German reunification—has been revived by the INF affair.[10]

The basic (although seldom acknowledged) reason American Atlanticists cling tenaciously to the transatlantic status quo is their reluctance to come to grips with the German Question, which encompasses the issues of German reunification and Germany's future political and military role in Europe. Such an attitude, however, is shortsighted and self-defeating because the German Question lies at the heart of NATO's nuclear dilemma and the broader issues of European security. The interplay of strategic factors with its own national aspirations makes Bonn's relations with the West inescapably ambivalent. Committed to the long-term goal of reunification, Bonn takes as its top foreign policy priority what is called *Deutschlandpolitik*, its political, economic, and cultural outreach to East Germany. To allow this policy to flourish, West Germany seeks to relax political tensions in Europe and to avoid any moves that could heighten East-West tensions. Inevitably, Bonn's policies cause friction within NATO, but in recent years both former Social Democrat chancellor Helmut Schmidt and Christian Democrat chancellor Helmut Kohl have made it plain that West Germany's national policy will not be subordinated to Washington's definition of NATO solidarity.

NATO's nuclear dilemma is a second factor undergirding Bonn's delicate balancing between East and West. Implicitly, the West

[9]James M. Markham, "Under Pressure, Kohl Eases Short-Range Missile Stand," *New York Times*, May 24, 1987, p. 9; Thomas F. O'Boyle, "German Neutrality Is Gaining Ground Among Right Wing Upset by Arms Talks," *Wall Street Journal*, June 2, 1987, p. 22.

[10]For an extended analysis of the link between the INF deployments and the revival of German nationalism, see Christopher Layne, "Toward German Reunification?" *Journal of Contemporary Studies* 7 (Fall 1984): 7–37. This article also analyzes at length the German Question's implications for U.S.-Soviet relations.

Germans have concluded that the U.S. nuclear guarantee cannot be relied upon and that a substantial lessening of the U.S. commitment to NATO is inevitable. American Atlanticists want to allay these concerns and reassure the West Germans by reinforcing the nuclear coupling between the two countries. Their approach is doubly flawed, however. First, U.S. interests require that Washington lower, not increase, the nuclear risks of U.S. NATO commitments. Seemingly, West Germans understand this better than many U.S. policymakers, which leads to the second point: Nothing the United States says or does is likely to convince the West Germans that America would really put its national existence on the line for their sake.

The alliance's strategic anomaly has always been that its most vulnerable and vital European member is a nonnuclear power that must rely upon others for its security. Consequently, as former French president Valéry Giscard d'Estaing has said, West Germany "is a target without a shield." As long as this remains true, Bonn has powerful incentives to seek a political accommodation with Moscow that will resolve its security dilemma as well as preserve its interests in more intimate relations with the other Germany. Bonn is convinced that there is no military solution to West Germany's strategic dilemma (either because the United States would not use nuclear weapons to defend West Germany or because it might indeed use them). Consequently, a new consensus is emerging in West Germany that seeks security in a "second phase of détente" involving comprehensive arms control and closer economic relations with Moscow.

The Kremlin is well-positioned to take advantage of West Germany's nuclear angst and rising national neutralism, and the growing friction in U.S.–West German relations.[11] The Soviets have a great deal of leverage because they can link progress in intra-German relations to Bonn's willingness to make political security and economic concessions to Moscow. Moreover, as Milan Svec argued in *Foreign Policy*, Gorbachev's greatest opportunity to "sway the West"—indeed to break up NATO—"is to take on the so-called

[11]See Christopher Layne, "Deutschland Uber Allies," *New Republic*, September 28, 1987, pp. 12–14.

German question."[12] Merely by flashing the German card, the Kremlin pulls Bonn eastward, thereby sharpening the strains between the United States and West Germany. If the Soviets ever did decide to play the reunification gambit, they would bring about NATO's sudden collapse. Notwithstanding conventional wisdom in Washington that the Soviets will never allow German reunification on any terms, it is not wise to base one's strategy on the assumption that one's adversary isn't smart enough to make an obvious winning move. Moreover, the Soviets can effectively use the German card even without offering outright reunification. There are indeed signs that Gorbachev may soon offer to tear down the Berlin Wall in exchange for a central European nuclear-free zone and/or withdrawal of all foreign troops from East and West Germany. If such an offer is made, it is hard to see how a West German government that refused it could survive politically. Yet Bonn's acceptance of a deal like this would shatter the alliance.[13]

Toward a Post-Yalta Settlement

The post–World War II (Yalta) settlement is crumbling. This is evidenced by the growing disarray in NATO; the resurfacing of the German Question; and the simmering discontent in Eastern Europe, where *glasnost*'s uncertain effects, economic difficulties, and anti-Soviet nationalism could spell trouble. Increasingly, the European situation is characterized by fluidity and potential volatility. Evolutionary forces are at work there, and they will determine the future course of the triangular relationship between the United States, Europe, and the Soviet Union. Change cannot be prevented but it can be directed. Washington's challenge in the post-INF environment is to formulate policies that will smooth the transition from the present European security system to a post-NATO world.

American Atlanticists are pursuing a policy that lacks vision and has no objective other than preserving the postwar security struc-

---

[12]Milan Svec, "Removing Gorbachev's Edge," *Foreign Policy* (Winter 1987–88): 158; also see Layne, "Atlanticism Without NATO," pp. 30–31.

[13]In the fall of 1987 French officials speculated about the possibility that Gorbachev might propose removing all foreign forces from the two Germanies. The French lamented the absence of a coherent Western strategy for coping with the Soviet leader's supple diplomacy. See Rowland Evans and Robert Novak, "But NATO Is Worried," *Washington Post*, September 25, 1987.

ture for its own sake. Yet, more than two decades ago, then-professor Henry A. Kissinger warned that it is an illusion to regard NATO as the "natural" structure of Atlantic relations and to think that sound policy consists only of attempts to improve the alliance.[14] The objective of the United States' European policy should not necessarily be to preserve NATO intact but to maintain peace and stability in Europe and to prevent the Soviet Union from gaining political ascendancy over the Continent. U.S. policymakers should be asking whether the postwar arrangements still serve their intended purposes and whether those purposes would be better met through new structures.

The United States' post-INF European policy should start by recognizing the obvious: Because the credibility of extended deterrence cannot be restored at an acceptable cost to the United States, NATO's long-term cohesion is seriously (perhaps fatally) compromised. At the same time, a U.S. policy of reducing the nuclear danger to America by increasing it for West Germany risks triggering a bitter divorce between Washington and Bonn—a turn of events that would benefit only Moscow. It is necessary, therefore, to seek a diplomatic solution to West Germany's security dilemma. And because West Germany's strategic difficulties are intertwined with the geopolitical effects of Germany's partition, U.S. policy must confront the German Question head-on. Although it grates on the sensibilities of certain U.S. foreign policy circles, West Germany has legitimate concerns and national interests that the United States ignores at its peril.

As the postwar era draws to a close, it is obvious that the United States needs a new European security policy. Washington's objectives should be the reduction of the nuclear exposure that extended deterrence imposes on the United States; enhancement of West Germany's security; alleviation of tensions in Eastern Europe; and the blunting of Gorbachev's West European "peace offensive." These goals can be advanced by pressing for a U.S.-Soviet agreement providing for the superpowers' mutual political and military disengagement from central Europe.

In coming years the United States' European interests would be

---

[14]Henry A. Kissinger, "Central Issues of American Foreign Policy," in Kermit Gordon, ed., *Agenda for the Nation* (Washington: Brookings Institution, 1968), p. 596.

159

served equally by mutual U.S.-Soviet disengagement from central Europe or by a gradual U.S. policy of devolution/Europeanization.[15] However, a determined U.S. effort to secure mutual disengagement is a prerequisite for any long-range policy of Europeanizing the alliance. Europeanization will remain a chimera as long as West Europeans view the Soviet Union as a relatively benign power and as long as West Germans believe something substantive might lurk behind Soviet hints of flexibility on the German Question. On the other hand, if the Soviets were unrelenting on the German Question and clung stubbornly to their East European position while the United States sought an interim solution to Germany's partition and manifested its willingness to leave Western Europe, reasonable people could have no doubt as to which superpower had embraced Europe's aspirations and which was blocking them. At that point the United States would be in a strong position to negotiate a new transatlantic compact that ultimately would lead to the alliance's Europeanization. Only if Gorbachev's overtures were revealed as a hollow propaganda ploy would Western Europe have reason to confront the difficult problems of West Germany's nuclear and political roles in a Europeanized alliance and only then would Bonn be persuaded to anchor itself firmly in the alliance.

Washington, however, should not use mutual disengagement merely as a public relations gimmick. Mutual superpower disengagement is a vehicle both for shifting the political momentum in Europe and for promoting U.S. interests. By championing new European security arrangements, the United States could turn the tables on Moscow and put the Soviet Union on the defensive. Washington could neutralize the Soviets' German card because the advocacy of mutual superpower disengagement would cast the United States—not the Soviet Union—as the champion of Germany's national aspirations. Such a U.S. initiative would have widespread popular appeal in West Germany, unlike current U.S. policies that have resonance only among a narrow (and shrinking) spectrum of politically conservative West Germans. Unlike the current Atlanticist policy of drift, the inexorable loosening of U.S.-West German bonds would be offset by the tangible improvement in Western

---

[15]For contrasting views of what devolution/Europeanization entails, compare Layne, "Atlanticism Without NATO," with Calleo.

Europe's security position that would accrue from mutual disengagement.

Moreover, by standing pat in Western Europe, the United States would allow the Soviet Union to exploit the centrifugal stresses in Atlantic relations. A more imaginative U.S. policy would force the Soviet Union into an agonizing reappraisal of the ambivalence imbedded in its own European political strategy. For example, do the Soviets really want to take on the German Question? Do they really want to break up NATO and drive the United States out of Europe and thereby risk the emergence of a powerful Western Europe that could be an irresistible political and economic magnet for Eastern Europe and that could include a nuclear West Germany? Mutual superpower disengagement would also make Western Europe more, not less, secure.

Far more than any attainable nuclear or conventional arms control agreement, disengagement would radically reduce the chances of war in Europe because it would lower the political tensions that could lead to conflict. Disengagement would neutralize Moscow's conventional superiority in Europe by reducing the Soviet army's size and putting it back where it belongs—in the Soviet Union (thereby making the nuclear threshold problem much less acute for Western Europe). Moreover, a Soviet pullback from Eastern Europe would lessen the stresses caused by the Continent's partition and help ensure that it does not become the Sarajevo of the 1990s. Washington and Moscow have a common interest in achieving Eastern Europe's Finlandization by reconciling legitimate Soviet security concerns with Eastern Europe's desire for greater autonomy, political pluralism, and economic reform. Unlike current proposals for conventional arms control, disengagement would not get bogged down in discussions about proper units of account, definitions of "offensive" versus "defensive" weapons, and the problem of reducing forces that are asymmetrical both quantitatively and qualitatively. Unlike the technical minutiae of arms control, the pristine simplicity of mutual disengagement could easily be grasped by the West German public (and by other Europeans), which would politically and morally strengthen the U.S. position in Europe.

It could be argued that the Soviet Union's geographical proximity to central Europe would give it a big edge if it broke an agreement and moved back into the region. This argument is superficially

161

plausible but does not hold up under scrutiny. The Soviet Union would pay an extremely high political price if it reentered central Europe after implementation of a mutual disengagement accord. This would be an important constraint because the Soviet Union's internal economic restructuring will depend heavily on access to West European trade, technology, and credits. By breaking a mutual disengagement agreement, the Soviets would cause a rupture of their economic ties with Western Europe and spur the West Europeans into taking concrete steps toward creating a formidable West European defense community. Militarily, mutual superpower disengagement would enhance Western Europe's strategic depth (now one of its real weaknesses) by putting Soviet forces hundreds of miles to the east of their present positions—and thus well away from West Germany's now-vulnerable industrial and population centers. Moreover, if the Soviets did want to attack Western Europe, their forces probably would first have to fight their way through Poland and East Germany. In any event, a Soviet move westward would be an unambiguous signal, providing Western Europe with strategic warning and ample time for mobilization.

No doubt, danger is inherent in the process of moving toward a new political dispensation in Europe, but danger is abundantly present in the status quo too. Diplomatically, Washington's present European policy is the equivalent of the death of a thousand cuts because it allows Moscow to orchestrate the process of NATO's gradual but steadily creeping paralysis. U.S. policymakers have not grasped that the critical dimension of European security is political. The basic problem with Washington's traditional Atlanticist European policy is that it leaves the geopolitical initiative entirely in Moscow's hands. Under Gorbachev's leadership, Moscow has developed a subtle and appealing *Westpolitik* that plays both to Western Europe's insecurities and to its pan-European aspirations. The Kremlin is able to manipulate West European perceptions of the Soviet threat and undercut support for new NATO defense initiatives and neutralize West European incentives to move concretely toward the alliance's Europeanization. Indeed, hardly a month now passes without some superficially attractive arms control proposal emanating from Moscow (most recently a call for an all-European summit to discuss security issues and an offer to withdraw Soviet combat aircraft in Eastern Europe if NATO forgoes redeployment of U.S. F–16s from Spain to Italy), or Soviet references to the fact that all Europeans dwell in a common house. Gorbachev's domestic program of openness and revitalization bolsters West European perceptions of a vastly reduced Soviet threat. Finally, by repeatedly dangling the German card, the Soviets keep West Germany uneasily suspended between East and West and encourage Bonn to slide toward a de facto neutrality, notwithstanding its NATO membership.

The United States stands by, helplessly bewildered by Gorbachev's dazzling diplomatic virtuosity. With no overarching European blueprint of its own, Washington is locked into a posture of reacting belatedly on an ad hoc basis to a succession of Soviet demarches. Kremlin hints that both superpowers "weigh anchor" and leave central Europe, and intimations that the Soviet Union has repealed the Brezhnev Doctrine and is prepared to accept pluralism in Eastern Europe, must be tested by constructive U.S. initiatives.[16] The lack of a creative U.S. European policy allows the Soviets to score a lot of uncontested diplomatic points by making such proposals.

The time has come to put the Soviet Union's intentions and sincerity to the test and force Moscow to fish or cut bait. The dangers of U.S. rigidity are apparent. The United States' political standing in Western Europe has slipped badly.[17] And, as a May 1987 article in Die Welt described, there is a real danger in yielding the political initiative on European security matters to the Soviets:

> Both the German domestic debate and the Euro-American debate show how the Russians can make military, political and psychological gains by disarmament proposals involving partial U.S.

[16]In this regard it is interesting to note that at a July 1988 Washington conference on East European affairs, the Soviet delegation admitted that the Soviet Union violated that 1945 Yalta agreement to allow free elections in Eastern Europe. See Robert C. Toth, "Soviets Concede Stalin Violated Yalta Agreements in East Europe," Los Angeles Times, July 10, 1988, p. 12.

[17]This fact is reflected in public opinion polls showing that West Germans believe Mikhail Gorbachev is more interested in peace than Ronald Reagan and that West Germans want Bonn to cooperate equally with the United States and the Soviet Union. See James M. Markham, "Gorbachev Gains in West Germany," New York Times, May 17, 1987, p. 6. See also the important survey "America and the Germans" conducted by the Munich-based Sinus Organization on behalf of the Stern magazine and the Friedrich Ebert Stiftung.

withdrawals from Europe. What is lacking is the grand design, the offer that can't be refused.

If Mr. Gorbachev establishes a link of any substance between military disengagement and political solutions for continental Europe—a link the Americans at present fail to establish—progress . . . might be made. It certainly would be in Germany. . . . It alone could be enough to make the national debate in Germany come to a head over the country's elected representatives.[18]

As demonstrated by the speculation about the unilateral withdrawal of Soviet forces from Hungary, the possibility that Gorbachev may make even more dramatic gestures in Europe cannot be discounted.[19]

The attempt to put European security on a new footing must be made because the United States' traditional Atlanticist policy seems destined to produce a bitter rupture between the United States and West Germany—NATO's keystone relationship. The post-INF agenda being pushed by American Atlanticists will not advance U.S. interests in Europe. One reason is that it will lead to further estrangement between Bonn and Washington because West Germany will reject nuclear modernization and a conventional buildup as being contrary to its strategic and national interests. A second reason is that by leaving West Germany's security dilemma unresolved, the Kremlin will continue to reap the advantages it now gains from manipulating extended deterrence's contradictions and thereby sowing discord in U.S.–West German relations. U.S.–West German relations are locked into what is now a ritual exchange of hollow assurances. Washington promises it will risk nuclear war to defend West Germany; Bonn tells the United States it is not a wanderer between the superpowers. Neither can mean what it says and still be faithful to its own national interests. Mutual disengagement is the one policy that offers the hope of reconciling U.S. and West German differences.

Until the United States tests Moscow, it cannot be known whether

[18]Herbert Kremp, "Soviet Proposal on German Reunification Fires Imaginations and Illusions," German Tribune, May 31, 1987, p. 5 (English language reprint of article in Die Welt, May 15, 1987).

[19]Michael R. Gordon, "U.S. Says Soviets May Pull Troops Out of Hungary," New York Times, July 9, 1988, p. 1; and Robert C. Toth, "Kremlin May Remove Forces from Hungary," Los Angeles Times, July 9, 1988, p. 1.

the Soviets would be interested in mutual superpower disengagement from central Europe. However, a negative response should not be assumed. The generational power transfer in the Kremlin may present the next administration with heretofore unimaginable diplomatic opportunities. There are important concrete Soviet interests that might dispose the Kremlin to agree to mutual disengagement. In this regard, whether the Soviets are merely seeking a breathing space to regroup for renewed conflict is a much less important question than asking whether—regardless of the Kremlin's intentions—opportunities exist to reach mutually beneficial political agreements that the Soviets would have difficulty in subsequently breaking. Clearly, U.S. interests would be served by the superpowers' subsequently joint disengagement from central Europe, and Washington should engage the Soviets on this issue. Although the Soviet Union and the United States are rivals, they have congruent as well as antagonistic interests. As Walter Lippmann once observed, statesmen who believe unfriendly powers cannot reach agreements forget what diplomacy is all about.

The next administration will take office at a delicate moment. If it stumbles, Gorbachev could capitalize on the resulting transatlantic discord. To meet Gorbachev's challenge at a time when U.S.– West European relations are evolving into a new phase, Washington must outthink the Kremlin. Unlike the current stagnation in the United States' European policy, change in Europe contains the seeds of opportunity—and U.S. statesmen need to be wise enough to nurture them. Washington holds the high cards in the political struggle for Europe and needs only the boldness and imagination to play them.

Policy Recommendations

The next administration should adopt a new European security policy for the United States based on the following.

- Removal of both superpowers' military forces and nuclear weapons from central Europe (the two Germanies, Poland, Hungary, and Czechoslovakia).
- A pledge that neither superpower will be the first to reintroduce its forces into central Europe ("no first reentry").
- Asymmetrical demobilization of the Soviet and U.S. forces withdrawn from Europe. That is, both superpowers would

disband the bulk of their forces removed from the Continent, but the Soviets, because of their numerical superiority, would be required to demobilize a proportionately greater number of troops. In addition, as a hedge against violation of a disengagement accord, the United States would be permitted to leave in place in West Germany prepositioned equipment for two U.S. divisions.

- As part of this broader disengagement package, Washington would press for the "third zero"—elimination of Soviet and U.S. short-range nuclear weapons in Europe—because the U.S. tactical nuclear weapons in Europe are a danger for this country and a source of poison in U.S.–West German relations.
- An interim solution to the German Question short of reunification but guaranteeing unhampered travel between the two Germanies.
- To help the United States regain the diplomatic upper hand in the political struggle for Europe, immediately on taking office the next administration should challenge the Soviets by unilaterally withdrawing from Europe (and demobilizing) one U.S. division and 1,000 of the shortest-range U.S. nuclear weapons.

10. Beyond U.S. Paternalism: A New Security Strategy for the Pacific Basin

Ted Galen Carpenter

Since the end of World War II, the United States has exercised unquestioned political, economic, and military dominance throughout the Pacific basin. Until recently the Soviet Union barely even bothered to contest U.S. influence in the region. During the 1950s and 1960s Communist China was more adventurous, but following the bloody Korean conflict, Beijing too appreciated the limits of its ability to challenge Washington's hegemony. The various noncommunist powers willingly followed America's lead, both accepting Washington's protection and deferring to its wishes on a wide range of policy concerns. The enormous gap in military and economic strength between the United States and the other members of the so-called free world coalition in the area essentially precluded any other course.

It is increasingly evident, however, that this state of affairs is coming to an end. Washington's failure to secure its objectives in Southeast Asia in the 1960s and early 1970s alerted nations in the Pacific region to the fact that even a superpower was not omnipotent. More significant has been the tremendous economic changes that have occurred throughout the Pacific basin during the past two decades. Japan has emerged to supplant the USSR as the world's number two economic power, and such nations as South Korea, Taiwan, Singapore, Malaysia, and Indonesia have become significant economic players. Finally, Beijing's decision to move away from the disastrous policies of centralized planning in favor of market reforms has awakened Asia's slumbering giant. China is already a major regional power and certainly has the potential to become one of the world's great powers within a few decades.

The growth of economic multipolarity in the Pacific basin, which is merely one manifestation of a global trend, has significant political and military implications. There are now several nations that are capable of assuming far greater security responsibilities and, with the cessation of U.S. willingness to undertake that task in their stead, would have every incentive to do so. Fears that gradual U.S. disengagement from East Asia and the western Pacific would open the door to Soviet domination of the region are misplaced. China already confronts the Soviet army along the lengthy border between the two states, and it refused to be intimidated even in the early and mid-1970s when it was far weaker both economically and militarily than it is today. Nor is it likely that such proud and capable nations as Japan, South Korea, Australia, or Indonesia would tamely accept Moscow's domination. Even if the USSR sought to achieve hegemony—and recent events point to a more accommodationist strategy—nations in East Asia and the western Pacific would be more likely to coalesce into an anti-Soviet formation than to be "Finlandized." As various scholars have shown, medium-sized powers when faced with an aggressive, expansionist state typically move to "balance" that country rather than "bandwagon" with it.[1]

Economic change in the Pacific basin not only creates an opportunity for the United States to devolve many of the security burdens it has borne for four decades, it underscores the urgent need to do so. American firms that once dominated global markets now must contend with increasingly ferocious competition—often from companies located in Far Eastern nations. Washington's insistence on subsidizing the defense requirements of those nations penalizes American firms and gives an artificial advantage to their foreign competitors. Among the adverse economic consequences are high taxes, the diversion of research and development funds into the military at the expense of civilian products, and the siphoning off of engineering and managerial talent into military work.[2] Such

[1]A concise discussion of the balancing and bandwagoning processes is found in Stephen M. Walt, "Alliance Formation and the Balance of World Power," *International Security* 9 (Spring 1985): 3–41. See also Kenneth Waltz, *Theory of International Politics* (Reading, Mass.: Addison-Wesley, 1979).

[2]For discussions of such problems, see Seymour Melman, *The Permanent War Economy*, rev. ed. (New York: Simon and Schuster, 1985); Lloyd Jeffrey Dumas, *The Overburdened Economy* (Berkeley: University of California Press, 1986); Robert W. DeGrasse, Jr., *Military Expansion, Economic Decline* (New York: M. E. Sharpe, Inc., 1983); and Richard Rosecrance, *The Rise of the Trading State: Commerce and Conquest in the Modern World* (New York: Basic Books, 1986).

developments would be distressing even if the United States had no option but to persist in its role as global policeman. But in an increasingly multipolar world, other options do exist, and the Pacific basin is one region where a change in U.S. security strategy is overdue.

Unfortunately, there is little indication that U.S. leaders understand the import of the vast changes that are sweeping through the area. Especially in the realm of security policy, officials cling to arrangements that were established in the late 1940s and early 1950s to meet the perceived problems of that era—arrangements that are now hopelessly out of date, ineffectual, and in many cases counterproductive. Indicative of such ossified thinking was the assurance by Secretary of State George Shultz that American troops will remain in South Korea for as long as Seoul believes they are necessary.[3] Implicit in that comment is the view that South Korea remains a war-ravaged waif utterly incapable of staving off the communist north without U.S. protection. That may have been the reality when the "mutual" defense treaty was concluded between Washington and Seoul in January 1954, but today South Korea is an economic dynamo with a population twice that of North Korea and a gross national product nearly five times as large. One would think that U.S. leaders might at least consider the possibility that a nation with those characteristics should be able to provide for its own defense instead of continuing to be an American protectorate.

Opportunity for the New Administration

The incoming administration has the opportunity and the obligation to restructure U.S. security policy in the Pacific basin. Instead of ignoring or vainly resisting the political and military implications of the region's growing economic multipolarity, the United States should adjust to the new realities. That adjustment will not prove easy since it involves an implicit admission that U.S. predominance has ended, and it means the devolution of defense responsibilities to other nations that may be none too eager to assume such burdens. Nevertheless, it is in both the financial and the security interests of

[3]Don Oberdorfer, "Secretary Pledges Support for Asian Democracies," *Washington Post*, July 18, 1988.

169

the American people that the process of devolution take place. And that objective should be the lodestar of the new administration.

Devolution does not imply either total indifference to the affairs of the Far East or the adoption of a "Fortress America" military strategy. Indifference would be unwise, given this country's increasingly pervasive economic ties to the East Asian nations. Economically, the Pacific basin nations rival Western Europe in significance as trading partners of the United States. Japan's importance in that regard is well known, but South Korea, Taiwan, and the members of the Association of Southeast Asian Nations (ASEAN) are also major factors, and in the early years of the next century China is likely to figure prominently in our commercial calculations. And in the military realm, a strict Fortress America strategy, whatever its emotional appeal, is simply not feasible, given the nature of modern warfare.

A decision to devolve security responsibilities must not become a pretext for the adoption of protectionist trade policies or other xenophobic measures. It is desirable for the United States to maintain and even expand its diplomatic and commercial activities throughout the Pacific basin. Militarily the United States would be able to demobilize air, naval, and ground units that exist primarily for the protection of East Asian nations that are now capable of defending themselves. (And we certainly should demobilize units whose sole justification is for the projection of U.S. power beyond the Pacific basin and into the Indian Ocean and Persian Gulf.) At the same time, the republic must maintain a significant "blue water" naval capability along with adequate conventional air power in the central and eastern Pacific to protect Hawaii and U.S. territories. That in turn implies the existence of air and naval installations as far west as Guam. A serious threat to America's Pacific territories is an exceedingly remote possibility, but adequate air and naval power constitutes a worthwhile insurance policy.

America's Burdensome Obligations

Washington's existing military commitments in the Pacific basin are multifaceted and expensive. Defense analyst Earl C. Ravenal has estimated that the forces needed for the protection of allies and clients in the Far East cost American taxpayers some $40 billion per

170

year—nearly 15 percent of the nation's annual military budget.[4] The most important commitment is the 1951 defense treaty with Japan, and a large portion of U.S. air and naval assets in the western Pacific exist to deter a Soviet move against that country. Moreover, under the doctrine of extended deterrence, the U.S. strategic nuclear umbrella covers Japan as well as the NATO signatories.

There are lesser but still significant treaty obligations with regard to other Pacific nations. Not only does the United States have a security pact with South Korea but that commitment is reinforced by the presence of more than 43,000 American troops, four squadrons of advanced fighter aircraft, and several hundred tactical nuclear warheads. Furthermore, an American officer commands the joint U.S.-South Korean force. Washington is also pledged to defend the Philippines, and that promise is underscored by the U.S. military installations at Clark Air Base and Subic Bay Naval Base. The United States is a signatory to the ANZUS treaty with Australia and New Zealand—although the ongoing dispute with the latter country over nuclear weapons policy has essentially converted that pact into a bilateral U.S.-Australian association. In addition, the United States maintains informal but entirely real security arrangements with other nations in the region, most notably Indonesia and China.

Japan's Free Ride

Although it is increasingly difficult to justify any of those commitments and the financial burdens they entail, it is especially so concerning the protection afforded Japan. There is little question that Tokyo could relieve the United States of most of its heavy security burden in the Far East. Japan is already an economic superpower, and with even a modest effort it could certainly become a daunting regional political and military power if not actually join the exclusive superpower club. Yet, because of domestic political factors and perverse incentives created by U.S. foreign policy, Japan has consistently failed to make the requisite effort.

The paucity of the Japanese military contribution is apparent in the level of defense spending. Whereas the United States is currently devoting nearly 6.9 percent of its GNP to the military—and has averaged 7.5 percent annually throughout the Cold War period—

---

[4]Earl Ravenal, *Defining Defense* (Washington: Cato Institute, 1984), p. 16.

171

Japan spends slightly more than 1 percent.[5] Tokyo's performance compares poorly even to the anemic efforts of the European allies, who spend barely 3.5 percent.[6] Although the trend in Japanese defense spending has been upward in recent years, the increases have been exceedingly modest, and at this rate it would take many years before Japan would become a serious military factor. Defense analyst Edward Olsen has accurately described the situation in noting that

> Japan's defense contributions remain decidedly minimalist, parsimonious, and inordinantly cautious. Japan is, indeed, getting a cheap ride. It benefits from an international security system predicated on collective security, but refuses to pay its fair share of the costs or bear a fair share of the risks.[7]

Olsen's last point is especially pertinent. It is not merely the huge disparity between U.S. and Japanese defense spending that underscores Tokyo's inadequate military role. Except for helping to defend the immediate air and oceanic approaches to the home islands, Japan does precious little to protect the security of the Far East, much less assume more far ranging defense responsibilities. Although South Korea is much more relevant to Japan's security interests than it is to the United States, it is U.S. forces—not Japanese forces—that help defend that country. The Soviet naval buildup in the western Pacific during the past decade has been countered by Washington, not Tokyo. U.S. ships in the Persian Gulf guard oil routes that are Japan's petroleum lifeline, and they are incurring severe risks in the process, while Japan's naval forces are conspicuous by their absence.

---

[5]Department of Defense, *Report on Allied Contributions to the Common Defense* (April 1987), p. 72. To minimize domestic opposition, the Japanese government disguises the actual extent of its military spending by calculating it in a manner different from that of the United States and the other NATO countries. Even taking that difference into account, Tokyo spends no more than 1.5 percent of GNP. See Reinhard Drifte, "Japan's Defense Policy: How Far Will the Changes Go?" *International Defense Review* 18, no. 2 (1985): 153–58.

[6]*Report on Allied Contributions*, p. 72.

[7]Edward A. Olsen, "U.S.-Japan Security Relations After Nakasone: The Case for a Strategic Fairness Doctrine," in *Collective Defense or Strategic Independence? Alternative Strategies for the Future*, ed. Ted Galen Carpenter (Lexington, Mass.: Lexington Books, forthcoming 1989).

Defenders of the status quo cite numerous reasons for Tokyo's lack of military responsibility. Among the most prominent reasons given are that the Japanese constitution prohibits a more vigorous role; that there is intense domestic opposition to even the current level of defense spending, much less to more ambitious objectives; and that Japan's neighbors, still recoiling from the memories of World War II, do not want to see a resurgence of Japanese power.[8] Such explanations are uncompelling. Article 9 of the Japanese constitution, imposed by the United States after World War II, renounces war as a sovereign right of the nation and theoretically prohibits even the existence of military forces.[9] But as interpreted by the Japanese government this article has had little practical effect other than to require the Orwellian euphemism of "self-defense forces" to describe the military establishment. Operationally, the government can define Japan's defense needs and create the forces required to implement them without restraint.[10]

The other reasons given are partially valid but still fail to justify Japan's willingness to accept a free ride on the U.S. defense guarantee. There is a strong pacifist strain in Japanese public opinion, and taxpayers in that country undoubtedly are not eager to pay more to support a military buildup. Strong resistance exists to increased military spending in other countries as well, including the United States. But Washington's willingness to heavily subsidize Japan's defense has spared Japanese leaders and voters from making the difficult choices about what level of military spending—and what force structure—is needed to adequately protect the security of their nation. Washington's generosity, moreover, has been an excessive and unjustified burden on U.S. citizens.

The observation that the other peoples of East Asia still recall the horrors of Japanese imperialism and would object to Tokyo having

[8]For discussions of some of these issues, see Taketsugu Tsurutani, "Old Habits, New Times: Challenges to Japanese-American Security Relations," *International Security* 7 (Fall 1982): 175–87; Masashi Nishihara, "Expanding Japan's Credible Defense Role," *International Security* 8 (Winter 1983–84): 180–205; and William T. Tow, "Japan's Rearmament: The ASEAN Factor," *Asia Pacific Community* (Winter 1984): 11–28.

[9]Amos Jenkins Peaslee, *Constitutions of Nations* (Boston: Martinus Nijhoff Publishers, 1985), p. 415. See also Theodore McNelly, "The Renunciation of War in the Japanese Constitution," *Armed Forces and Society* 13 (Fall 1986): 81–106.

[10]See, for example, the evolution of Japanese defense policy since 1976 discussed in Nishihara.

primary responsibility for the defense of the region cannot be dismissed lightly. Both the governments and the populations of those countries undoubtedly prefer the current situation, with the United States playing the role of protector. But the pertinent question from the standpoint of U.S. foreign policy is not whether the status quo is more comfortable for those regional states, but whether it is in the best interests of the American people. It is difficult to justify the view that the United States must continue to bear an expensive—and potentially dangerous—set of military commitments indefinitely merely to spare Japan and its neighbors from forging new security arrangements, however difficult it might be for them to overcome old animosities. World War II ended more than four decades ago, and it is time for the East Asian nations to put its ghosts to rest.

In an increasingly multipolar world, Japan is a logical candidate to assume substantial responsibility for the security of the Far East. It has the population (121 million) and the economic base to play an important leadership role. That role might be played in conjunction with other nations in the region—especially China and South Korea—that also have an incentive to deter any hegemonic aspirations harbored by the USSR. Conversely, Japan might prefer to adopt a more independent posture and act as the "balancer" in the region, especially if the Soviet-Chinese rivalry became unusually contentious. The decision on force structure could involve a purely conventional military buildup, or if domestic opposition can be overcome, the creation of a modest nuclear deterrent as well. These are matters that should be decided by the Japanese through their own political processes; it is not for Washington to dictate what they need for the defense of their country. In any case, Japan has a far greater stake in the security of the Far East than does the United States, a fact that underscores the inequity and illogic of Washington's continuing status as the gendarme of East Asia.

Time to End South Korea's Dependency

Just as Japan has reached the point where it should cease being an American protectorate, so too has South Korea. Again, a U.S. security commitment established in another era to meet a specific threat has become an expensive anachronism. South Korea has a significant advantage in population, technological sophistication,

174

and economic strength over communist North Korea. Furthermore, the technological and economic disparities are accelerating as the south enjoys rapid growth while the north stagnates because of its blind adherence to collectivist policies.[11] North Korea does maintain a larger army and has more tanks and combat aircraft, but it is questionable whether such factors actually translate into a meaningful military advantage. Most experts agree that South Korean forces are better trained and their equipment is newer and of higher quality. Moreover, since the south would be in a defensive rather than an attacking mode, it would not have to match its enemy in either manpower or material; an attacking force normally needs a significant edge in both categories to succeed, especially if it must confront highly motivated defenders.[12]

There is also little doubt that Seoul could close the quantitative gap in military power quite rapidly if it chose to do so. Yet South Korea spends under 6 percent of its GNP on defense—less than its distant American protector—despite occupying a front-line position in the Cold War. South Korea's numerical inferiority in certain weapons systems, especially aircraft, is also largely attributable to an explicit reliance on the United States for that aspect of its defense. It is not that Seoul could not fully counter Pyongyang's military power; rather, there has been no incentive to do so while the United States has been willing to bear a sizable portion of the burden.

Such U.S. paternalism is extremely costly to American taxpayers. The direct marginal cost of stationing the 43,000 troops in South Korea is relatively modest—about $3 billion per year, of which Seoul offsets some $1.8 billion—but that is merely the tip of the financial iceberg. The cost of various military units that are earmarked for a Korean conflict must also be included, as must their share of the

---

[11]Charles Wolf et al., *The Changing Balance: South and North Korean Capabilities for Long-Term Military Competition*, Rand report R-3305/1-NA (Santa Monica, Calif.: Rand Corporation, December 1985). See also Doug Bandow, "Korea: The Case for Disengagement," Cato Institute Policy Analysis no. 96, December 8, 1987.

[12]Stephen D. Goose, "The Military Situation on the Korean Peninsula," in *Two Koreas—One Future?* ed. John Sullivan and Roberta Foss (Lanham, Md.: University Press of America, 1987), pp. 55–94. Several years ago the authoritative International Institute for Strategic Studies in London concluded: "The opposing forces on the Korean peninsula are roughly equivalent. Neither is capable of a successful major offensive against the other without significant foreign assistance." See International Institute for Strategic Studies, *The Military Balance 1985–86* (London, 1984), p. 118.

Pentagon's overhead. Calculated in that manner, the defense of South Korea accounts for nearly half of the expense associated with the U.S. role as security guarantor of the Far East, or approximately $20 billion per year.[13]

America's continuing military presence on the Korean peninsula not only entails unnecessary financial burdens, it is poisoning U.S. relations with major portions of the South Korean population. The United States has been blamed for supporting a succession of military dictators that have ruled that country, for complicity in specific outrages such as the 1980 Kwangju incident in which the South Korean army brutally suppressed anti-government demonstrations, and even for the continuing political division of the Korean peninsula. Although the recent emergence of a democratic regime in Seoul has reduced the virulence of anti-American sentiment, the U.S. presence continues to be an irritant in that country's domestic politics. It reminds Koreans of all political persuasions that their nation is dependent for its defense on an external power, and such factors as nominal U.S. command of the country's armed forces offend national pride.[14]

It would be better for all concerned if South Korea gradually assumed responsibility for its own defense. The republic has both the population and the economic base to create whatever military force structure is deemed necessary to deter aggression from the communist north. The only plausible argument for a continuing U.S. role is if China or the USSR were likely to provide active support for a war of conquest by Pyongyang (as China did in 1950). Even then, U.S. intervention would be ill-advised since South Korea is not intrinsically essential to U.S. security interests. But that point is largely academic in that neither Beijing nor Moscow gives any indication of encouraging North Korean adventurism. Indeed, relations between China and South Korea have been improving steadily

---

[13]Stephen D. Goose, "U.S. Forces in Korea: Assessing a Reduction," in Carpenter, Collective Defense or Strategic Independence? Even the "offset" is misleading: $1.5 billion of that amount consists of "rent-free" real estate provided by the Korean government to the U.S. military. Since those forces are there for the protection of South Korea, the notion that American taxpayers should have to pay rent for the privilege and that Seoul is doing them a great favor by forgoing such charges borders on the perverse.

[14]Bandow, pp. 6–9, 12–13.

176

in recent years, and even the USSR now seems ready to acknowledge the legitimacy of South Korea.[15] In short, Seoul is fully capable of handling the only threat it is ever likely to confront.

Opportunity for Mutual Disengagement

America's other major security commitments in the Pacific basin are perhaps even more obsolete and unjustified than the protectorate status accorded Japan and South Korea. A succession of U.S. administrations have gone to great lengths to preserve the U.S. military bases in the Philippines. That policy included warm endorsements and lucrative economic and military aid packages for dictator Ferdinand Marcos as he systematically oppressed and looted that unhappy country for two decades.[16] As in the case of South Korea, Washington's support for a "friendly" authoritarian ruler has engendered considerable bitterness that was only partially assuaged by the last-minute assistance given to Corazon Aquino's revolution. And the U.S. military presence has become a highly controversial issue in the domestic politics of the Philippines.

Worst of all, U.S. leaders have engaged in morally dubious conduct to retain bases that are largely irrelevant to the security interests of the republic. Indeed, as several experts have noted, the Clark Air Base and Subic Bay installations are not even particularly useful in defending Washington's other clients in the Far East. Their principal utility is to enhance U.S. naval operations in the Indian Ocean and to implement a policy of forcing a "back door" opening into the Persian Gulf and the Middle East.[17] Contrary to the hysteria surrounding the promulgation of the Carter Doctrine in 1980 and the U.S. naval buildup in 1987–88, the defense of the Persian Gulf has never been essential to America's well-being.[18] Consequently,

[15]Roy Kim, "Gorbachev and the Korean Peninsula," *Third World Quarterly* (July 1988): 1267–99; and Bandow, pp. 17–19.

[16]For an incisive analysis of U.S. policy, see Raymond Bonner, *Waltzing With a Dictator: The Marcoses and the Makings of American Foreign Policy* (New York: Times Books, 1987).

[17]Paul Kattenburg, "New Strategies for U.S. Security Interests in Southeast Asia, the Indian Ocean, and the South Pacific Region," in Carpenter, *Collective Defense or Strategic Independence?*

[18]Sheldon L. Richman, "Where Angels Fear to Tread: The United States and the Persian Gulf Conflict," Cato Institute Policy Analysis no. 90, September 9, 1987.

the case for retaining the bases in the Philippines as support facilities becomes even more questionable.

In addition to their marginal military relevance, the bases are rapidly depreciating geopolitical assets. The current agreement covering Clark Air Base and Subic Bay expires in 1991, and a renewal is most uncertain. Powerful political elements (including a vocal antinuclear component) in the Philippines vehemently oppose the U.S. military presence, and the Aquino government has remained carefully noncommittal.

Rather than risk losing the bases and getting nothing in return, the next administration should explore the possibility of mutual superpower disengagement from the southwestern Pacific. A prime concern of U.S. officials over the past decade has been the buildup of the USSR's naval power in the western and central Pacific, as symbolized by the major Soviet base at Cam Ranh Bay on the coast of Vietnam. That buildup, combined with a more vigorous Soviet diplomacy, has created alarm among conservatives in the United States and elsewhere; they portray every commercial agreement or diplomatic mission that Moscow established with nations in the Pacific basin as evidence of a menacing strategic offensive.[19] Although such concern has been excessive (Moscow's power in the Pacific basin still is insignificant compared to that of its potential adversaries), it would do no harm to seek ways to reduce the profile of the Red Navy.

There may be a low-cost method of achieving that goal. In a major address on Asian policy delivered in Vladivostok in July 1986, Mikhail Gorbachev tacitly offered to give up the base at Cam Ranh Bay if the United States withdrew from Clark Air Base and Subic Bay. More recently, he explicitly proposed such an agreement.[20] From the U.S. standpoint Gorbachev's proposal has considerable appeal, although clearly the Soviet air base facilities at Da Nang should also be part of the bargain. We would be trading away installations that have little relevance to American security, that create needless turbulence in our relations with the Philippines,

[19]See, for example, Colin Rubenstein, "The USSR and Its Proxies in a Volatile South Pacific," Heritage Foundation Lecture no. 161, March 8, 1988.

[20]*Soviet Daily Press*, July 29, 1986, pp. 16, 18; Michael Dobbs and David Remnick, "Gorbachev Unveils Initiative," *Washington Post*, September 17, 1988.

and that we may not possess after 1991 in any case. If the Soviets are serious about the offer, it is one we should not refuse.

The ANZUS Anachronism

Of the various U.S. security arrangements in the Pacific basin, ANZUS is the most bizarre and pointless. The creation of that alliance with Australia and New Zealand in 1951 epitomized the observation that statesmen typically prepare to fight the last war. ANZUS was a perfect device for preventing the domination of the central and southern Pacific by the Imperial Japanese Navy. Its relevance to protecting Australia and New Zealand from the USSR was not entirely clear, especially since Moscow's naval power in the region was minuscule. The alliance actually represented little more than a U.S. expression of solidarity with two other democratic nations, and it symbolized the "pactomania" that came to dominate the 1950s when it often seemed that U.S. officials wanted allies for the sake of having allies.

Until the mid-1980s, ANZUS remained a congenial association, albeit largely meaningless from the standpoint of U.S. security interests. That situation began to change in July 1984, when New Zealand's Labour party came to power with David Lange as prime minister. One crucial plank in Labour's political platform was a commitment to ban all nuclear-powered or nuclear-armed warships from New Zealand as an initial step toward making the nation a "nuclear-free zone." A confrontation developed the following year when the Lange government announced that New Zealand's ports would be closed to U.S. ships unless Washington certified that they did not carry nuclear weapons. The Reagan administration refused, citing a longstanding policy and noting that such information would give potential enemies an intelligence bonanza.

This port-access dispute soon escalated into a diplomatic cold war, as the United States canceled joint military training operations with New Zealand, restricted the sharing of intelligence data, and took other steps to coerce its recalcitrant ally. An angry David Lange denounced Washington's tactics as "akin to the very totalitarianism that we're supposed to be fighting against."[21] The confrontation

---

[21]"New Zealand Leader Criticizes U.S. Tactics," *Dallas Morning News*, March 1, 1985. Discussions of the controversy include Ted Galen Carpenter, "Pursuing a Strategic Divorce: The U.S. and the ANZUS Alliance," Cato Institute Policy Analysis

became even more acrimonious in June 1987, when New Zealand's parliament enacted the port ban into law. The United States promptly suspended its pledge to defend New Zealand, essentially converting ANZUS into a de facto bilateral security treaty with Australia.[22]

Such harsh U.S. actions were motivated less by concern over the intrinsic importance of ANZUS, which is minimal, than by a fear that the "New Zealand disease" might infect more significant allies, especially Japan and the NATO signatories. The same worry underlies the U.S. opposition to the Treaty of Rarotonga negotiated by Australia, New Zealand, and other members of the South Pacific Forum, which established a nuclear-free zone in the South Pacific. That intransigence and the coercive actions already taken against New Zealand—plus the recurring threats of economic sanctions against Wellington made by some members of Congress—are meant to demonstrate that Washington will brook no opposition to its military policies, especially on nuclear matters. As in the case of the Philippines and South Korea, a superfluous, U.S.-dominated security arrangement threatens to damage relations with otherwise friendly countries.

The next administration should dissolve ANZUS rather than continue coercing New Zealand to return to membership on U.S. terms. ANZUS has never been important to U.S. security interests, and today it is truly an alliance in search of a purpose. New Zealand and Australia (to a lesser extent) do not perceive a serious threat from the USSR or any other power outside the region, and that is a reasonable conclusion despite the modest Soviet naval buildup. Hence, they do not need—and increasingly they do not desire—U.S. protection, particularly if that protection might someday embroil them in a superpower nuclear confrontation arising from issues irrelevant to the South Pacific. It is time for the United States to respect their wishes.

---

no. 67, February 27, 1986; and Stuart McMillan, *Neither Confirm Nor Deny: The Nuclear Ships Dispute between New Zealand and the United States* (New York: Praeger, 1987). On more general ANZUS problems, see Joseph A. Camilleri, *The Australia, New Zealand, U.S. Alliance: Regional Security in the Nuclear Age* (Boulder, Colo.: Westview Press, 1987).

[22]Don Oberdorfer, "U.S. Withdraws New Zealand's ANZUS Shield," *Washington Post*, June 28, 1987.

180

Conclusion

The incoming administration has unprecedented opportunities and incentives to reassess U.S. security commitments throughout the Pacific basin. What has been aptly termed the "economic miracle" of that region has profound implications for the post–World War II security system established by the United States, and the foremost implication is both the feasibility and the desirability of a much lower U.S. military profile. There is no longer any justification for America to be the Atlas of the Pacific basin, bearing the security burden of the entire region on its shoulders. Clinging to an obsolete policy of U.S. paternalism entails both excessive risks and costs to the American people. It is a prime example of what historian Paul Kennedy has accurately described as "imperial overstretch."[23]

The incoming administration should devolve security responsibilities to the other Pacific basin nations in an orderly but inexorable fashion. Important steps in that process include the following:

- Immediate termination of the ANZUS alliance.
- A phased withdrawal of all U.S. forces from South Korea over a five-year period and termination of the mutual security treaty at the end of that time.
- Proposing to the USSR a mutual withdrawal from all military bases in the Philippines and Vietnam.
- Signing the protocols to the South Pacific Nuclear Free Zone Treaty.
- A phased withdrawal of U.S. forces from Japan over a ten-year period and termination of the defense treaty at the end of that time.
- The demobilization of U.S. military units no longer needed for the military commitments noted above, to realize the full financial savings from the devolution process.
- Development of adequate air and naval facilities on the U.S. possessions of Guam and Wake Island as an insurance policy in the unlikely event that U.S. military power must be employed in the central Pacific to meet a serious threat from the USSR or another hostile state.

---

[23]Paul Kennedy, *The Rise and Fall of the Great Powers: Economic Change and Military Conflict From 1500 to 2000* (New York: Random House, 1987).

11. A New Central America and Caribbean Policy

Alan Tonelson

Nowhere in the world can the United States employ more military and economic power than in Central America and the Caribbean basin, and nowhere does it enjoy greater superiority over its adversaries. Yet U.S. policy in the region during the 1980s has surely joined Vietnam, Iran, and Lebanon on the list of abysmal post–World War II foreign policy failures. Practically everywhere in Central America and the Caribbean basin, Washington today is at least as far or farther from its stated political, social, and economic goals than at the decade's beginning, and its policy engines seem stuck in reverse. Worse, U.S. missteps have magnified, not reduced, regional threats to U.S. security, whether in the form of an increased Soviet bloc military presence in Nicaragua or the emergence of a narco-militaristic regime in Panama.

Moreover, singly or in combination, all of the major alternative policies suggested thus far—more diplomacy, more economic aid, or more military support for the contra rebels in Nicaragua and for pro-American regimes—have either failed already or fortunately lack public support.

Why does the United States seem to have only unacceptable or demonstrably inadequate options left in its own backyard? Both principal sides of the Central America–Caribbean policy debate trot out their favorite clichés to explain this mess. To many on the left, the region once again shows the "inutility of force" and the limits on U.S. power in the post-Vietnam era. To most on the right, U.S. bungling is simply the latest sign that the country has lost the will to defend itself.

Yet neither the ironies in which liberals delight nor the sour grapes of conservatives can explain so utterly absurd a situation, and especially its Nicaraguan core: a continent-spanning state tied up in knots by a tiny, impoverished, left-wing banana republic deep within that state's sphere of influence but halfway around the world from the only conceivable source of protection. The roots of the problem must lie elsewhere.

More importantly, neither set of explanations is of any help in developing a more effective policy. Liberals forget that international relations is not a philosophy seminar. There are certain dilemmas that a country cannot just stoically accept or admire—no matter how perfect. For neither diplomacy nor development alone or in tandem can guarantee U.S. national security. Conservatives, meanwhile, forget that the American public in which they have lost faith is the only American public they have. If conservatives' policies cannot attract public support, they would do better to return to the drawing board rather than lament the "new appeasement"—or rationalize law-breaking by the executive branch.

Instead, the problem with U.S. policy in Central America and the Caribbean today is the assumption underlying all the failed alternatives listed above: that the region presents the United States with a complex security challenge that requires an equally complex, multidimensional, and largely indirect response. For all the impassioned debate that has surrounded Central America in recent years, a broad consensus has emerged that the United States must not only aid friendly regional forces militarily (be they national governments or insurgents) and protect the region against external military threats but also must promote democracy and modernization as well. Only the precise mix of ingredients still provokes widespread debate.

Yet the security problem that has led to deep and extensive U.S. involvement in Central America and the Caribbean is relatively simple and narrowly defined—that of keeping out any hostile foreign military presence. And the best solution for the United States should be equally simple—and tightly focused on that security problem. Specifically, Americans should realize that they possess ample military might to achieve their security goals in Central America and the Caribbean without bothering with the complicated, costly, and usually fruitless task of nation building. Washington should abandon the utopian strategy of linking its security to a wholesale transformation of this chronically misruled region and should end its obsession with the nature of the domestic economies and soci-

184

eties of local states—which in themselves have no effect on America's security or well-being. The United States should concentrate on handling its highly specific security problem the way great powers have always protected their interests in neighboring regions: through the threat and, if necessary, the direct unilateral use of military might. To conserve lives and precious resources, and to exploit its greatest strengths vis-à-vis the region (which are military and material more than moral and intellectual), U.S. policy in Central America and the Caribbean needs to get back to security basics.

A Litany of Failure

For all the time, energy, and resources that the United States has lavished on the region, and particularly on Central America, its policies today are in a state of near collapse. And despite signs that the Soviet Union is losing interest in Third World backwaters such as Central America and the Caribbean, Soviet bloc influence in the region today—particularly in Central America—stands at an all-time high. Meanwhile, anti-Americanism is on the rise nearly everywhere.

The contra war to topple Nicaragua's leftist Sandinista regime, democratize that country, and thus reduce Soviet bloc influence in Central America has all but petered out. Despite more than seven years of legally and illegally funding the insurgents and frantic efforts by Washington to sanitize their image, the contras spent more of this period in Honduran base camps than in their homeland, never seized significantly populated territory in Nicaragua, and advanced no coherent political program. Although the contra war has clearly helped cripple Nicaragua's economy and the Sandinistas' modest efforts to foment revolution throughout Central America, the Sandinista regime will remain firmly in power in Nicaragua well after President Reagan leaves office. Moreover, more than seven years of war and economic stagnation have plainly left the Sandinistas less, rather than more, willing to widen the narrow bounds in which a political opposition may operate and dissenting views may be expressed.

In addition the Reagan administration's desperate attempts to reform the contras by supporting ostensible "authentic democrats" such as Arturo Cruz and Alfonso Robelo over the movement's more conservative wing have come to naught. The contras are still deeply

185

split along ideological, tactical, and personal lines. Moreover, contra military commander Enrique Bermudez, a senior officer in ex-dictator Anastasio Somoza's hated National Guard, has recently won one of the five seats on the movement's governing political directorate.

Far more importantly, Soviet military aid to Nicaragua and the presence there of advisers from countries hostile to the United States have all increased during the contra war, while the construction of infrastructure needed to permit Soviet bloc military use of Nicaraguan facilities continues unabated. According to a June 1988 Pentagon report, the potential for Soviet military use of Nicaragua continues to rise.[1]

The Reagan administration's widely praised policy toward El Salvador is in shambles today as well. The tiny nation has now received more than $3 billion from Washington since 1980, and it currently depends on that source for between 60 and 80 percent of its national budget.[2] El Salvador has held several national and municipal elections, and once-rampant killing by right-wing death squads fell dramatically during the mid-1980s.

Yet El Salvador is no closer to defeating leftist insurgents today than it was in 1982. Moreover, the massive U.S. effort to neutralize the far right and advance social and economic justice is falling apart. Further, Jose Napoleon Duarte, the Christian Democratic president of the country who is as popular in Washington as he has been ineffective at home, has stomach cancer that gives him only a few months to live. And his party lost control of the National Assembly in March 1988 to the Republican Nationalist Alliance (Arena), the far right's latest political vehicle. With the Christian Democrats deeply split over choosing Duarte's successor, the party is likely to lose the presidency in the next scheduled election as well. More disturbingly, statistics compiled by El Salvador's Roman Catholic

[1]John McCaslin, "Threat from Nicaragua Grows, Pentagon Warns," *Washington Times*, June 27, 1988.

[2]Douglas Farah, "El Salvador's Ruling Party Is Dogged by Failures," *Washington Post*, May 24, 1988; and Paul E. Sigmund and William Potter, "Central American Journey: Will Peace Break Out?" *Princeton Alumni Weekly* 88, no. 4 (October 28, 1987): 13.

Church show that death-squad–related killing for the first third of 1988 nearly equaled the total for 1987.[3]

Panamanian strongman Gen. Manuel Antonio Noriega, indicted by two U.S. federal grand juries for drug trafficking, has humiliated the United States since mid-1987 by defying concerted U.S. pressure to yield power. In addition the ineptly imposed U.S. sanctions of 1988 have been roundly criticized by most Latin American governments and have created a sizable anti-American backlash in Panama itself. Meanwhile, Noriega is moving ever closer to Cuba and Nicaragua. For example, Nicaraguan president Daniel Ortega Saavedra visited the Panamanian strongman in the summer of 1987 in a show of solidarity.[4]

In Honduras, usually described as one of America's staunchest allies in the region, the government's delivery of an accused local drug kingpin to U.S. authorities in probable violation of Honduran extradition laws touched off several days of anti-American protests. These culminated in an April 7 attack on the U.S. embassy in which as many as five people died and damage estimated at $6 million was done. Guatemala's civilian president Vinicio Cerezo continues to be little more than a figurehead of that country's all-powerful military. In all, Costa Rica remains the only Central American country that has achieved genuine democracy—or anything close to it. And its president, Oscar Arias Sanchez, has since early 1987 been pushing a Central American peace plan that, for all its virtues and good intentions, ignores U.S. security interests, and that the Reagan administration clearly mistrusts.

Among the Caribbean islands, the United States is faring little better. The U.S.-assisted demise of the kleptocratic Duvalier dynasty in destitute Haiti has not yet moved the country noticeably closer to democracy—or even to competent authoritarianism. In Jamaica the economically beleaguered pro-Western government of President Edward Seaga seems likely to lose the next election to the socialist Michael Manley, an ardent admirer of Fidel Castro and

[3]Douglas Farah, "Salvadoran Officials Say U.S. Military Aid Cuts May Weaken Democracy, Help Rebels," *Washington Post*, February 12, 1988; and Anne Manuel, "Blood and Money in Salvador," *New York Times*, June 11, 1988.

[4]Larry Rohter, "Most Latin Nations, Ending Reticence, Back Deposed Panamanian," *New York Times*, February 27, 1988, p. 5.

champion of radical Third World economic causes as president in the 1970s.

Problems and Perils of the Arias Plan

Through the spring of 1988, many Americans believed that an effective diplomatic blueprint for ending Central American wars, building democracy, and addressing U.S. security concerns had finally been found—the Arias peace plan. Arias's diplomacy undeniably achieved some successes. A handful of exiled rebel and opposition leaders from El Salvador and Guatemala were able to return briefly to their homelands to engage in politicking, and lived to tell of it. The Sandinistas negotiated a cease-fire with the contras, invited them to enter Nicaragua's political life once they disarmed, and eased many controls on political activity and free expression. Perhaps most importantly, despite widespread noncompliance, none of the Central American presidents wished to take responsibility for scuttling Arias's initiative once and for all.

However, as country after country missed deadline after deadline for implementing the plan's provisions, its future became bleaker. And in the United States, liberal opponents of the administration's Central American policy had endorsed the plan so enthusiastically that holding signatories to concrete results became far less important than fostering the illusion of progress and the feeding of increasingly groundless hopes. As a result, harping on shortcomings such as the plan's lack of any verification of enforcement provisions came to be viewed by Arias's supporters as a sign of naiveté, impatience, and even opposition to the very aim of peace. The process became an end in itself, regardless of where it was heading and what that boded for the United States.

In addition, the plan's failure to limit external military aid to governments (as opposed to insurgents) worked however inadvertently against U.S. interests by sanctioning Soviet bloc arms and even personnel flows into Nicaragua—the primary raison d'être for deep U.S. involvement in Central America in the first place. Indeed, the Soviets, Cubans, and Americans were all lumped together by the Arias plan under the heading of "outside powers" whose influence in the region needed to be reduced. This formulation may satisfy abstract principles of equity and evenhandedness, but it completely ignores the fact that the shape of Central America's

188

future is vastly more important to the United States than to the Soviet bloc.

By the early summer of 1988, nowhere was the failure of the Arias plan more apparent than in Central America's most dangerous trouble spot, Nicaragua. The cease-fire is most accurately seen as the product of the collapse of U.S. congressional support for the contras, a collapse largely triggered by the promise perceived in the Arias plan. The Sandinistas' crackdown on peaceful opposition activities in the summer of 1988 at the very least shows that Nicaragua is no closer to democracy than it has been since the overthrow of Somoza. Worse, since the Arias plan's approval, the United States has made no progress toward reducing the Soviet bloc's military presence in the region. Indeed, despite Nicaragua's crumbling economy, the near-neutralization of the contras has ensconced the Sandinistas in power more firmly than ever.

Ineffective Options

That U.S. policy toward Central America has reached a dead end is clear from examining the principal alternatives advanced to date. In the wake of Managua's summer 1988 crackdown, many in Congress were looking again to the contras. Yet, not even much higher levels of military aid for the contras will turn this strategy into a winner. The rebels still lack a political program to present to the Nicaraguan people, and their recent setbacks on Capitol Hill have widened several splits in a leadership that has held together only because of intense U.S. pressure. For all the popular Nicaraguan resentment of Sandinista repression and the regime's disastrous economic policies, Col. Bermudez's growing influence in the contra movement will surely further dim the prospects that masses of Nicaraguans will rally to the rebels' cause. In fact, the contras' complete reliance on U.S. aid contrasts sharply with the records of other Latin American rebels such as Fidel Castro, who triumphed without significant outside help. And, Reagan administration rhetoric notwithstanding, the Sandinistas' repressive machinery is hardly world-class.

The biggest problem with the contras, however, is that they cannot be realistically expected to help the United States achieve either of its essential security goals in Central America: preventing the establishment of hostile foreign military presences and defend-

189

ing the Panama Canal. How, for example, can supporting Honduras-based rebels fighting the regime in Managua help the United States keep the Panama Canal open? If an unfriendly Panamanian regime shuts down the canal, would creating a force of Panamanian contras do the United States any good? Only if Washington were prepared to wait several years until the new rebel army felt ready to march into battle.

Moreover, continuing the contra war will only increase the numbers of unfriendly foreigners and their facilities in Nicaragua as the Sandinista regime seeks Soviet bloc support. Even the rebels' most ardent and optimistic backers have cautioned that it would take several years for an adequately funded insurgency to force decisive political change by the Sandinistas, much less to oust them. During this period, Managua will seek help from wherever help is available.

Nor is diplomacy likely to advance U.S. interests in Central America, for reasons that go beyond the specific flaws of the Arias plan. Any conceivable regional peace treaty would prohibit Washington from responding to hostile foreign presences unless local states agreed. In fact, requiring such a consensus would be any treaty's raison d'être. Yet, most local governments are so fragile politically that they would have every reason to close their eyes to mounting levels of Soviet bloc personnel and weapons. What would be the chances of getting Noriega on board? How, for example, could any Mexican politician endorse a U.S. retaliatory strike against Nicaragua?

Even if the will existed among Central American countries and their neighbors to enforce such a quid pro quo, legal constructs such as treaties raise the prospect of complicated procedures that conflict with America's need to respond to violations quickly, before they become dangerous—lengthy deliberations to document charges, protracted appeal processes, the filing of countercharges, and so on. For these reasons, resolving America's specific Nicaragua-related concerns through a bilateral treaty would be unsatisfactory as well.

Least promising of all is containing present threats to U.S. security and nipping future challenges in the bud by promoting modernization and democracy in Central America. Such an approach might solve U.S. security problems in the long run; however, if the United States has learned anything about the Third World it is that modernization is a process that can destabilize countries as easily as stabilize them, at least in the all-important short run. But even the most skillfully designed and generously funded development program can only be a long-term solution. The impact on America's security interests would be small for many years.

Faulty Assumptions

Policy dead ends as complete as that encountered by the United States in the Central America–Caribbean region can often be traced to erroneous root assumptions, especially when those assumptions are shared by all major contending domestic factions. And at the heart of U.S. policy toward the region today is the belief that U.S. national security ultimately requires turning local countries into viable, prosperous democracies immune to domestic or foreign policy extremism.

In fact, a determination to solve U.S. security problems in the hemisphere through nation building dates back to the early 20th century. Then, internationally minded Americans were most concerned that their Latin neighbors' inability to handle international economic relations properly or preserve domestic order would jeopardize the Monroe Doctrine. European powers, they feared, would be endlessly intervening in the Western Hemisphere to punish delinquent debtor governments or seize their assets, or to protect their nationals during the periods of civil strife forever bedeviling Latin America.

In theory the United States could have preserved the Monroe Doctrine by simply amassing the military strength needed to keep Old World powers out of the hemisphere, by force if necessary. But although U.S. naval strength continued to grow impressively during the first two decades of this century, Presidents Theodore Roosevelt, William Howard Taft, and Woodrow Wilson rejected so direct an approach in favor of what they called a civilizing mission.

As Roosevelt wrote to his trusted adviser, Secretary of State Elihu Root, "If we intend to say 'Hands off' to the powers of Europe, sooner or later we must keep order ourselves."[5] Taft's secretary of state, Frank Knox, believed that the Panama Canal made "the safety, the peace, and the prosperity of Central America and the

---

[5]Albert K. Weinberg, *Manifest Destiny: A Study of National Expansion in American History* (Chicago: Quadrangle Books, 1963), p. 430.

191

zone of the Caribbean of paramount interest to the United States."[6] Taft himself deemed it essential that the region's countries "be removed from the jeopardy involved by heavy foreign debt and chaotic national finances and from the ever-present dangers of international complications due to disorders at home."[7]

The comprehensive approach came most prominently back into vogue late in the Eisenhower administration, and it blossomed in the early 1960s during John F. Kennedy's presidency. Washington became convinced that the only way to prevent future Cubas was to eliminate the destitution and repression that communism fed on. Thus there came to be the Alliance for Progress, which envisioned nothing less than a complete overhaul of Latin America through a mind-boggling mix of development assistant programs and sweeping sociopolitical reform programs.

From the mid-1960s to the mid-1970s, the U.S. preoccupation with Vietnam, the Middle East, the energy crisis, and the Soviet military buildup pushed Latin America far down the ladder of foreign policy priorities. Not until the Panama Canal treaty battle and the Nicaraguan revolution did the region return to the spotlight. Today's often obscured but pervasive Central America policy consensus has been shaped largely by the 1984 report of the National Bipartisan Commission on Central America.[8] Chaired by former secretary of state Henry A. Kissinger, the commission was charged by President Reagan with bridging the gap on Central American policy that divided the administration and its liberal opponents. The commission concluded that the only effective U.S. strategy had to reflect both the human rights and socioeconomic reform concerns of the left and the security concerns of most conservatives.

Consequently the introduction to the commission's report emphasized that "the roots of the crisis are both indigenous and foreign" and asserted that "unless rapid progress can be made on the political, social, and economic fronts, peace on the military front will be elusive and would be fragile. But unless the externally supported insurgencies are checked and the violence curbed, prog-

[6]Ibid., p. 432.
[7]Ibid.

[8]*Report of the National Bipartisan Commission on Central America* (Washington: Government Printing Office, January 1984).

ress on those other fronts *will be elusive* and would be fragile."[9] The report viewed threats to U.S. security as direct outgrowths of Central America's domestic ills and the opportunities they created for "aggressive outside powers" to exploit "local grievances to expand their own political influence and military control."[10] Consequently, the commission assumed that the United States could never be safe until the six principal Central American countries were all well on the way to almost millennial change.

The program recommended by the commission rivaled the Alliance for Progress in scope and complexity. In addition to more and better military aid for friendly governments and the contras, the commission recommended an infusion of $8 billion in U.S. economic aid between 1985 and 1990; an immediate increase in economic aid of $400 million; new trade credits; technical and financial support for export promotion; land reform; more efficient agricultural pricing policies; better rural infrastructure; expanded Peace Corps activities; aid to Central American schools; scholarships for Central American students; better training for the region's judges and law enforcement officials; new training programs for health care professionals; attacks on malaria, dengue fever, and infant mortality; continuation of family planning programs; expanded funding for new urban housing; and many other efforts.[11]

And notwithstanding the widely recognized failure of the Alliance for Progress almost 20 years earlier, the Kissinger Commission's Alliance-style analysis and recommendations soon became gospel in Washington. Congress endorsed the commission's work in 1985 with an amendment to the Foreign Assistance Act that declared:

> The building of democracy, the restoration of peace, the improvement of living conditions, and the application of equal justice under law in Central America are important to the interests of the United States.[12]

In June 1986 Assistant Secretary of State for Interamerican Affairs

[9] Ibid., p. 4.
[10] Ibid.
[11] Ibid., pp. 48, 49, 53, 58, 70–72, 74, 76–78, 80.
[12] Elliot Abrams, "FY 1987 Assistance Requests for Latin America and the Caribbean," *Department of State Bulletin* 86, no. 2112 (July 1986): 86.

Elliot Abrams underscored the current policy's philosophical debt to the Alliance for Progress, and he argued that the Reagan administration was pursuing an even more comprehensive policy:

> Twenty-five years ago, when the Alliance for Progress was first launched, the entire hemisphere seemed to discover that there could be no long-term security without economic development. Today, we are learning a new lesson: in addition to the nexus between security and development, there is a second nexus—this one between security and democracy.[13]

The new consensus analysis was summarized in more detail in an April 1986 speech by one of Abrams's chief deputies, James Michel. U.S. strategy, Michel stated, recognized "that the political, economic, social, and security dimensions of the situation are dynamic and intertwined." Therefore, Washington needed "a sophisticated strategy to address simultaneously the range of political, economic, social, and security concerns within each nation and within the region."[14]

Yet, the record indicates that this painstakingly thought out strategy has overemphasized complexity and produced policy paralysis. By now the reasons should be obvious. The consensus strategy holds that the United States can never be secure in its backyard unless it creates something that has never existed before—successful democratic nation-states in Central America.

Nor is there any reason to view Central American countries as promising candidates for modernization and democracy. They lack not only democratic traditions but also cohesive national political and social structures. As in much of the Third World, most loyalties in Central America are to the clan or locality, the rule of law is unheard of, sporadic at best, and public office is usually prized as an opportunity to plunder the treasury or physically eliminate opponents.

The consensus approach is completely ahistorical as well. The degree of democracy and prosperity in Central America has had no bearing on U.S. well-being whatever. Save for post–World War II

[13]Elliot Abrams, "A Democratic Vision of Security," *Department of State Bulletin* 86, no. 2113 (August 1986): 86.

[14]James H. Michel, "U.S. Policy on Central America: The Need for Consensus," *Department of State Bulletin* 86, no. 2113 (August 1986): 89.

Costa Rica, the Central American countries have been impoverished and oppressed by dictators for most of their histories. And the territorial integrity, political independence, and prosperity of the United States has not suffered in the slightest. Both individually and collectively, the region's countries are too small, too weak, too poor, and too disorganized to pose any threat to the United States on their own.

What is new and dangerous to the United States in Central America is the possibility of local states becoming platforms for Soviet bloc military power. But the consensus approach and its preoccupation with modernization and democracy has distracted U.S. attention from this primary security concern and has obscured the strengths that can be used to handle this difficulty.

Going Back to Security Basics

U.S. policy in Central America and the Caribbean in the 1990s should therefore focus tightly on highly specific security concerns. The United States should announce that it is no longer concerned with either the domestic makeup of any of the countries of the region or with the outcome of any of the military conflicts embroiling them. It should establish or maintain diplomatic relations with any political faction that it believes meets the admittedly fuzzy criteria for sovereignty that Washington uses as a standard with other Third World countries. U.S. military aid should be withdrawn and economic assistance, at the very least, drastically reduced. And Washington should use naval and air power if necessary to control the flow of foreign weapons and military supplies into Central America and the Caribbean.

At the same time, the United States should use whatever means are necessary to exclude from the region any foreign presence that Washington deems threatening. By employing discrete doses of air and sea power, the United States would stand a good chance of enforcing this edict without bogging itself down fighting Central Americans on the ground. And a demonstrated determination to use force should inhibit any Central American country or faction from threatening the Panama Canal.

Such a policy should be able to compel outside powers and local forces to respect U.S. foreign policy and security interests in the region. Even in an age of superpower strategic nuclear parity, the

U.S. Navy rules the Caribbean. The United States clearly has ample military power in that region to handle any conventional military challenge to a Pax Americana from the Soviet Union, Nicaragua's only conceivable protector. Thus Moscow has continuously abided by the agreement forced on it after the missile crisis of 1962 to restrict the types of weapons provided to Cuba. The Soviets have pointedly made no promises to ride to Nicaragua's rescue in the event of U.S. attack. And they watched helplessly as U.S. forces overwhelmed Grenada, an action that sent shudders through the ruling circles in Havana and Managua. Of course, if the Soviets are completely deranged, they will threaten nuclear retaliation to save local clients. But if they are that deranged, then productive negotiations on any subject will be impossible, and nuclear confrontation could occur whatever force-backed policies the United States adopts.

As for the Sandinistas themselves, they are all but defenseless against U.S. air and sea power. If the regime has a healthy sense of self-preservation, the United States should be able to bring Nicaragua to heel without slogging through its jungles—especially if it is clear that Managua's reward for good behavior would be a postponement of that regime's rendezvous with the ash heap of history. The same quid pro quo should appeal to any forces thinking of interfering with the Panama Canal's operations: The United States will leave them alone if they stay away from the waterway.

This back-to-basics policy also should satisfy the primary concerns of all the major domestic U.S. parties to the Central America dispute, even though it would require them to sacrifice prominent but superfluous portions of their agendas. By preventing the establishment in Central America and the Caribbean of threatening foreign presences and by protecting the Panama Canal, the policy would protect U.S. national security, which all sides say is their top priority. The policy should also please all sides by greatly reducing the odds that the United States will be trapped in a long, dirty land war in Central America.

Conservatives in particular should be happy that the proposed policy recognizes the central importance of military power in confronting the challenges posed by the region. Liberals should derive satisfaction from the proposed policy's requirement that Washington abandon its obsession with overthrowing the Sandinistas and let Central Americans decide their own domestic futures.

196

In addition, the back-to-basics policy should give the public what it wants as well. Both liberals and conservatives in Washington seem to believe that the American people in the aftermath of Vietnam have shown themselves to be dead-set against any use of force abroad, except against the rare pushover target such as Grenada. But the public is much more intelligent and sophisticated. Poll results indicate that the message it has been trying to send since Saigon's fall is a demand for competence, not a plea for pacifism. Americans are not insisting on staying out of all wars or nasty "gray-area" situations (as Secretary of State George Shultz defines them) if there is a discernible connection to the U.S. security interests. They primarily want to stay out of senseless wars and operations that consume American blood and treasure for the slightest of strategic stakes—as in Vietnam, as in Angola in 1975 and 1976, as in Lebanon in 1982 and 1983.

This position is anything but contradictory, irrational, or irresponsible. It is a demand that U.S. leaders preserve or enhance the country's security without blundering into a new Vietnam, that they defend U.S. interests without plunging wildly into civil wars between morally indistinguishable belligerents. The wonder of it is that these twin goals have always been immediately assumed by the experts to be all but irreconcilable, and that the contras were always thought to be the key to solving U.S. problems in Central America.

Important objections to the back-to-basics policy are easy to imagine. A policy that could send U.S. warplanes on mission after mission over Central American targets could reawaken bitter memories of past Yanqui imperialism (memories not sleeping too soundly to begin with), increase anti-Americanism in the hemisphere, destabilize fragile democracies and pro-Western regimes, and compound Washington's security difficulties.

However, such an objection lumps all conceivable U.S. uses of force against radical regimes under one heading and assumes that Latin Americans will be equally angered by all of them. What the United States's neighbors are most determined to prevent are the classic interventions of the early 20th century and the cold war years, when U.S. troops or U.S.-aided forces plus the Central Intelligence Agency toppled governments and replaced them with U.S. military rule or surrogate regimes. The contra war evidently strikes many Latin Americans as more of the same.

197

The back-to-basics policy, however, would entail no such U.S. invasions, no lingering U.S. military presence or indirect mechanisms of control of any kind—no interference whatever in the domestic affairs of the region's countries. The policy is neither interventionist nor imperialistic. Rather, the back-to-basics approach is a policy of self-defense. If, as they proclaim, Latin American governments are sensitive to America's special security interests in the region, this policy should give them few serious problems. And Washington should pay little heed if they do object. Just as it is unreasonable to expect Latin Americans to continue to sit back and watch the United States trample all over their sovereignty, it is unreasonable to expect Washington to await a favorable consensus to develop among its politically weak neighbors before acting to protect U.S. security interests. The outlines of a new hemispheric bargain based on power realities but also permitting a modicum of self-respect are visible. All the hemisphere's leaders have to do is recognize it.

The other principal set of concerns is operational. What would be the definition of unacceptable Central American behavior? How would the U.S. government decide? Wouldn't this policy trigger an endless series of disputes over how to define a Soviet base, or over interpreting ambiguous reconnaissance photos and other intelligence? The answer, of course, is yes. A determined minority in Congress could easily block any U.S. use of force and defang the policy at the start.

Regarding definitions, the criteria for unacceptable behavior would be entirely up to the United States. But for maximum flexibility, Washington should not make public an exhaustive list of do's and don'ts, but rather present general guidelines. Vagueness can keep hostile elements in Central America off balance, and thereby more likely to err on the side of caution.

As for avoiding paralyzing domestic debates about genuine violations, the only way out of this bind will be very difficult for the Reagan administration's critics to swallow, but swallow it they must. Within the context of an explicitly agreed upon, security-focused policy such as outlined above, the decisions must be left up to the president. In fact, liberals in Congress are already on record that they will (in House majority leader Thomas S. Foley's words) "support any action to repel Nicaraguan aggression against

198

its neighbors, or to prevent the introduction of advanced weaponry or to prevent the use of Nicaragua as a base for Soviet and Cuban main forces."[15] Giving the president the last word is the only way to make such a posture credible.

Two factors, however, should help prevent abuses of this authority. First, limiting U.S. goals is the best guarantee of limiting the means used to achieve them. Having renounced the goal of overthrowing the Sandinistas, the executive branch would have no need to engage in secret, foolish, and illegal shenanigans that could make deeper and dirtier military involvement more likely. And Congress would still retain the investigative authority to rein in an administration determined to have it both ways. Second, the American people have never tolerated wanton brutality by their government. Any president appearing to order air strikes cavalierly will pay politically.

This proposed great-power approach does fail on one ground: political aesthetics. It is not a pretty policy in theory, and it would not be pretty in practice. It exudes none of the elegance of the Arias plan or the Kissinger Commission blueprint, with national governments, societies, and rebel forces responding on cue to intricate diplomatic or economic initiatives. Nor would the policy be as neat and painless for the United States as the contra war is billed by its supporters, who blithely argue that the Nicaraguan rebels can do America's dirty work at bargain-basement prices. Finally, the back-to-basics approach has little potential to undergird a sweeping new U.S. foreign policy doctrine applied on a global scale. It responds solely to a set of circumstances that probably do not exist anywhere else, although some of its animating insights might benefit U.S. policy in other regions.

But the policy would return some badly needed proportion and perspective to U.S. policy in Central America and the Caribbean. U.S. policymakers seem to cherish the belief that it is possible for the United States to mold all states and societies in its own image. But given the manifest problems still afflicting the nations of Central America and the Caribbean after decades of independence, U.S. officials should realize that turning those societies into success stories would require a prohibitive expenditure of American blood

---

[15]Thomas S. Foley, "Contra Aid: An Act of War," *Washington Post*, April 15, 1986.

and treasure, and it may be beyond the ability of the United States in any case. By returning to security basics, the United States would be able to treat the problems in that region, appropriately, as a minor nuisance and to preserve precious resources and energies for more important and promising tasks.

The next administration's policy for Central America and the Caribbean basin should be based on the following measures and initiatives:

- An immediate halt to all forms of aid to the Nicaraguan contras.
- A phased suspension of all economic and military aid to El Salvador and other nations in the region over a six-month period.
- A declaration by the U.S. government to all other governments in the region outlining the basics of America's new security-oriented policy toward the hemisphere. Washington will refrain from interfering in the affairs of its neighbors if they refrain from establishing certain kinds of ties with governments deemed unfriendly to the United States. The requirements would include a sharp limit on the size of embassy staffs and economic aid missions from those countries, a prohibition on the receipt of heavy weapons from such states through either purchases or aid programs, and most importantly, a prohibition on the establishment of bases or other military facilities by hostile powers. Washington should stress that it will enforce the terms of this covenant unilaterally, and with military force if necessary.
- Private meetings with representatives of governments in the region to explain the policy in greater detail, but without providing excessively specific requirements concerning permitted or prohibited conduct or the nature of the U.S. response in the event of violations.
- Private meetings with representatives of the Warsaw Pact countries, Vietnam, Libya, North Korea, Iran, and other unfriendly states, outlining the terms of permissible relations those governments may have with Central American and Caribbean nations.
- An official diplomatic note to the government of Nicaragua insisting on the prompt withdrawal of the great majority of Soviet, Cuban, and other foreign personnel from that country.

- Adoption of a hands-off policy with respect to the internal political arrangements, economic policies, and human rights practices of governments in the region.

12. Leaving the Third World Alone
Doug Bandow

A misguided concept of realpolitik has governed U.S. policy toward the Third World during both Republican and Democratic administrations since World War II. The overriding goal has been to enhance U.S. power through almost constant interference with the affairs of other nations. Many U.S. diplomats have treated poorer states almost frivolously, acting as if influence with foreign governments was a common commodity to be bought and sold at will and as if moral values had no place in international relations. Indeed, even as it has rhetorically promoted liberty and democracy abroad, the United States has constantly applied enormous economic, political, and even military pressure to achieve its own geopolitical ends. Thus, while millions of Third World people clamor to emigrate to a nation they see as a beacon of freedom, millions of others demonstrate against heavy-handed U.S. government meddling.

Foreign Aid

The mainstay of U.S. intervention in the Third World is so-called foreign aid. Since the end of World War II, Washington has provided roughly $825 billion in current dollars to other nations. Although the Reagan administration has demonstrated an increased willingness to use military force abroad, and past Democratic presidents have placed ceaseless diplomatic pressure on other states to do Washington's bidding, large-scale financial transfers to foreign countries have been a bipartisan constant of U.S. policy. The bulk of these funds is transmitted bilaterally, although international organizations—most notably the United Nations, the World Bank, and the International Monetary Fund—also play a major role in shaping U.S.–Third World relations.

Ironically, U.S. foreign aid expenditures increased substantially under self-proclaimed fiscal conservative Ronald Reagan. In constant 1987 dollars, foreign assistance rose from $13.6 billion in 1981 to $19.8 billion in 1985. Although military aid showed the greatest jump, spending in every other category, including development and food aid, also climbed. For years, conservative and liberal members of Congress who disagreed over program priorities solved the problem by simply voting more money for every category of aid.

Only when the huge federal deficit was compounded by the Gramm-Rudman-Hollings legislation, which provided for across-the-board spending cuts to bring the deficit within prescribed limits, did this high-budget compromise end. Then, despite frantic lobbying efforts by Secretary of State George Shultz, legislators turned on a program that was unpopular with voters, reducing outlays by 14.7 percent in 1986. In early 1988 the State Department even announced that it was cutting off some small recipients of foreign aid, such as Fiji.

Nevertheless, Congress approved $14.3 billion in foreign assistance for 1989, a $700 million jump over 1988. And the United States still generously provides for its major clients: In 1989 Israel was slated to collect $3 billion, Egypt $2.1 billion, Turkey and Greece $550 million each and the Philippines $250 million. And if deficit pressures eventually ease, advocates of foreign aid will undoubtedly press even harder for significant spending increases.

Most U.S foreign assistance since World War II—that is, $196.5 billion of a total of $315.1 billion (in 1987 dollars) in bilateral outlays, plus $58 billion or more in contributions to multilateral agencies—theoretically was intended to either mitigate suffering or foster development in Third World states. Whether or not U.S. policymakers actually believe their rhetoric, they defend foreign aid in terms of traditional humanitarian goals. The programs "express our humanitarian interest and help alleviate poverty by promoting self-sustaining growth," declared the Commission on Security and Economic Assistance, chaired by Frank Carlucci, now secretary of defense.[1]

Yet the sad reality is that U.S. assistance has done little to promote these goals. Even the Carlucci commission, which advocated

[1] The Commission on Security and Economic Assistance, *A Report to the Secretary of State* (November 1983), p. 31.

increased foreign aid outlays, conceded that despite its "broad endorsement of the overall impact of U.S. assistance, it is far less clear that specific programs have been consistently effective with regard to any one objective."[2] In fact, four decades of experience suggest that foreign aid is more likely to harm rather than help recipients.

Ostensibly humanitarian assistance has often been motivated by objectives other than kindness. The Food for Peace program, for instance, purports to feed the starving. But the program was devised largely as a means of unloading surplus U.S. produce abroad; only one out of every seven dollars in food aid goes to disaster areas. Most crops are routinely given or sold at below market cost to perennial aid recipients: Food for Peace, or Public Law 480, outlays run between $1.5 billion and $2 billion annually.

Unfortunately this constant flood of cheap food has ruined indigenous farmers, preventing many Third World nations from developing healthy agricultural sectors. P.L. 480's disincentive effects have been felt in countries as diverse as India, Guatemala, Haiti, Indonesia, Jamaica, Pakistan, and Peru. In fact, in 1982 the Peruvian agriculture minister even requested the United States to stop shipping rice, but Washington, at the behest of domestic producers, responded that Peru had to accept the rice or receive no food at all. As policy analyst James Bovard has concluded, P.L. 480 "has been one of the most harmful programs of aid to Third World countries."[3]

Moreover, humanitarian aid, to the extent that it is directed at man-made disasters, creates perverse incentives by insulating Third World governments from their own folly. Ethiopia, for instance, greatly aggravated the consequences of a drought by forcibly collectivizing its farmers; in 1984 the Ethiopian government squandered as much as $200 million to celebrate its tenth anniversary in power. What might have been a manageable problem turned into a catastrophe. Yet Western food aid bailed out the communist regime. Four years later, with its rural policies unreformed, Ethiopia again faced mass starvation.

Development aid has often had even less-salutary effects than

[2] Ibid.

[3] James Bovard, "How American Food Aid Keeps the Third World Hungry," Heritage Foundation Backgrounder no. 665 (Washington, August 1, 1988), p. 1.

humanitarian programs. Bilateral economic assistance generally flows through the Agency for International Development; multilateral aid is provided by several international agencies, including the World Bank and the International Monetary Fund. Grants and loans from these bodies both fund individual projects and provide general financial support for recipient governments.

Despite the tremendous flow of resources to the Third World—official U.S. assistance has been augmented by aid from other Western governments, the OPEC nations, and $1.2 trillion in private lending by commercial banks—there is no calculable relationship between aid and development. Third World growth rates have fallen steadily over the last two decades despite continued financial flows; between 1968 and 1987 the economies of developing states were stagnant, with some sub-Saharan and heavily indebted countries moving backward. Major aid recipients such as Ethiopia, Sudan, Tanzania, Bangladesh, and India are still among the poorest nations on earth.

Why Foreign Aid Fails

One reason foreign assistance does not produce economic growth is that by attempting to plan and structure development in poor countries, aid officials have exhibited what Nobel laureate F. A. Hayek has called the "fatal conceit," the belief that they can amass, analyze, and use information better than the overall marketplace. In fact, their understanding and thus their policy programs are inevitably limited and flawed. The consequences include industries without markets, roads without traffic, and machines without fuel.

Another problem is that aid, as a largely government-to-government transfer, reinforces the primary cause of Third World poverty: statist domestic economic policies. When governments such as that of Ethiopia steal from their farmers, crop production falls. Other debilitating policies include stultifying regulations, which favor established elites while blocking development of small business; price and production controls, which discourage indigenous industry; bloated state enterprises, which waste scarce financial resources; counterproductive fiscal, credit, and monetary restrictions, which disrupt the economy; and onerous limitations on foreign investment, which deny Third World states access to needed capital.[4]

---

[4] For a more detailed discussion of the causes of Third World poverty and the

Indeed, as economists P. T. Bauer and B. S. Yamey have argued, aid "accelerates and aggravates the disastrous politicization of life in the Third World" by increasing the resources available to largely authoritarian and corrupt regimes.[5] Politics already dominates life in developing states because, in contrast to pluralistic Western societies, there are so few alternative power structures; thus, control of the political apparatus results in domination of virtually every social institution worth controlling. Foreign aid centralizes power to an even greater degree.

Of course, AID, the International Monetary Fund, and the World Bank all ostensibly promote market-oriented reforms, but in practice policy conditionality has been a grievous failure. The problems are many—one World Bank review of its highly publicized structural adjustment lending program, for example, concluded that the loans' "seemingly hard and all-encompassing conditionality is largely illusory."[6] Bank officials are unwilling to enforce loan covenants, and borrowers know that additional funds will be forthcoming whatever they do. The result continues to be lots of lending but little policy reform.

Moreover, the attempt of Western states to force particular policy changes, however desirable, on Third World societies often creates enormous political opposition to needed reform. Domestic failure, not a foreign bribe, generates the strongest pressure on developing states to abandon the statist economic policies that make them poor: China and the Soviet Union have moved away from collectivism because they could not feed their people, not because of the availability of World Bank structural adjustment loans.

The illusion that aid actually aids Third World states nevertheless persists. And policymakers—who consistently disregard the disastrous consequences of their actions—are only too happy to maintain the illusion because doing so provides a humane gloss to a program

effects of foreign aid, see Doug Bandow, "The U.S. Role in Promoting Third World Development," in Doug Bandow, ed., *U.S. Aid to the Developing World: A Free Market Agenda* (Washington: Heritage Foundation, 1985), pp. vii–xxxii.

[5] P. T. Bauer and B. S. Yamey, "East-West/North-South: Peace and Prosperity?" *Commentary*, September 1980, p. 61.

[6] Elliot Berg and Alan Batchelder, "Structural Adjustment Lending: A Critical View," World Bank CPD Discussion Paper no. 1985–21 (Washington, January 1985), p. 47.

that is primarily designed to achieve far less altruistic geopolitical goals.

The Real Rationale

America's distribution of foreign aid is largely based on a blunt assessment of U.S. national interests. Washington wants to expand U.S. political influence around the globe, promote U.S. commercial activities, and strengthen U.S. military power. Although these goals are neither unimportant nor necessarily unreasonable, policymakers focus too frequently on the tactical and the short-term aspects, ignoring both the moral dictates of a just society and the often-counterproductive practical consequences of U.S. interference in other nations' affairs. At times U.S. officials seem oblivious to the existence of fundamental social forces abroad that are beyond Washington's control. As a result the United States usually tries to block change rather than encourage reforms consonant with human freedom and dignity; the Reagan administration's convenient conversion to democracy as the Marcos and Duvalier regimes were collapsing was a welcome if belated exception to past policy.

The goal that dominates the State Department is gaining influence and ensuring smooth relations with other nations. Virtually all foreign aid—whether labeled humanitarian, economic, or military—is intended as a de facto bribe to bring about foreign support of U.S. policies. As the Carlucci commission, an Establishment entity, explained, "The United States seeks international political relationships that promote U.S. national interests."[7] In its report the commission paid due deference to the principles of democracy and development, but it is evident that political interests were the commission's most important concern. The report's unstated assumptions were that any foreign leader can be bought and that no expense should be spared to enhance Washington's political reach.

There are undoubtedly some cases—a South Vietnam or El Salvador for instance—in which a combination of U.S. aid, military intervention, and political support has gained enormous clout for the United States. However, political power gained in such a fashion may be lost even more quickly; for example, North Vietnam's

[7] The Commission on Security, p. 9.

208

conquest of South Vietnam extirpated U.S. influence, and a victory for the conservative opposition in El Salvador could severely circumscribe U.S. power in that nation.

Moreover, from a purely nationalistic standpoint, attempts to purchase influence, even if successful in the short term, can have disastrous long-run consequences. U.S. assistance in support of Anastasio Somoza's venal dictatorship in Nicaragua, for example, failed to keep Somoza in power but did tie Washington to a hated autocracy. Whatever political benefits the United States once gained from its support of Somoza seem very small today compared to the damage that the Sandinistas have inflicted on U.S. regional interests in Latin America.

U.S. support for the shah of Iran led to similarly disastrous consequences. The shah prevented the formation of a vibrant moderate opposition, channeling dissent into a fundamentalist Islamic revolution. The United States was inextricably linked to the discredited past regime, which led to the sort of widespread popular hostility that resulted in the 1980–81 U.S. embassy takeover in Teheran. In addition the United States has lost influence in other nations, such as Sudan and the Philippines, when longtime U.S. clients have been ousted. Although in the Filipino case the United States switched sides in time to salvage some of its reputation, there is nevertheless growing pressure on the Aquino government to close the U.S. bases in the Philippines.

New disasters waiting to happen include Zaire, ruled by the insatiably corrupt Mobutu Sese Seko. If Mobutu, whose country is torn by regional and tribal strife, falls, there is no guarantee that his successors will forgive the United States for supporting his autocracy. Moreover, *Wall Street Journal* reporter Jonathan Kwitny has argued that even now the United States gets very little for its foreign aid to Zaire: "The government we had established . . . continued to impose a murderous tyranny on its people. And instead of guaranteeing our mineral supplies, it daily held them hostage to a great economic and moral ransom. At considerable cost, we had achieved nothing and done great harm."[8]

The United States appears to secure remarkably little influence

[8] Jonathan Kwitny, *Endless Enemies: The Making of an Unfriendly World* (New York: Congdon & Weed, 1984), p. 5.

209

for its money elsewhere as well, even in the short term. In 1988, for instance, the Reagan administration proposed aiding 87 countries that had voted against the United States two-thirds or more of the time in the United Nations and 13 that had done the same at least half of the time. Although most of the UN votes involved were of little consequence, they do provide at least a rough gauge of the state of America's bilateral relations with other countries.

Even supposedly close friends of the United States often demonstrate nothing but contempt for American wishes. For example, repressive Somalia, which received some $41 million in U.S. aid in 1988, is a U.S. ally by virture of its position as a neighbor of Soviet client-state Ethiopia. Nevertheless, the Somali government would not allow the U.S. embassy to use a plan to evacuate Americans from war-torn northern Somalia. "Foreign assistance gives very little leverage when you want one-for-one results," acknowledged one State Department official.[9]

Some foreign aid cases are simply bizarre. Why, for example, has Washington subsidized Warsaw Pact member Poland? Why has Washington simultaneously underwritten both the Marxist MPLA government and the anti-Marxist UNITA insurgency in Angola? Washington almost reflexively lavishes money on foreign nations irrespective of their actions or the state of their relations with the United States.

Moreover, there is a fundamental moral issue that rarely is discussed in terms of foreign policy: Is it right for the United States to support largely autocratic Third World governments? Washington should be concerned about U.S. security, of course, but relations with few Third World nations seriously threaten U.S. security. Instead, the clout supposedly achieved with foreign aid is used for the most prosaic purposes—such as gaining support on a UN resolution or aiding a U.S. firm. These goals, however worthy, are not compelling enough to justify forcing U.S. taxpayers to subsidize often-corrupt and brutal foreign regimes.

Of course, not all aid recipients are repressive; everyone from President Reagan to liberal Democratic senator Alan Cranston has endorsed the idea of a massive "Marshall Plan" for the Philippines'

[9] As quoted in Linda Feldmann, "Critics Charge US Policy Fuels Conflict in Somalia," *Christian Science Monitor*, August 10, 1988, p. 4.

Aquino government. But that nation needs new economic policies, not new funds. For reasons noted earlier, the act of pouring billions of dollars into another country is likely to do more harm than good; in this case it would likely corrupt a fragile democracy in which the previous president, Ferdinand Marcos, used U.S. assistance to create a kleptocracy. Aid to Third World democracies may be less offensive than support of dictatorships, but it is rarely more justified.

Helping American Business

Another but largely unstated purpose of U.S. foreign aid is to assist American manufacturers. The Export-Import Bank of the United States explicitly subsidizes exports, and the Overseas Private Investment Corporation insures U.S. investments in foreign nations. Though officially treated as development-related agencies, both Ex-Im and OPIC are just open petty cash drawers for American companies—comparable to, for instance, the Small Business Administration, which provides loans and loan guarantees for domestic firms with primarily domestic markets.

Foreign economic aid has often been sold politically in the United States as a means of enriching influential business interests. Although such aid is supposed to help spur development in Third World states, most of it must be spent on U.S. goods or services. And in lobbying for increased foreign assistance, groups such as the Citizens Network emphasize the amount of U.S. aid that ends up in the hands of U.S. firms—and in which congressional districts. Business publications also have been quick to point out the profit opportunities from foreign assistance; for example: "AID programs can provide an opportunity for American companies to venture into the international marketplace with the secure knowledge that the bill will be paid, not left to the whims of a debt-ridden Third World nation."[10] As a result, many U.S. companies, which hope to sell more of their products overseas whether or not the buyers need them, lobby vigorously in favor of increased foreign aid.

Such foreign aid programs help selected businesses, not the United States as a whole. British development economist P. T. Bauer offers the analogy of a shopkeeper who gives away money in the hope

[10] Stephen Simurda, "Breaking into the U.S. Foreign Aid Market," *Northeast International Business*, July/August 1988, p. 6.

211

that some of the proceeds will be spent in his store. Direct business aid through Ex-Im and OPIC and indirect subsidies through foreign assistance drain resources away from other productive enterprises in the United States, thereby slowing domestic economic growth. The losses far outweigh the gains achieved by the few lucky businesses that collect the money that filters back into the United States.

Foreign Aid and Military Strategy

The third major objective of foreign aid policy is to enhance America's strategic position. Although military intervention is the most powerful means of asserting U.S. influence, it is also the most costly; therefore, policymakers tend to look at foreign aid as a relatively inexpensive way to achieve national security goals.

Most obviously related to defense is direct military assistance—credit for purchase of U.S. weapons, for instance, as well as grants and training. In this way the United States directly augments the military strength of other nations. However, security assistance has often gone to nations that can easily finance their own defense efforts. South Korea, for instance, collected hundreds of millions of dollars annually in low-interest loans until 1986, even though it had the world's fastest-growing economy at the time.

Moreover, in many cases the United States derives no palpable advantage from having reinforced the beneficiaries' military establishment. Washington has provided security assistance to more than 100 nations annually, including communist Yugoslavia, neutral Austria, irrelevant Luxembourg, and isolated Fiji. In fact, military aid is largely just another form of bribery used to obtain political influence. However, this sort of bribe can be particularly pernicious since it strengthens the military in countries that usually are either military oligarchies or unstable democracies. Even the Carlucci commission, in between its many cheers for foreign aid, admitted "the possibility that the assistance supplied will be used to suppress democratic forces."[11]

A less direct security benefit that is thought to flow from economic as well as military aid is the undergirding of allied states. The United States provides vast amounts of money to the governments of nations—such as Egypt, Pakistan, El Salvador, Zaire, and the Phil-

[11] The Commission on Security, p. 33.

ippines—that are considered to be strategically important. U.S. aid undoubtedly does bolster recipient governments in the short term; they can use U.S. funds to buy off opponents, enrich allies, and augment security forces. In the longer term, though, ruling elites that are heavily subsidized by the United States probably feel less pressure to reform either their economies or their political systems. In the Philippines, for instance, the corruption, brutality, and incompetence of the Marcos regime, all generously underwritten by U.S. aid, allowed a dangerous Marxist insurgency to develop. It will take years for that nation to rebuild its economy, political structure, and military forces.

At least there is hope for the Philippines. U.S. aid almost certainly had a negative impact in Nicaragua and Iran, where U.S.-supported autocrats brought their countries down; from the rubble emerged virulently anti-American regimes. A little less U.S. enthusiasm for Anastasio Somoza and the shah of Iran might have led to moderate democratic governments, or at least to revolutionary governments that nevertheless did not view the United States as the Great Satan.

Even in a nation such as El Salvador, where U.S. aid appears to have helped contain a communist insurgency, that same assistance has had some destabilizing effects. It has strengthened an often brutal military, subsidized a land-reform program that did not give peasants ownership of their land, encouraged tax hikes, ameliorated the effect of the government's nationalization of the banks, and supported a doddering ruling party that may lose the next election.[12] In fact, El Salvador well illustrates the limits of foreign aid. U.S. money cannot reform foreign political systems or resolve deep-seated social resentments.

Other Foreign Policy Tools

Although foreign aid is the dominant method used by Washington to deal with Third World governments, U.S. relations with foreign states are also affected in three other important ways: military force, multilateral diplomacy, and commercial trade.

---

[12] The agricultural collectivization program has been particularly disastrous. See, for example, James Bovard, "The Continuing Failure of Foreign Aid," Cato Institute Policy Analysis no. 65 (Washington, January 31, 1986), pp. 6–8; Agency for International Development, *Agrarian Reform in El Salvador: A Report on its Status*, Audit Report no. 1-519-84-2 (Washington, January 18, 1984).

Direct military intervention is far more heavy-handed than foreign aid. The conflicts may be short, such as in Grenada, or long, as in Vietnam. The intervention may be intended to protect abstract international rights, as with U.S. Navy patrols in the Persian Gulf; block communist subversion, as in Vietnam; stabilize a chaotic society torn by civil war, as in Lebanon; or enforce America's will in political or economic disputes, as in the frequent use of the U.S. Marines in Central America and the Caribbean earlier this century.

Washington's willingness to forcibly reorder the affairs of other nations stems from the same realpolitik philosophy that motivates it to use foreign aid to buy influence. The ultimate objective is to advance the U.S. national interest, narrowly defined to mean gaining some political, economic, or military advantage for the United States. The use of almost any means, irrespective of its impact on other nations, is considered justified; basic moral principles are at most treated as secondary considerations.

Military force is not even viewed as a matter of last resort. Rather, as foreign policy analyst Ted Galen Carpenter has observed, U.S. officials choose "the military option not when other tactics proved insufficient, but when rapidly changing events precluded the use of more subtle techniques."[13] However, the efficacy of military force varies widely with the conflict. In the short term, U.S. intervention throughout Latin America has reshaped a number of governments, most recently that in Grenada, at relatively little cost. The long-term impact has been less salutary, though. The specter of Yankee, imperialism haunts the United States' relations with countries as diverse as Nicaragua and Mexico. The gains achieved by sending in the marines decades ago have long since dissipated; the tensions that afflict Washington's relations with a number of Latin states today are a more painful, and immediate, reality.

Far more costly and futile was U.S. intervention in Lebanon and Vietnam. In the former case U.S. policy never made sense, since a few marines could not bring peace to a region beset by centuries of sectarian strife. In Vietnam the United States realized both the limits of its power and the American people's unwillingness to compel their neighbors to fight and die for goals that were less than critical.

[13]Ted Galen Carpenter, "The Ultimate Interventionist Tool: Direct Use of Military Force," in Peter Schraeder, ed., *Intervention in the 1980s: U.S. Foreign Policy in the Third World* (Boulder, Colo.: Lynne Reinner Press, 1989).

Although Washington's evident readiness to use force to oppose communism may have enhanced its relations with a few Third World countries—such as Thailand, which sees U.S. power as a counterbalance to Chinese and Vietnamese influence in Southeast Asia—U.S. intervention has mostly been viewed abroad as heavy-handed interference in the affairs of other nations, and has thus encouraged widespread hostility to the United States.[14]

Ironically, U.S. participation in international organizations, most notably the United Nations, has been equally devoid of principle, but more as a result of a refusal to advance U.S. interests than a willingness to use any means to achieve them. In fact, throughout the 1970s the United States calmly acquiesced as the Third World pulled virtually every UN agency into its campaign for a New International Economic Order—the collectivist restructuring of the global economy. The United States largely contented itself with damage-control efforts, moderating the rhetoric contained in UN resolutions and watering down restrictive proposals. In some areas the United States helped draft vast new regulatory schemes; in the late 1970s, for instance, former Republican cabinet member Elliot Richardson led the Carter administration's U.S. delegation to negotiate the Law of the Sea Treaty, which would have established a UN "Authority" to regulate private seabed mining and an "Enterprise" to engage in mining for the UN.

This policy of accommodation—in essence, seeking to gain influence and ensure smooth relations by not fighting to protect the fundamental moral values upon which the United States is based—is similar to the use of foreign aid to buy influence. For in both cases the United States eschews principle to make political gains.

For a time the Reagan administration departed from the bipartisan example of its predecessors. Taking the international war of ideas seriously, it killed the Law of the Sea Treaty; resisted new regulatory proposals in a variety of UN agencies, ranging from the Food and Agriculture Organization to the International Telecommunications Union; and pulled out of the UN Educational, Scientific

---

[14]Intervention often involves the danger of escalation to a superpower confrontation. This risk, argues Carpenter, has limited U.S. military intervention in the Third World: "It is difficult to imagine, for example, the United States continuing to tolerate a communist regime in Cuba were it not for the restraint required in a thermonuclear context." Ibid.

and Cultural Organization, which had served as a forum for proposals to license the international press. The Reagan administration and then Congress also cut U.S. contributions to the UN, forcing that organization to undertake a major financial retrenchment.

Near the end of Reagan's second term, though, the administration returned to Washington's more traditional policy of accommodation. Secretary of State George Shultz, for instance, simultaneously lobbied for increased foreign aid outlays and larger U.S. payments to the UN. His interest was in trying to buy more friends abroad.

Finally, domestic mercantilistic pressures can have an important impact on U.S. relations with foreign lands. For example, although ever ready to preach the virtues of free enterprise abroad, the Reagan administration steadily shut Third World states out of the U.S. market through tariffs and quotas. In early 1981, for instance, the administration and Congress revived sugar import quotas, and they steadily tightened the limits each year thereafter. The result has been to disrupt economies throughout the Caribbean despite the much-heralded Caribbean Basin Initiative, which was supposed to spur trade and thus economic growth throughout the region. The Dominican Republic, Costa Rica, St. Kitts, and Jamaica—countries that receive hundreds of millions of dollars in U.S. foreign aid annually—have been particularly hard hit by the sugar restrictions.

Similarly the Reagan administration's "voluntary" steel quotas have damaged heavily indebted Brazil and other industrializing Third World states. Under pressure from a Democratic Congress, the administration also tightened restrictions on textile imports, reducing sales of a commodity of critical importance to such impoverished Third World nations as Bangladesh. Foreign aid, at least, is theoretically supposed to help both U.S. firms and foreign citizens; no one makes any pretense that protectionism is anything other than a subsidy for domestic business.

New Directions for U.S.–Third World Relations

U.S. relations with much of the Third World range from wretched to awful. While people around the world look to the United States as the exemplar of freedom—a Shining City on the Hill that offers hope amid global tyranny and poverty—Washington busily subsidizes assorted corrupt autocracies. The United States preaches democracy while militarizing poor societies and advocates free enterprise while closing off U.S. markets to foreign goods. In international forums in which ideas actually matter, Washington frequently concedes the high ground, attempting to use its acquiescence to buy foreign friendships. And when it finds itself unable to achieve its goals any other way, Washington resorts to military force, acting as if America's national interest was the planet's highest moral law.

This is not to suggest that U.S. misbehavior is either unique or worse than that of other states. The Soviet Union has fomented totalitarian insurgencies and backed bloody dictatorships around the globe; its military intervention in Afghanistan lacked even the gloss of good intentions that attended America's war in Vietnam. And some democratic states, such as France, have always managed their relations with other nations with a cynical realism unmatched by the United States.

Nevertheless, Americans have control over the international conduct of this country, not the Soviet Union, France, or any other. Thus the incoming administration has a responsibility to fundamentally refashion U.S. policies toward the Third World. Among the goals that should be pursued are the following:

- All U.S. policies should be developed within a moral framework that emphasizes the principles underlying the founding of this nation—particularly respect for political, civil, and economic rights and commitment to peace and justice. Although the realities of international politics may require a willingness to compromise, some fundamental values grow out of the United States' creation and define its proper role in the world; they should not be sacrificed.

- Absent compelling circumstances, Washington should avoid trying to buy access and friendship with foreign aid. Forcing American citizens to pay for bribes to foreign dictators in exchange for a few petty favors neither is morally right nor pays off practically in the long term.

- Military intervention can be justified only in the most extreme circumstances, when the nation's fundamental security is at risk. Otherwise the United States should pledge not to interfere with the internal affairs of foreign states or intervene in conflicts between nations. They should be left free to develop as they wish, however foolish or misguided their policies.

217

- Washington should slash so-called humanitarian and development assistance programs, including contributions to the multilateral aid agencies. Aside from the few programs that provide temporary relief for countries suffering from natural disasters, foreign aid is not even expected to help people in other nations; instead, the assistance is primarily intended to buy influence with recipient governments. And by strengthening the ruling elites that are often holding their countries in economic and political bondage, U.S. aid is more likely to harm than help the poor.
- U.S. policymakers should take the war of ideas seriously, vigorously opposing authoritarian and collectivist schemes advanced in such international organizations as the UN. Washington should also defund global agencies that are working to undermine principles of economic and political freedom. At best the UN provides a forum in which politicians from other nations can let off steam; there is no reason for the United States to pay so much for something of so little value.
- The United States should promise better economic and cultural relations by bringing down its barriers to foreign trade and immigration. International commerce both ties disparate nations together and provides poor countries with needed income. The global flow of citizens also creates an important cultural link between states that are thousands of miles apart. The United States could provide poorer nations with no more important benefit than to open its borders to their goods and people.

It will take years to repair America's frayed ties with a host of Third World states. In the short term, cutting off financial subsidies and forswearing military intervention may make some nations less likely to support any particular U.S. policy initiative. In the long run, however, the values and ideas represented by the United States are more likely to triumph if they are not tied to a policy that relies on usually officious, and often brutal, meddling in other countries' affairs. Such a world would be a better place for people in the United States as well as those in other countries.

PART III

DOMESTIC POLICY

13. Social Security: A New Compact between the Generations

Peter J. Ferrara

Social security expenditures dominate federal domestic spending. In fiscal 1989, total spending for old-age, survivors, disability, and retirement hospital benefits, which are all financed by the payroll tax through special trust funds, will amount to about $300 billion. This total equals almost half of all federal spending on domestic nondefense programs.[1]

Private Alternatives

This huge burden of social security spending should be particularly surprising because, of all government programs, social security has the most widely recognized and used private-sector alternatives. Pensions, individual retirement accounts (IRAs), 401(k) plans, Keoghs, and other retirement savings plans perform in the private sector the same basic functions as social security cash retirement benefits. Private life insurance performs the same basic functions as social security survivors benefits for workers under 65. Private disability insurance performs the same basic functions as social security disability insurance. Private health insurance performs the same basic functions as the government's retirement health insurance program.

In the beginning, tax payments into social security were quite modest. The maximum annual social security tax on both employer and employee for an individual worker was just $60 for the first 13 years of the program, through 1949. In 1958, the maximum annual tax was still only $189. Even as late as 1965, the maximum tax was only $348. But this year (1988), the maximum annual employer/

---

[1]Domestic nondefense programs include all federal spending except that spent on national defense and interest paid on the national debt.

221

employee payroll tax for an individual worker is $6,759. By 1990, it will be almost $8,000, continuing to grow thereafter.

Why must we require today's workers to rely so heavily for their retirement and insurance needs on social security, rather than allowing them to choose from the broad spectrum of private alternatives?

Such heavy, mandated reliance on social security greatly restricts the economic freedom of workers. It deprives them of the freedom to control major portions of their own incomes and to choose the means of providing for their retirement and insurance needs in ways best suited to their personal needs and circumstances. It also deprives workers of the opportunity to develop a substantial ownership stake in America's business and industry through the investments of the private alternatives. In effect, the social security program socializes a large portion of the nation's financial sector, as it takes over more and more of the role of the private alternatives, with a public government displacing a private array of services offered in a competitive market. This mandated program also naturally involves an enormous spending burden for the federal government, in effect forcing virtually all Americans to be dependent on the government for the bulk of their income for what is now a major portion of their lives—their retirement years.

This dependency and the program's socialization of a major portion of the financial industry amount to a radical departure from a general economic system of free markets, private property, and free exchange. Moreover, total federal spending clearly cannot be sharply reduced without addressing social security. For those who want to see an expanded role in our society for free markets, the private sector, and individual economic freedom, and a reduced role for coercive big government, social security clearly cannot be ignored. It must be reformed.

An Outdated Status Quo

Mandating such heavy reliance on social security is making less sense every year because the program is outdated for today's young workers. The social security tax burden for these young workers is now so high that even if they receive all the benefits currently offered to them by the program, they will still be receiving low, below-market returns—or effective interest rates—on the taxes paid into the program over their careers. This is documented in a recent study for the National Chamber Foundation.[2] The study finds that for most young workers now entering the work force, the real rate of return paid by social security will be less than 1.5 percent, with the returns to many workers virtually zero or even below zero.

The study also finds that if these young workers could invest the social security taxes that they and their employers will pay over their careers in private investments earning the average return in the stock market over the last 60 years, then most workers would be able to receive from such investments three to six times the retirement benefits offered by social security, while still matching the pre-age-65 survivors and disability benefits promised by the program. Calculations in the study made at a range of different private investment returns show that even at much lower returns, today's young workers could expect much higher benefits than offered them by social security. Indeed, most could expect higher benefits at any real private investment return above 1.5 percent.

Besides these higher benefits, the system of private market investments supporting them would also generate substantial additional tax revenues to finance other government goods and services and/or general tax reduction. Social security generates no revenue available for these purposes.

What sense can it possibly make to require today's young workers to rely so heavily on social security in the face of the low returns offered to them by the program? How can we require some workers to pay, along with their employers, almost $7,000 a year (in 1988) into a system that offers them basically zero or even below-zero returns on this huge payment?

Moreover, it remains quite questionable whether social security will actually be able to pay the benefits promised to today's young workers. Under the most recent, most widely cited intermediate projection made by the Social Security Administration (SSA) itself, if we add all of the system's trust funds together[3] and assume each can draw from the others as needed, then the entire combined program would run short of funds to pay promised benefits by the

[2]Peter J. Ferrara, *Social Security Rates of Return for Today's Young Workers* (Washington: National Chamber Foundation, 1986).

[3]These include the Old-Age and Survivors Insurance Trust Fund, the Disability Insurance Trust Fund, and the Hospital Insurance Trust Fund.

223

year 2030, just before today's young workers will be retiring.[4] Thereafter, paying all benefits promised to today's young workers would require a 50 percent increase in current payroll-tax rates, to 23 percent for employers and employees combined (compared to 15 percent today).[5]

Under the so-called pessimistic projections, the entire system would run short of funds to pay promised benefits by the year 2011.[6] Paying all benefits promised to today's young workers would require that today's total payroll-tax rate be more than doubled, to about 35 percent.[7] This would mean a total social security annual tax split between employer and employee of $7,000 for a worker making $20,000 per year. (At such a tax rate, the maximum social security tax for 1988 would be $15,750.)

The payroll tax is already far too high, seriously hampering economic growth and limiting job opportunities for today's young workers. For most workers, the total employer and employee payroll tax is greater than the worker's income-tax liability.[8] By FY 1990, total annual social security payroll-tax revenues are projected to reach $384 billion, approaching the $482 billion for the personal income tax.[9] While increasing the payroll tax to keep pace with benefit expenditures, Congress has apparently overlooked the heavy burden the sharply increased tax now places on low-income jobs. A married worker with two children earning poverty-level wages of $10,000 in 1988 will pay about $751 in payroll taxes, with another $751 from his employer that probably comes out of his wages as

---

[4]Calculated from *1988 Annual Report of the Board of Trustees of the Federal Old-Age and Survivors Insurance and Disability Insurance Trust Funds* (Washington, April 29, 1988) (hereinafter *1988 OASDI Trustees' Report*); *1988 Annual Report of the Board of Trustees of the Federal Hospital Insurance Trust Fund* (Washington, April 29, 1988) (hereinafter *1988 HI Trustees' Report*).

[5]Ibid.

[6]Ibid.

[7]Ibid.

[8]Indeed, under the 1986 tax-reform legislation, 80 percent of workers are supposed to be in the 15 percent income-tax bracket, assessed after the standard deduction and personal exemption shelter a substantial portion of their incomes. But the total payroll-tax rate is now 15.02 percent, without any standard deduction or personal exemption to shelter wages from the tax.

[9]Office of Management and Budget, *Budget of the United States Government, FY 1989* (Washington: Government Printing Office, 1988).

well, for a total of $1,502 out of the productive capacity of this needy, low-income worker.

The payroll tax is simply a tax on employment. To the extent the tax is borne by employers, it discourages them from hiring. To the extent it is borne by workers, it discourages them on the margin from working as much as otherwise. The overall result is fewer jobs and reduced economic growth. Here as elsewhere the result of taxing something is that there is less of it. One study estimates that just the payroll-tax rate increases scheduled for 1988 and 1990 ultimately will eliminate over one-half million jobs and reduce the gross national product (GNP) by $25 billion per year.[10] In a society supposedly deeply concerned about employment opportunities, the incredible payroll-tax burden on employment is ludicrous.

The social security benefit structure is also riddled with haphazard inequities. Workers are not paid equal returns on past taxes paid into the program. Blacks and other minorities with below-average life expectancies tend to receive discriminatorily lower returns, as they tend to live fewer years in retirement to collect benefits.[11] A white male at birth today can expect to live 50 percent longer in retirement than a black male, and consequently to receive 50 percent more in retirement benefits. Moreover, blacks as a group are significantly younger than whites, and since social security offers a worse deal the younger one is, the program disadvantages blacks on this account as well.

A Social Security Surplus?

The 1990s could be expected to be a relatively rosy time for social security. The huge baby-boom generation will be growing into its prime earning years, swelling social security tax payments. At the same time, the relatively small generation born during the low-fertility years of the Great Depression and World War II will be entering retirement, imposing relatively smaller benefit obligations in the aggregate. Because of these factors, the SSA's intermediate projections show payroll-tax revenues substantially exceeding program expenditures each year for the next two decades.

[10]Aldona Robbins and Gary Robbins, *Effects of the 1988 and 1990 Social Security Tax Increases*, Economic Report no. 39 (Institute for Research on the Economics of Taxation, February 3, 1988).

[11]National Center for Policy Analysis, *Social Security and Race* (Dallas: 1987).

Recent recognition of these long-projected surpluses has led to much commentary suggesting that the surpluses are so enormous and overwhelming that they will lead to decades of surpluses in the total federal budget and ultimately pay off the national debt.[12] However, this commentary is based on a misreading of official U.S. government social security projections and a lack of understanding of federal budget accounting.

Four major points can be made about this misreading. First, the commentary discusses government projections of social security financing over the next 75 years that are published in nominal dollars. But the commentary fails to adjust the nominal-dollar projections for inflation and the relative effects of economic growth over time. This leaves a badly distorted impression of the relative magnitude of the projected dollar amounts. For example, an analysis published by Arthur Laffer's California consulting firm states that the social security trust funds will total $12 trillion in 2030.[13] But under the same projections, GNP in that year would be $54 trillion, a total federal budget of the same size relative to GNP as today would be about $12.5 trillion, total expenditures out of all the social security trust funds would be $5 trillion, and these expenditures would exceed OASOHI taxes in that one year by $1.4 trillion.

Second, the commentary fails to include the large projected deficits in the Hospital Insurance Trust Fund. But analysis of likely future budget surpluses and deficits must include all of the accounts in the federal budget that are now projected, not just those that are in better shape.

Third, the commentary includes interest on the social security trust fund bonds as income to the federal government for reducing the deficit and even paying off the national debt. But the social security trust funds exclusively hold federal government bonds, and consequently the interest they earn is an expenditure of the federal government as well as income to it through the trust funds, effectively canceling out as an intragovernmental transfer. Consequently, to determine the impact of social security on the federal budget, the interest on the trust fund bonds must be subtracted out

[12]See, for example, Stuart J. Sweet, "Growing Year-By-Year: The Incredible Social Security Surplus Emerges" (Lomita, Calif.: A. B. Laffer Associates, February 18, 1988).

[13]Ibid., p. 1.

of social security income, and the surplus only of social security tax revenues over expenditures must be calculated.[14]

Finally, the analysis included in the commentary is based on the argument that the Gramm-Rudman-Hollings legislation will require the federal budget apart from social security to be balanced by 1993, and that the social security surpluses thereafter will consequently amount to a surplus in the entire federal budget each year, thereby reducing and ultimately eliminating the national debt. But Gramm-Rudman-Hollings requires a balanced budget including the social security surpluses, not a balance in the budget apart from social security.

Correcting for all these errors shows that the annual net social security trust fund surplus available to reduce the total federal deficit, under the most widely cited intermediate projections of the SSA, will be less than 1 percent of GNP (about 0.8 percent) from now until 2005. After that, the annual surplus starts declining, ultimately turning negative in 2013. In recent years, by contrast, federal budget deficits have been as large as 3.5–6 percent of GNP. These projected trust fund surpluses are substantial, but they are not nearly large enough to eliminate recent large federal deficits by themselves.

The trust fund surpluses are substantially reducing the total federal deficit by about $40 billion in the current fiscal year (1989) (assuming that other federal spending has not been allowed to remain higher than otherwise because of the offsetting social security surpluses). But a deficit of 6 percent of GNP, as we had in 1983, would be $300 billion today, so the trust fund surpluses are at most offsetting only a minor fraction of such large recent deficits. The primary factors reducing the deficit have been overall spending restraint resulting from Gramm-Rudman-Hollings and other presidential policies, and sustained economic growth, rather than the annual social security surpluses. Indeed, these surpluses have already had the real deficit-reduction impact they are going to have, as the surplus is already about 0.8 percent of GNP and will remain at or near that level through 2005 and then decline.

The surpluses are clearly not so overwhelming as to be likely to

---

[14]Sweet's analysis claims to recognize this, but its quantitative statements show no adjustment for it. See Sweet.

cause large annual surpluses in the total, unified, federal budget. Without such a total budget surplus, there can be no reduction in the national debt. To the extent that the trust fund surpluses reduce the deficit, and other federal spending is not simply allowed to increase because of the offsetting surpluses (which seems likely over the long run), the surpluses will slow down the rate of growth in the net national debt held by the public.

Moreover, without the superior economic performance and sustained economic growth of the Reagan years, these annual trust fund surpluses will not continue. The more pessimistic SSA projections show the impact of a return to the weak economic performance and inflation and recession cycles of the 1970s. Under these projections, the annual surpluses fall to trivial amounts by 1995 and turn negative by 1997, despite the favorable demographic trends during this period.[15]

The larger, long-term problem is that after a couple of decades of favorable population trends, social security will face a demographic wind shear, as the underlying trends will reverse far more powerfully. The huge baby-boom generation will begin entering retirement, dramatically increasing benefit demands on the system. At the same time, the relatively small generation born during the low-fertility years following the baby boom will be in the work force, producing relatively small amounts of revenue.

As a result, under the intermediate projections, the deficit of total trust fund taxes compared to expenditures starting in 2013 will grow to 1 percent of GNP by 2019 and close to 3 percent by 2035, when today's young workers will be retiring, and will continue at that level through 2060 (the last year given in the projections).[16] As a percentage of GNP, these latter deficits are more than three times as large as the earlier surpluses and would alone create annual federal budget deficits for each of these years as large as current federal deficits.

Under the more pessimistic projections, the trust fund deficits starting in 1997 will reach about 1 percent of GNP in 2009, 7 percent

---

[15]Calculated from *1988 OASDI Trustees' Report*, Appendix G; *1988 HI Trustees' Report*.

[16]Ibid.

in 2035, and 8.5 percent in 2060.[17] As a percentage of GNP, the trust fund deficits from 2035 on would alone create total federal budget deficits two to three times as large as current federal deficits.

The meaning of the social security trust funds themselves, and the balance projected to be accumulated in them over the years owing to the annual trust fund surpluses, have also been badly misunderstood. As long as there is not a surplus in the entire, unified federal budget, social security income not needed to finance current benefits is lent to the federal government in return for new, specially issued federal bonds, which are held by the trust funds. The federal government then spends this money borrowed from the social security trust funds on other programs. In the process, outstanding federal debt held by the public is not bought up by social security or reduced in any way. Such outstanding federal debt can be reduced only when there is a surplus in the entire, unified federal budget. With no real prospect of such total budget surpluses on a sustained basis, there is no danger that social security will buy up all, or even a substantial portion, of outstanding federal bonds, or that these bonds will be otherwise retired, regardless of the accumulated balance of the social security trust funds.

When social security income falls short of expenditures, the trust fund bonds are turned into the federal government for the cash needed to finance benefits. The government holds no cash or other assets to back up these social security bonds. The trust fund assets are consequently just further claims against the federal government that will have to be financed out of federal revenues and/or borrowing when they are cashed in to finance social security benefits.

The trust fund bonds are in fact part of the gross national debt, and this gross debt grows as the trust funds grow. The net national debt held by the public remains unchanged. The trust fund assets are indeed potential additions to the real, publicly held debt when they have to be cashed in to pay promised benefits. The social security trust fund balance, therefore, does not in any sense represent an offset to the national debt.

As a practical matter, the social security trust funds themselves are nothing more than a statement of the legal authority social security has to draw from general revenues in the future. In other

[17]Ibid.

words, the larger the trust fund balance, the more social security has a claim against income-tax revenues as well as payroll-tax revenues. When we hear that the trust funds will accumulate $12 trillion, that does not mean that the federal government will be rolling in dough. Quite to the contrary, it means that social security will have an additional $12 trillion claim against federal taxpayers, besides their payroll-tax liability. Because the social security trust funds do not hold any real assets, but just claims against future federal revenues, a growing trust fund by itself does not mean that paying for the retirement of future generations will be any easier economically. It just means that more of this burden will be met out of income taxes and federal borrowing rather than payroll taxes.

Short- and Long-Term Reform

In January 1988, a large payroll-tax increase went into effect, increasing the total employer/employee payroll-tax rate from 14.3 to 15.02 percent. In January 1990, another scheduled increase will raise the payroll-tax rate to 15.3 percent.

Under the SSA's intermediate assumptions, social security will be able to pay all promised benefits for the next three decades, until about 2020, even without these 1988 and 1990 tax increases, because of the positive demographic factors during this period (as discussed above).[18] This is even assuming that the large projected deficits in the hospital insurance program are covered by the surpluses elsewhere in social security.

Consequently, the 1988 and 1990 payroll-tax rate increases should be repealed. This will free today's young workers from an unnecessary tax burden and create over one-half million new jobs. Maintaining the large tax increases could in fact undermine the very economic prosperity that is essential for the financial health of social security. These tax increases could lead to the weaker economic performance assumed under SSA's more pessimistic projections, under which the surpluses will soon end and the entire system will run short of funds soon after the turn of the century.

But without more fundamental reform, payroll taxes will eventually have to be raised to much higher levels to pay all promised benefits to the baby-boom generation and today's young workers.

[18]Ibid.

230

As discussed above, even with the 1988 and 1990 tax increases, the system as a whole will be unable to pay all promised benefits by 2030, just before today's young workers will retire. Eliminating the tax increase would merely accelerate that date a few years, to 2020.

To make the tax reductions permanent, and provide for a better overall system for today's young workers, Congress should adopt a new compact between the generations: The elderly would be assured that they would receive all promised benefits in full, and workers would be allowed the freedom to choose to rely more on private-sector alternatives for their retirement and insurance needs and less on social security.

The stumbling block to allowing workers a private option to social security always used to be the argument that if workers were allowed to invest their social security tax funds in private alternatives, there would not be enough money flowing into social security to pay benefits to the elderly today. But this problem can be avoided by offering workers a rebate on their income taxes, rather than their social security payroll taxes, for payments into a private system.

For example, each worker and his or her employer could be allowed to contribute to a private investment account up to some limit in return for income-tax credits equal to the amount of such contributions. To the extent a worker exercised this option over his career, he would receive proportionally less in social security benefits in his retirement, relying on benefits from his private account instead. The worker and his employer would continue to pay social security taxes in full, but to the extent they exercise the private option, these taxes would be completely offset for them by the income-tax credits.

This private-sector option could be expanded gradually over time and extended to the full range of social security benefits. Workers and their employers could be allowed to contribute additional amounts to their private accounts for the purchase of private life insurance, again in return for income-tax credits. To the extent such contributions were made, the worker would forgo social security survivors insurance benefits and rely instead on private insurance benefits. Workers and employers could similarly be allowed to contribute additional funds for the purchase of private disability insurance, in return for income-tax credits, substituting the private insurance for their social security disability benefits. Workers could similarly be allowed to contribute additional funds to purchase private medical insurance to substitute for Medicare in retirement.

Ultimately, each worker would have the complete freedom to choose how much to rely on private accounts and how much to rely on social security. Those who thought social security was better than the private alternatives would be completely free to continue to rely on the program in full, with no participation in the private system.

This private-account option would in fact sharply strengthen social security financially, improving the ability of the program to pay promised benefits. The program's revenues would be maintained in full, as workers exercising the private-account option would receive credits against income taxes rather than the payroll taxes that finance social security. Yet, expenditures would be reduced as workers relied more and more on the private accounts and less and less on social security. The need for future payroll-tax increases could consequently be eliminated altogether, and payroll taxes could potentially be cut even more as the program's expenditures were reduced.

Those workers who did opt for private accounts could today expect higher returns and benefits. These benefits would also be completely equitable, with each worker facing the same market investment returns.

Workers would also have much greater freedom of choice and control through the private-accounts system. They would each be able to tailor their own individual package of investments and insurance coverage to suit their personal needs and preferences. In addition, they could be allowed complete freedom to choose their retirement age, and they could also choose to leave some of their private-account funds to their children or other heirs, which they cannot do with social security.

The private-account option would also give average- and lower-income workers their only real chance to accumulate and control some substantial capital. Through private accounts, each worker would have the opportunity to develop a significant ownership stake in America's business and industry. The relatively substantial resources that even lower-income workers could accumulate would provide a sturdy foundation to help their families break out of the cycle of poverty. The reform could consequently do more to help the poor than all the recent talk about welfare reform put together. The reform could also ultimately reduce federal spending sharply, as workers start to rely more and more on their private accounts and less and less on social security.

The reform could begin by allowing workers an option to substitute the private alternatives for only a part of their retirement benefits. Or the reform could start by allowing workers an option only for social security survivors insurance, disability insurance, or Medicare. Each of these possibilities would be desirable in itself.

By starting with an option for only one relatively small piece of the entire system, the income-tax revenue loss resulting from the tax credits would be kept within manageable limits. This revenue loss would eventually be offset completely by reduced social security expenditures. For options focused on the program's survivors and disability insurance for workers, these expenditure offsets would in fact occur relatively quickly.[19]

Workers in the transition under this reform would not "pay twice" for their retirement, as some critics have erroneously suggested. Workers paying into the private system would receive 100 percent income-tax credits proportionately offsetting their payment of social security taxes—in effect nullifying those taxes to the degree they choose to rely on the private sector. To the extent the revenue loss from these tax credits would be financed by additional spending reductions or offsetting taxes, workers would simply be bearing the cost of providing for the increased savings of a private, fully funded system.[20]

The reform basically would involve shifting from social security's pay-as-you-go system, under which each worker's payments are immediately paid to current recipients, to a private, fully funded system whereby each worker's payments would be saved to finance

---

[19]For further discussion of the private-sector option, see Peter J. Ferrara, ed. *Social Security: Prospects for Real Reform* (Washington: Cato Institute, 1985, Chapter 11; idem, "Social Security and Super IRAs," in David Boaz and Edward H. Crane, eds., *Beyond the Status Quo: Policy Proposals for America* (Washington: Cato Institute, 1984); idem, "Social Security and the Private Sector," in Steven H. Hanke, ed., *Prospects for Privatization* (New York: The Academy of Political Science, 1987).

[20]To the extent that the transition would be financed by reductions in wasteful and/or counterproductive government spending, then it would involve no real costs to workers at all.

his or her own benefits. The advantages of the higher returns on this increased saving compared to the low, even negative returns of social security, the improved economy resulting from such savings increases, and the other benefits of the shift to the private sector would be well worth the cost of providing for such increased saving.

To the extent that the revenue loss would be financed by increased government borrowing, no savings increase would result during the transition, but workers would not bear any added costs either. Such borrowing would simply amount to an explicit recognition of the implicit government debt that already exists in the unfunded liability of social security. The government borrowing to finance the tax credits would be equal to the increased savings in the private retirement accounts, resulting in no net increase in the government-borrowing drain on the private sector. As social security expenditures would be reduced over the years owing to reliance on the private accounts, net government borrowing to finance the transition would decline as well, leading to a slowly rising increase in savings and the eventual shift to a true, fully funded system.

Private Alternatives Around the World

Similar reforms have been adopted in Great Britain and Chile in recent years.[21] In 1978, British employers were allowed to choose to substitute their own company-wide pensions for half of that country's social security system. About half of all British workers exercised this option. Under Thatcher administration reforms that went into effect in July 1988, all British workers are now able to opt out of half the public system this year on an individual basis. Workers will be able to contribute to individual investment accounts in return for substantial tax rebates. In retirement, they will rely on the benefits payable from these accounts in place of half of the public benefits.

In 1981, all workers in the public system in Chile were given the option of switching to a new private system. All workers under the private system are required to make tax-deductible contributions equal to 10 percent of wages to an individual pension savings account. Workers are required to choose one of twelve government-

[21]See John C. Goodman and Peter J. Ferrara, *Private Alternatives to Social Security in Other Countries* (Dallas: National Center for Policy Analysis, 1988).

authorized, specially created private investment companies to manage their pension account investments. Each company is required to pay a minimum return on the funds equal to a percentage of the average return earned by all twelve companies. This minimum return is government-guaranteed. In retirement, workers will rely on the funds payable by these private accounts rather than on public retirement benefits. The government guarantees a substantial minimum retirement benefit.

Chilean workers under the private system are also required to pay another 3 percent of wages for purchase of private life and disability insurance, and 6 percent for health insurance. The total 19 percent fee under the new system compares to a 26 percent average tax under the old system. Benefits under the new system are also targeted at substantially higher levels than under the old system.

Workers who switch to the private retirement system receive special, nontransferable government bonds representing past contributions to the old system. These bonds will pay a sum equivalent to the real value of such past contributions plus interest at retirement into each worker's private pension account.

The Chilean reform has been highly popular, with over 90 percent of workers switching to the new private system. The government credits the reform with substantially increasing national savings and investment through the private investment accounts. It also cites the reform as improving the attitudes of workers toward private business enterprises, in which they are gaining a larger and larger ownership share each year through their private retirement investments. The system is unnecessarily rigid, however, with a high mandated payment of 19 percent of wages designated in fixed percentages for particular benefits, and retirement investments channeled through particular, highly regulated, investment intermediaries. Future liberalizations of the new system would likely result in even greater benefits for the workers and retirees of Chile.

Such private-sector–based reforms are not unique to Great Britain and Chile. A recent study by the National Center for Policy Analysis found already existing private-sector options or analogous components built into the social security systems of about 20 percent of all noncommunist countries.[22]

[22]Ibid.

235

There is no reason why such reform could not be highly popular in the United States as well. It would simply modernize and liberalize the current system, providing the freedom and flexibility best suited to today's workers. These workers need not be forced to rely so heavily on social security for their retirement and insurance needs. There is no reason why they cannot be allowed to provide for some and eventually all of such needs through the private sector if they prefer. The currently mandated heavy reliance on social security is simply imposing a huge unnecessary spending burden on the federal government, as well as a heavy and unnecessary restriction on the economic freedom of all U.S. workers.

Recommendations

The following policies should be adopted by the new administration:

- *Repeal the 1988 and 1990 payroll-tax rate increases*
  As discussed above, these tax increases are not needed to pay social security benefits to today's elderly. Repealing the tax hikes would remove an unnecessary tax burden on today's workers, providing them some relief from years of relentless payroll-tax increases. It would also provide new jobs and economic opportunities, particularly for lesser-skilled workers who have limited opportunities.
- *Allow workers the freedom to substitute private savings and insurance accounts for a portion of their social security retirement benefits*
  As discussed above, the current system is outdated for today's young workers, who can now get a better deal through the private sector. These workers can be given a private option while ensuring that all promised social security benefits will be paid to today's elderly. Similar private options have been adopted recently in Great Britain and Chile and have been highly popular. Over time, the private option can be expanded so that workers will have the complete freedom to choose how much to rely on social security and how much to rely on the private sector.
- *Restore the IRA*
  IRAs offset the harsh, discriminatory, multiple taxation on savings that still exists in our income-tax code. Such an offset is needed if workers are to be able to effectively accumulate

236

supplemental private savings to meet retirement needs. All workers and their spouses, whether or not employed outside the home, should be able to contribute $2,000 each to an IRA annually. Moreover, this $2,000 annual cap should be indexed to increase with the growth in wages, as are social security taxes, to maintain its relative value over time.

• *Repeal the catastrophic-illness health care tax on the elderly*
In the so-called catastrophic-illness health care legislation enacted in 1988, an income-tax surcharge of 15 percent was imposed on the elderly to fund supposed Medicare catastrophic-illness health care benefits. The tax is indexed to grow with the new expenditures, and the Treasury estimates that by 1993, the surcharge will have risen to 28 percent. The monthly Medicare premiums were sharply increased as well. These harsh taxes and premiums on the elderly should be abolished. To offset the revenue loss, an up-front deductible of $1,000 per year or so could be added to Medicare. This would leave the elderly responsible for more routine medical expenses, for which insurance only produces perverse incentives for overutilization, while maintaining true catastrophic-illness protection for retirees. Medicaid can provide additional benefits for the poor elderly to ensure that they are able to obtain essential medical care.

14. Education in America: The Opportunity to Choose

Pete du Pont

Twice during the past five years I have had the opportunity to visit the North Carolina School for Science and Mathematics, a public high school in Chapel Hill devoted exclusively to providing the best possible education to gifted students from throughout the state of North Carolina.

That school is an example—and there are many others—of how good education in America can be. It is an example of what happens when families are allowed to choose where their children go to school, and when the entire school system and its personnel focus their attention on the needs of the students and look for ways to increase their learning capacity.

It is also an example of what Americans *must* do if we are to compete effectively in a world in which education is playing an increasingly important role. Maintaining our high standard of living will require maintaining a comparative advantage in labor-intensive, high-technology fields such as computer science, communications, health, and business services—and that comparative advantage will depend, more than ever before, on our having a highly skilled, well-trained work force.[1]

The Sorry State of American Education

Five years have now passed since the publication, in 1983, of *A Nation at Risk* which focused the country's attention on the unacceptable state of its schools.[2] If anyone ever doubted that ideas have

---

[1]See, for example, William B. Johnston, *Workforce 2000*, (Indianapolis: Hudson Institute, 1987), which estimates that more than half of all jobs created in the year 2000 will require more than a high school education.

[2]National Commission on Excellence in Education, *A Nation at Risk: The Imperative for Educational Reform* (April 1983).

consequences, the *Nation at Risk* report should have laid those doubts to rest. Its unforgettable indictment ("If an unfriendly foreign power had attempted to impose on America the mediocre educational performance that exists today, we might well have viewed it as an act of war."[3]) provoked a nationwide debate on the state of American education, a debate that is still going on today.

That debate already has resulted in some movement in the right direction. Forty states now have competency tests for students, and 35 states require teachers also to demonstrate competency as a condition of certification.[4] With the strong support of the National Education Association (NEA), school districts have raised teacher salaries dramatically. Over the objections of the NEA, many states and school districts have tied those increases to better performance through merit pay plans.

We should not minimize the importance of these changes, but after five years, there is painfully little evidence that they have had any real impact on student performance.

In 1982, researchers under contract to the Department of Education conducted a series of tests comparing the performance of U.S. students with those from two dozen foreign countries in mathematics and science. The results garnered nationwide attention because U.S. students did quite poorly. Not only did our students place far below the Japanese, but for most of the categories tested, they were not even among the top ten nationalities.[5]

Five years later, *after implementation of many of the reforms mentioned above*, researchers from the University of Northern Iowa administered those same test questions to a group of advanced mathematics students in Iowa. Before considering the results, it should be noted that Iowa has one of the best education systems in the United States. It consistently ranks in the top five states in graduation rates, and its students generally place first or second in average scores on the standardized ACT test for college admission.

But Iowa's schools are still far from being the best in the world. In the 1987 tests, Iowa's eighth graders placed second behind Japan's.

[3]Ibid., p. 5.

[4]Joyce D. Stern and Mary Frase Williams, *The Condition of Education*, 1986 ed. (Washington: Government Printing Office, 1987), pp. 92–96.

[5]F. Joe Crosswhite et al., *Second International Mathematics Study: Summary Report for the United States* (Washington: National Center for Education Statistics, 1985).

However, Iowa's best twelfth graders placed far behind the students from nine other countries, including Hong Kong and New Zealand. As one of the researchers put it, "It appears Iowa is doing one of the finer jobs in the United States, but by international standards, you are just approaching mediocrity."[6]

Unhappily, Iowa's schools are not alone in failing to show the kind of dramatic improvement called for in A Nation at Risk. The most recent National Assessment of Educational Progress (NAEP) shows achievement levels in science remaining significantly below those achieved in 1969, and NAEP's executive director has noted that while "we hit bottom in the 1970's, it is an open question whether the glimmers of recovery we have seen in recent years will translate into positive trends."[7] As for verbal skills, SAT verbal test scores leveled off in 1986 and 1987 after several years of gains, and actually fell two points in 1988, leaving them far below their 1963 peak.[8]

The conclusion that emerges from this evidence is that the reforms implemented to date are not producing the kind of dramatic improvement needed in American education. The question is, What further changes need to be made? And the answer, it seems, depends on which education "expert" one happens to ask: get the government out, get it in, teach more classics, teach more job skills, pay teachers more, lengthen the school year, and so forth. Everyone seems to have an answer. The problem is, all the answers are different—and most of them have already been tried, with few noticeable improvements.

Why Current Reforms Cannot Succeed

The remarkable thing about our elementary and secondary education system today is that we have any private schools at all. The government provides education free of charge at government schools, and still people choose to pay thousands of dollars in tuition to send their children to private schools. It is the biggest case of

[6]Quoted in Linda Lantor, "Iowa High Schools Slipping Behind World in Math Education," Des Moines Register, May 17, 1987.

[7]Quoted in Carol Innerst, "American Students Found Illiterate in Science Fields," Washington Times, September 23, 1988.

[8]Carol Innerst, "SAT Scores Fall 2 Points—First Decline in 8 Years," Washington Times, September 20, 1988.

predatory pricing in history, and still the government has not been able to drive its competition out of the marketplace.

The reason, of course, is that government-run and monopoly enterprises are notoriously inefficient. They tend to become complacent and satisfied, bureaucratized and ossified, with high labor costs, low rates of innovation, and little if any accountability for results. They produce shoddy, second-rate products—which is why private-sector competitors such as Federal Express, MCI, and the Catholic schools have been growth enterprises in America over the past decade.

The educational bureaucracy, of course, has a different view. It believes we are not feeding it enough, and it points in particular to alleged cuts in education funding by the Reagan administration. The facts are, first, that federal funding for elementary and secondary education has risen from $7.2 billion in FY 1981 to over $9.3 billion in FY 1989, keeping real spending approximately constant during a time of stable (or slightly falling) enrollment.[9] Second, and perhaps more importantly, federal funding makes up only about 7 percent of elementary and secondary education funding, with the rest coming from state and local funds. When we look at the total education budget, we see that real per-pupil spending has risen more than 20 percent since 1981.

This increase in funding for elementary and secondary education reflects the continuation of a long-term trend. Since 1960, real spending per pupil in elementary and secondary education has more than doubled. We can learn a great deal about why government schools are failing if we look at what has happened to that extra money. Teacher salaries have gone up only about 30 percent, and class sizes have gone down only about 40 percent. Spending for administrators, by contrast, has risen dramatically, and today there are more than twice as many administrators per student as in 1960.[10]

It is tempting to look at these results and conclude that the appropriate policy is to monitor more closely the ways in which

[9]Office of Management and Budget, *Budget of the United States Government: Historical Tables* (Washington: Government Printing Office, 1988), pp. 65–67.

[10]Department of Education, Center for Education Statistics, *Statistics of State School Systems* (1983, 1988), *Fall Statistics of Public Schools* (1983, 1988), and *Digest of Education Statistics* (1983, 1988).

state and local school districts spend their money, and to force them to stop spending money on "wasteful" overhead and start spending it on smaller class sizes, "better" teachers, "improved" curricula, and so on. Indeed, this regulatory approach to school improvement is behind most of the reforms we have seen since *A Nation at Risk* was issued in 1983. But before taking this approach, we ought to ask ourselves how happy we have been with the way regulated monopolies have performed in other areas. Were we happy with regulated airlines, trucking operations, and telephone service? Would more stringent regulation—say, for example, trying to crack down on non-price competition among airlines—have been a better solution than introducing competition?

The answer, of course, is that regulation cannot substitute for competition as a means of fostering diversity and innovation, quality, lower cost, and sensitivity of producers to consumer demands. Two recent studies, taking very different approaches, come to very similar conclusions on this point. The first, by two sociologists, James S. Coleman and Thomas Hoffer, looks at the impact of communities on schooling performance.[11] The Coleman and Hoffer study is best known for its finding that private schools, and Catholic schools in particular, are far superior to government schools in terms of educational results.

What is far more interesting than their results, however, is Coleman and Hoffer's analytical framework. They argue that shared values are crucial to the success of individual schools and school systems, and that the traditional geographical organization of our school system—combined with a trend away from local control and toward so-called top-down management—has led to schools in which there is little consensus on values. In their words:

> A principal of a school today in which attendance is based on residence has no set of dominant community values to uphold. Instead, there are a number of contending values, each claiming legitimacy, and at least some of them capable of being backed up by suits in court.[12]

---

[11]James S. Coleman and Thomas Hoffer, *Public and Private High Schools: The Impact of Communities* (New York: Basic Books, 1987).

[12]Ibid., pp. 11–12.

The result, Coleman and Hoffer conclude, is either paralysis or pursuit of the lowest common denominator.

What the Coleman and Hoffer analysis clearly indicates will not work is to increase the extent of top-down regulation of standards, curriculum, personnel, and so forth. Precisely the same conclusion is reached, by a very different path, by John Chubb.[13] He undertook an in-depth study of 500 high schools, all of which had also taken part in the 1980 "High School and Beyond" study. The combination of the two data bases provides a detailed picture not only of student performance but of a wide variety of school characteristics as well.

What Chubb finds is very discouraging for the current round of school reforms. Looking at what he calls the "formal structure" of schools—characteristics such as class size, teacher salaries and experience, and teacher/pupil ratios—Chubb finds almost no difference between high-achievement schools (those in the top quartile of student achievement gains) and low-achievement schools (those in the bottom quartile).

On the other hand, Chubb finds some very important differences in what he calls "informal organization"—that is, the attitudes and informal interactions of school personnel. Compared with low-achievement schools, high-achievement schools

> have different goals. [They] place much more emphasis on academic excellence as opposed to "the basics," occupational skills, or good work habits. Their goals are also clearer. Their staffs are more likely to agree on priorities. . . . In a word, they are more likely to perceive the school as having a mission.[14]

To use Coleman and Hoffer's phrase, Chubb finds that schools with "shared values" produce better students.

Chubb next looks at how these differences in informal organization come about, and his findings can be summarized in one word: autonomy. Schools, government or private, that have a high degree of freedom to innovate tend to develop shared values and perform much better than schools in which rules are laid down from the outside. The superior performance of private schools is

---

[13]John E. Chubb, "Why the Current Wave of School Reforms Will Fail," *Public Interest* 90 (Winter 1988): 28–49.

[14]Ibid., p. 33.

244

explained by the fact that they "appear to provide autonomy as a matter of course."[15] And the danger in the current round of reforms—most of which Chubb concludes "are regulatory in nature,"[16]—is that they may quash autonomy.

The Case for Competition

What both of these studies indicate is that increased regulation is not the way to achieve better performance in the schools. They suggest that we cannot succeed, for example, by picking some successful model—Japan is often suggested[17]—and forcing all our schools to imitate it. Indeed, the path to better education lies in the opposite direction: where others pursue structure, we must pursue freedom; where others pursue regulation, we must pursue entrepreneurship and innovation; where others pursue monopoly, we must pursue competition and diversity.

In short, I do not believe there is any single answer to improving American education, at least not in the sense most people today are looking for an answer. We must look for an answer in diversity and initiative, and government does a very poor job of encouraging those qualities. Rather, they are qualities associated with competition and the marketplace.

For elementary and secondary education, competition means choice. But that does not mean just increased choice among government schools, and not just Title I vouchers for disadvantaged students as former education secretary William Bennett, to his credit, has proposed. It means allowing private schools to compete directly with government schools for students on an equal footing.

Today, over five million families are paying to send their children to private schools because they believe the children will get a better education. All the evidence, including both the Chubb and the Coleman and Hoffer studies discussed above, suggests they are right. Studies have shown that private schools, especially Catholic schools, produce better students. And the greatest beneficiaries are not well-to-do students from upper-income families; rather, they

[15]Ibid., p. 44.

[16]Ibid., p. 45.

[17]See Department of Education, *Japanese Education Today* (Washington: Government Printing Office, 1987).

are disadvantaged and poor students, the ones most in need of special help.[18]

The best evidence that private schools offer something better does not come from the researchers. It comes from public school teachers—the real experts—who send their children to private schools nearly twice as often as parents in general. In Chicago, for example, 46 percent of public school teachers who live in the city send their children to private schools, compared with a citywide average of 23 percent.[19]

The American people understand how much better off they would be if they could choose their schools. Most of all, minorities, the poor, and those with less education themselves understand it—they are the ones who continue to be the biggest supporters of vouchers.[20]

In the spring of 1988, the *Chicago Tribune* undertook an in-depth examination of the state of the public school system in Chicago, publishing its results in a two-week series of articles. The findings were shocking—perhaps as much to the *Tribune* as to its readers. In an editorial following the final article, it reached the following conclusions:

> The Chicago schools are so bad, they are hurting so many thousands of children so terribly, they are jeopardizing the future of the city so much that drastic solutions must be found. It's too late for easy changes, simple answers, painless posturing. . . .
>
> What's necessary first of all are radical changes to wrestle the schools away from the bureaucrats and the unions. . . .
>
> The quickest surest way to explode the bureaucratic blob, escape from the self-seeking union and develop schools that succeed for children is to set up a voucher system. That would bring new people into school management, assure local control, empower

[18]See, for example, Chester E. Finn, Jr., "Education Choice: Theory, Practice and Research," testimony before the Senate Subcommittee on Intergovernmental Affairs, Committee on Governmental Affairs, October 22, 1985.

[19]National Governors' Association, *Time for Results*, (Washington 1986).

[20]See "Voters Like Vouchers," *New York Times*, May 8, 1988, p. E29, reporting on a 1988 poll of 2,109 people. The group most strongly favoring vouchers is "Partisan Poor," which favors vouchers by a 62–17 margin, compared with 49–28 for the population at large. These data confirm several years' worth of data from the Gallup Poll. See also "The 19th Annual Gallup Poll of the Public's Attitudes Toward the Public Schools," *Phi Delta Kappan*, September 1987, pp. 17–30.

parents, squeeze out bad schools and put the forces of competition to work for improving education.[21]

Remember, this is not some theoretical economist writing those words. This is the leading newspaper in our nation's third largest city, calling for dramatic, fundamental change. And what the *Tribune* is saying has much broader implications because it means that the liberal, big-government system of education has failed in America's large cities—and, in fact, is destined to continue failing.

But even as the *Tribune* issues its indictment, I must say that I know from personal experience that the majority of parents in the United States are satisfied with their government schools. And indeed, in many cases they have good reason to be happy. Government schools have worked well for decades, and in thousands of communities across the country they continue to work well—not because they have better bureaucrats but because many schools still represent the community of values that is crucial to educational success.

The goal for federal education policy must be to provide incentives for competition—and remove disincentives—while avoiding the urge to mandate a nationwide policy. Elementary and secondary education is one of the few remaining areas in which the federal government plays a relatively small role. Competition—no matter how desirable a goal—would not be worth achieving if the price were the federalizing of our school system. Today's education monopoly is run at the state and local level, and it must be up to the governments at those levels to change it.

By the same token, communities that believe their schools need improvement ought to be able to do something about it by encouraging competition. And there are at least two specific federal roles here.

• First, the federal government should make federal assistance for disadvantaged students available through vouchers, as the Department of Education proposed under the leadership of William Bennett. This proposal, which probably requires congressional

[21]"How to Fix America's Worst Schools" (editorial), *Chicago Tribune*, May 29, 1988.

approval,[22] is only a small start in that it would affect relatively few students and relatively little money. However, it would accomplish two things: it would make the benefits of competition available to the disadvantaged students who are suffering the most from the monopoly, and it would set the right example.

• Second, the federal government should play a role in providing incentives and removing disincentives to greater competition. The most important step here would be to clear up the legal questions that surround federal assistance to parochial schools—questions that make it difficult for school districts to know precisely which forms of aid might be permissible under the Constitution.[23] At a minimum, the next administration ought to make clear its views on the issue and indicate a readiness to participate in litigation to defend the right of parents to use vouchers in the schools of their choice.

Conclusion

In pursuing the goal of a more competitive education system, it is important to be able to point to examples in which the process of choice already is succeeding. We can point to increasingly clear evidence that competition among government schools increases educational quality—including experiments in Cambridge, Massachusetts, in Harlem, and now the statewide program being implemented in Minnesota.[24] And we should not forget that we can point to a 100-year-old system in Vermont, where state and local governments combine to pay tuition—up to a set amount—regardless of whether families choose private or government schools.[25]

Competition will reward goods schools, force bad schools to get better, and provide every family in the United States with choices it does not have today. I believe our goal should be to encourage

---

[22]However, see Thomas Vitullo-Martin and Bruce Cooper, *Separation of Church and Child*, (Indianapolis: Hudson Institute, 1987), which argues that the Department of Education effectively could institute Title I vouchers administratively.

[23]See ibid., p. 9.

[24]See John K. Andrews, Jr., "Consumer Sovereignty in the Schools: Will Colorado Opt for School Choice as Minnesota Did?" (Denver: Independence Institute Issue Paper 17-88, August 5, 1988).

[25]See John McClaughry, *Educational Choice in Vermont* (Concord, Vt.: Institute for Liberty and Community, 1987).

universal educational choice—for all students, not just the poor or wealthy—by the year 2000. States and localities should be able to provide vouchers or other funding mechanisms so that all families can choose the education that best fits their children's needs.

15. Privatization: Better Services at Less Cost

Peter Young

Interest in privatization in America has been mounting over the last three years, at the same time as there has been an exponential increase in privatization around the world. However, actual privatization activity at a federal level in the United States has been low. The only major sales have been those of Conrail and loan portfolios. There has been more privatization at the state and local level, mainly involving the contracting out of services and the private development of new infrastructure projects.

Press coverage of privatization is increasing rapidly, indicating greater familiarity with the concept throughout America. The Nexis system, for example, a nationwide data base index of major periodicals, was queried for the appearance of "privatization" and derivative terms as key words in articles published in 1985 and 1986; there were 457 such articles in 1985 and 1,005 in 1986, an increase of 220 percent.

Greater federal interest in privatization was signaled by President Reagan's decision in August 1987 to appoint a President's Commission on Privatization and to create a new position in the Office of Management and Budget responsible for coordinating the administration's privatization initiatives.

Pressures for privatization are continuing to increase. Aside from the continuing federal deficit, factors that are having and will continue to have a positive influence on the growth of privatization in the states in particular include a decline in federally provided state revenues, a decline in oil tax revenues, the states' inability to achieve large tax increases, greater demands for state services, and a shift to the right in state governorships and legislatures.

State and local governments are finding it increasingly difficult to finance much-needed new projects and to upgrade existing

251

facilities by traditional public-sector methods. The declining availability of tax-exempt municipal financing and federal grants, therefore, creates great opportunities for innovative private financing of infrastructure projects. One of the primary roles for the federal government in privatization should be to use its power and influence to facilitate privatization at the state and local level.

Federal Privatization Policy to Date

Although privatization has long been a goal of the Reagan administration, it has not received the high-level attention accorded to other policy initiatives such as tax reform. In the early years of the Reagan administration, privatization efforts focused on federal lands (which cover a third of the total U.S. land area). These efforts, however, were handled clumsily and they failed.

The privatization concept was revived in the administration's January 1986 budget. The budget contained proposals to privatize Conrail; five power-marketing administrations, which wholesale 6 percent of all the electric power generated in the United States; two oil fields owned by the Department of Energy; property owned by the General Services Administration; the Federal Housing Administration, which insures real estate loans; the Overseas Private Investment Corporation; Export-Import Bank loans and other loan portfolios; and Amtrak. Apart from Conrail and federal loan portfolios, none of these proposals achieved congressional passage.

Most of the 1986 proposals were repeated in the administration's 1987 and 1988 budgets, but they came no closer to being passed by Congress. The 1988 budget proposals also added some new privatization projects, including studies of the privatization of the U.S. Postal Service, the Tennessee Valley Authority, uranium-enrichment facilities, and air traffic control; pilot projects in the contract management of federal prisons, customs services, and tax courts; and the immediate privatization of military housing, nonemergency Coast Guard services, and military commissaries.

Although substantial privatization of the federal sector has yet to occur in the United States, at least the arguments for privatization are now better understood in Washington. Politicians and others are now relatively well acquainted with the British privatization program, and they appreciate the variety of its successful techniques. The privatization proposals emanating from the Reagan administration in its latter days showed much greater political sophistication than the administration's earlier attempts. It is a pity that by that time the Reagan administration had insufficient political capital to achieve their adoption.

The federal government has a very strong influence on the extent of privatization at the state and local level. Federal tax policy and grant policy are vital factors in determining the appeal of privatization. In particular the private financing, construction, and operation of new assets were affected by the 1986 federal tax reform.

Tax reform, for example, significantly reduced the tax benefits associated with some forms of privatization. The cap on industrial development bonds, now known as private activity bonds, was significantly tightened, the investment tax credit was eliminated, and depreciation schedules were lengthened.

The primary restriction on tax-exempt financing of nongovernment projects is the volume cap on private activity bonds, $50 per capita starting in 1988. This represents a nationwide total of $13 billion, a decline of 60 percent since 1984. A few selected uses remain outside the volume cap if they are government-owned: airports, docks, ports, and solid-waste disposal facilities.

Some projects, if privately owned and operated, are not eligible for any tax-exempt financing, even under the volume cap. These are sports facilities, convention and trade show facilities, parking facilities, alcohol-fueled and steam-generating facilities, hydroelectric generating facilities, air and water pollution control facilities, industrial parks, and small issue bonds for nonmanufacturing projects.

Governmental activities—the construction of roads, bridges, schools, public buildings, parks, sewers in residential communities, and similar infrastructure projects—continue to qualify for tax-exempt financing. However, the percentage of use by people other than the general public cannot exceed the equivalent of 10 percent of bond proceeds without jeopardizing the tax-exempt status of the bonds.

Despite the tax changes, other factors continue to make privatization as attractive as it ever was. Since tax reform, companies have had to emphasize inherent private-sector advantages, including the private sector's greater technical and operating expertise, quicker access to the latest advantages in technology, ability to employ "fast track" construction methods, greater design flexibility, and ability to offer a full-service approach that encompasses design, construction, operation, and ownership of facilities.

Perhaps the most important pressure for more privatization is the declining attractiveness of public ownership. For example, in the wastewater field, the main advantage of public ownership—namely, free money—is rapidly disappearing. Under the Wastewater Treatment Construction Grants Program, maximum federal contributions have already declined from 75 percent to 55 percent of project cost, and appropriations have been pegged at $2.4 billion per year. The 1987 Water Quality Act provides for a complete phasing out of the federal grant program and its replacement by a federally capitalized, state-administered revolving loan program. Repayment rates may be as high as market rates.

Another important factor is the growing imposition of "high-quality/high-cost" service requirements by the federal government on state and local governments, especially in the areas of health care, energy, water purification, waste disposal, and transportation.

It should also be noted that tax reform has made tax-exempt financing generally less attractive. Because individual tax rates are lower, the public's interest in tax-free investments has been reduced. Furthermore, earnings from many tax-exempt bonds will be subject to the new alternative minimum tax. Tax reform, therefore, has resulted in a general reduction in tax-exempt municipal financing.

The decline in traditional methods of financing public works infrastructure has greatly increased the attractiveness of straightforward taxable financing of fully private projects. Tax reform has raised the cost of all infrastructure projects, but privatization in most cases is still the least-cost alternative.

Opportunities for Privatization

A future federal privatization program should involve all the targets already identified by the current administration and some others. Public policy should support the strategy of encouraging employee buyouts of public-sector bodies—a strategy that is particularly applicable to public bodies with large numbers of employees, such as the U.S. Postal Service, Amtrak, and mass-transit systems.

Experience with Employee Stock Ownership Plans in the private sector has been favorable. ESOPs can provide tax advantages useful in privatization, and employee ownership can widen support for privatization both among employee groups and across the political spectrum.

There are strong pressures for greater private involvement in the provision of new infrastructure projects. Accordingly the public policy task should be to encourage such involvement and allow the private sector to compete on a level playing field with traditional public-sector approaches.

Discrimination against the private sector through the tax system should be removed. It is unfair that in the provision of certain functions, only the public sector should have access to tax-exempt financing. This privilege institutionalizes a bias against the introduction of more efficient, competitive private-sector solutions.

The answer is either to restore the private sector's access to tax-exempt debt for those projects, or preferably, to phase out tax-exempt financing altogether.

The reduction of federal grants for public-sector projects in states and localities has had a very positive effect on the growth of privatization. Therefore, the policy objective in all fields should be the further reduction of these grants, and, if possible, their outright abolition.

Insofar as federal grants are still given for local projects, they should require that such projects be put out for competitive bidding before the grants can be paid. Thus, the grant system should be used to encourage privatization, not block it.

Following are several specific candidates for privatization that should be considered by a new administration seeking to improve service delivery and reduce the federal deficit.

The U.S. Postal Service

The U.S. Postal Service should be a prime privatization target, as it is a large, inefficient state monopoly that affects the lives of all Americans. Although the great numbers of USPS employees pose a political problem, they also represent an opportunity to use privatization to spread capital ownership.

The USPS employees could be interested in a buyout proposal in that USPS owns many valuable assets, as well as a complete nation-

255

wide distribution network. Were USPS to be transferred to its employees, many of them could become substantially richer.

However, any such privatization should also be accompanied by removal of the monopoly protection of the private express statutes. To calm the fears of rural voters that repeal would lead to sharply increased postal rates for remote areas, only firms offering single nationwide tariffs should be allowed to compete with USPS. In any case, current private courier firms such as Federal Express already charge only one rate.

Federal Land

Federal land could also be successfully privatized if a more politically astute approach was adopted. If nonprofit environmental groups were allowed to obtain development rights and encouraged to buy tracts of land at favorable prices, they might well be converted to the merits of privatization.

Some federal land holdings, such as Governor's Island in New York and that part of Waikiki Beach owned by the army, could be sold to the highest bidder for huge prices and with little political opposition. Western grazing land should be sold at reduced prices to those who currently have grazing rights. Sales of federal land of an environmentally sensitive nature should involve private environmental groups as described above. One aim of such sales should be to expand greatly the number of privately run environmental sanctuaries.

Public Housing

More emphasis should be given to the sale of public housing. That is an area in which there are major opportunities to increase capital ownership among the less affluent, but little has yet been achieved. In Great Britain, by contrast, over 1.2 million public housing units have been sold to their tenants.

The federal government need not abandon its role in housing assistance to the poor. Instead of building government-owned accommodations for the poor, it should provide housing vouchers so that eligible households can rent suitable housing from the competitive private sector.

Existing public housing units should be transferred to tenant ownership as fast as is feasible. The first step in housing projects

256

should be transfer of management to tenant groups, followed by sale to individual households or private tenant cooperatives.

Airports and Air Traffic Control

It is generally recognized that there is an acute shortage of aviation infrastructure in the United States. Since airline deregulation in 1978, passenger traffic has expanded dramatically—from 270 million passengers to 415 million in May 1987, and the demand for air travel continues to grow at a rate of more than 5 percent per year. Nevertheless the nation's airports and air traffic control system have not kept pace with that growth; the national airport infrastructure has only been able to accommodate an average 1 percent a year increase in air departures over the past seven years. The result is severe congestion and delays and increasing public and congressional anger.

In 1986, 16 major U.S. airports, which together handle 43 percent of all air passengers, were seriously congested and were experiencing high levels of delays. By the year 2000, 58 airports handling 76 percent of all passengers will be congested unless capacity is increased.

The need for new airports is clear, but new capacity is not forthcoming. Airports are unpopular with voters for locational reasons, and public funds are hard to get for airport construction. Denver has a major new airport in the planning stage, but the last large airport to be built was the Dallas–Fort Worth Airport in 1973.

There are very few privately owned commercial airports in the United States, although some airports are successfully managed under contract by private firms. This situation contrasts with that in Great Britain, where the major airports have been privatized. BAA (formerly British Airports Authority), which runs seven airports, has prospered since privatization, primarily through aggressive exploitation of all commercial opportunities at its airports.

Tax reform has not had any major effect on the privatization of airports. As before, tax-exempt bonds are available only for capital expenditure of government-owned airports. However, this does not rule out greater private involvement in the airport market for at least two major reasons. First, the private sector could become involved in the construction, financing, and operation of parts of airports for which governments wish to isolate risk—for example, the construction and operation of people-mover systems at airports.

257

There have been proposals made to this effect for both John F. Kennedy and Dulles International airports.

Second, private companies could build, finance, and operate airports using tax-exempt debt as long as they did not own the airports. Eastern Airlines, for example, is building a terminal in San Juan, Puerto Rico, using tax-exempt debt issued through a special facility of the Puerto Rico Port Authority. Eastern owns the facility initially, but ownership is gradually being transferred to the port authority.

Such innovative approaches to the construction of new airports or the expansion of existing ones that involve private financing, lease-back, and private management arrangements could prove attractive to some local governments. The federal government should encourage the private sector to become involved in airport construction, perhaps by selling suitable redundant military bases to private-sector groups for conversion to new civilian airports. Federal funding of airports should cease, and airport operators should be allowed to charge peak-time landing and takeoff fees, as well as passenger facility fees.

The tax bias against private airports should be removed. Whether publicly or privately owned, airports serve planes and passengers. Airports are not an inherently governmental function.

Similarly, government restraints on the expansion of the air traffic control system have led to an expensive and out-of-date service that cannot meet increasing service demands. Air traffic control at airports should be the first part of the service to be privatized. Competing private companies already provide this function more efficiently at some smaller airports.

Next, the remainder of the air traffic control system should be transferred to a private corporation, owned jointly by its users and current Federal Aviation Administration employees. This corporation should be financed by user charges. The FAA itself should be restricted to the function of safety regulation, which it will be able to carry out more efficiently if it is not also providing the air traffic control system.

Roads, Bridges, and Tunnels

Little privatization activity has yet occurred in this area (other than contracting out maintenance and repair work). For some time a private company has owned and operated the Detroit-Windsor Tunnel, under the Detroit River between Detroit and Windsor, Ontario. More recently the Municipal Development Corporation has concluded a deal to construct and operate a new private toll bridge on the Minnesota–North Dakota border.

MDC also has proposed to build a $35 million toll road in Northern Virginia near Dulles International Airport, but this project must clear some legislative hurdles before it can proceed. In the summer of 1986 the Front Range Toll Road Company was formed by a group of Denver businessmen. The firm proposes to construct, operate, and own a private four-lane highway from Fort Collins to Pueblo, Colorado. Under an 1883 Colorado law, private toll roads are permitted, subject to county approval of tolls.

There is a great need for increased expenditures on bridges in the United States. According to the Federal Highway Administration, almost 40 percent of U.S. bridges are deficient and in need of rehabilitation. The FHWA estimates that some $48.3 billion is needed nationwide to rehabilitate and replace deficient bridges, and there is increasing interest in private-sector financing of such work. Entrepreneur Jerry Janssen of Peoria, Illinois, has formed a company called Build-A-Bridge for the purpose of building privately financed bridges.

The federal government should encourage the construction of private toll roads by denying grant funds to those states that have legislative obstacles to the private sector owning roads and charging for their use. The private provision of new roads should be a primary goal of the FHWA.

Drinking-Water Treatment and Supply

Drinking-water treatment and supply are likely to experience significant increases in demand over the remainder of the century owing to changes in consumption patterns. The primary responsibility for meeting this growing demand will rest with state and local governments, and some of them are already turning to privatization as a solution. For example, San Diego is working with the Galloway Group in an attempt to buy between 300,000 and 500,000 acre-feet of drinking water. Estimates of the capital required to build a reservoir of such capacity range up to $700 million.

Private companies are introducing technological advances such as computerized monitoring and remote control of water supply and ozonation/direct filtration. Expansion in this area of privatization can be reliably expected.

The declining availability of federal funds for water supply improvements is an important factor in encouraging privatization. Further reductions in federal subsidies are required, as well as enthusiastic federal encouragement of this privatization option.

Transportation

The provision of mass transportation in the United States today is primarily a public-sector function. Since the 1960s, when substantial public funds began being spent on transit, the cost of service has increased sharply while ridership has declined. American Public Transit Association statistics show annual operating deficits of more than $5 billion for all mass transit systems nationwide.

Such privatization that has occurred is mainly of the contracting-out form, and this is the main focus of current administration policy. Increasing numbers of bus systems are being contracted out with resultant savings. There have been proposals for private transit infrastructure projects. The two of these that have advanced the furthest are the Orlando Southwest Corridor—which would connect the Disney parks and other attractions with International Drive and Orlando—and the Dulles International Airport light rail project.

There are a range of proposals for high-speed rail projects, all of which would involve the private sector to varying degrees, from private financing to private ownership and operation. The most developed proposal is for a 320-mile high-speed rail line linking Tampa/St. Petersburg, Orlando, and Miami.

Existing transportation systems can and should be privatized. After the successful privatization of Conrail, Amtrak should be next for transfer into the private sector.

Currently costing the taxpayer some $600 million a year in subsidies, Amtrak has a negative net worth. Its sale for even a negligible amount would be of benefit. There is evidence that sections of Amtrak—such as the Northeast Corridor—are potentially profitable, particularly if they were in the hand of employee groups that would have the incentive to eliminate restrictive practices and maximize productivity. The Northeast Corridor should be the first section of Amtrak sold to its employees at a nominal price. If this policy is successful, other sections should also be sold.

Section 13(c) of the Urban Mass Transportation Act essentially precludes any form of privatization that would harm current mass transit employees through layoffs or pay cuts. This ban is a serious obstacle to privatization and should be repealed at the earliest opportunity.

On the other hand, there are some incentives for privatization in the favorable tax treatment accorded to employee buyouts. Half the interest paid on bank loans used to finance such buyouts is deductible from the tax liability of the institution providing the financing. This and other tax advantages were strengthened in the 1986 tax reform and should be preserved. They would be particularly helpful in any buyouts of Amtrak sections.

Although the final policy objective should be the elimination of Urban Mass Transit Administration grants, the current obligation to spend 10 percent on the private sector should be extended, perhaps initially to 30 percent. Only projects that have been put out for competitive bidding should be funded.

Wastewater Treatment Facilities and Systems

Wastewater treatment plants have been among the most common privatization targets in the United States over the past few years. Communities all over the nation have turned to the private sector for urgently needed wastewater treatment facilities, and privatization has proven to be an efficient and financially sound solution. Some of the largest U.S. engineering and construction firms have taken an active role in this field, including the Parsons Corporation and Metcalf and Eddy.

Privatization of wastewater treatment (as noted above) does not seem to have been slowed by tax reform. The advantages of privatization are still legion. For example, a typical wastewater treatment facility funded by the Environmental Protection Agency takes four to six years to complete once funding is approved (itself a lengthy process). On the other hand, in Chandler, Arizona, the Parsons Corporation placed the first privatized wastewater treatment facility in service two years after the city first requested proposals from the private sector.

The tremendous need for improved wastewater treatment facilities throughout the United States suggests that privatization will continue to expand. In the Northeast, aging, poorly maintained plants need to be replaced. In the Southwest, growth is outstripping the ability of local governments to provide facilities where needed. At the same time, federal funds simply are not available to solve local problems.·

Local governments should be required to seek proposals from the private sector to be eligible for federal grants, and EPA should set up a special office to encourage privatization.

Prisons and Other Correctional Facilities

The use of the private sector to finance, construct, and manage prisons in the United States has been slowly growing over the past five years. There are currently some 1,200 adults being held in secure correctional facilities operated by the private sector. These include, for example, the Marion Adjustment Center, a minimum-security facility for 200 males in Kentucky; the Bay County Jail and Annex in Florida, a medium-security facility for 350 men and women; and the Silverdale Detention Center in Hamilton County, Tennessee, for 340 men and women.

Private involvement in this field does not always extend to actual operation of the jail; in many cases only the financing and construction are performed privately. This arrangement offers the advantage of much speedier construction at lower cost than public-sector construction. After examination of the favorable U.S. experience of prison privatization, Great Britain has now started to privatize its own prison system.

The U.S. prison system has a severe problem of overcrowding and lack of capacity. Forty states are under federal court orders to relieve overcrowding. New beds are required as soon as possible, and only the private sector can supply them quickly enough. Among the states now moving toward varying degrees of privatization in their prison systems are Texas, Arizona, New Mexico, and South Carolina. The trend is accelerating.

The federal government should encourage this trend by privatizing its own prison facilities and by providing help and advice to state and local governments that are considering this option.

Although some Immigration and Naturalization Service detention facilities have been privatized—all with very favorable results in terms of cost and service—the majority of such facilities are still in the public sector. All of them should be put out for competitive

262

bidding. Similarly the Federal Bureau of Prisons should put the management of its existing facilities out to contract, together with the construction and operation of new facilities.

Ports and Shipyards

There are 188 deep-draft ports located along the U.S. coast, all owned by government agencies. In a survey undertaken by the National League of Cities and the U.S. Conference of Mayors, 63 percent of the city officials who responded reported that their docks, wharfs, and port facilities needed repair, rehabilitation, or replacement. At some ports, particularly older ports along the Atlantic coast, deteriorating piers, wharfs, and other landside facilities are a serious problem.

Like airports, ports are still eligible for tax-exempt financing outside the volume cap if they are owned by government entities. Port improvements are usually financed by tax-exempt revenue bonds.

So far, unlike in Great Britain, there has not been any privatization of ports in the United States. Some state and local governments may be persuaded to move in this direction, however. As in Britain, ports could prosper under aggressive private management, exploiting real estate development opportunities to a greater extent. There is also the potential of private construction and operation of new port facilities. Ports under full private ownership would not have access to the tax-exempt bond market. Arrangements could be made, however, to lease a port from a port authority, thereby preserving the port's tax-exempt status.

There are also privatization possibilities within ports—that is, for selected parts of port operations. For example, the Port Authority of New York and New Jersey has issued a request for proposals for private participation in providing a trans-Hudson ferry service. Some shipyards are also possible privatization candidates. The U.S. Navy owns eight such shipyards, and they could be sold, perhaps by means of employee buyouts.

Conclusion

The experience of the Reagan administration shows that there are two main elements in a successful privatization program. One is the preparation of well-designed privatization proposals that are designed to meet the concerns of the interest groups associated

263

with the public-sector body to be privatized. The other is the organization of the substantial political effort that needs to be put behind the privatization program. This effort should involve commissions, privatization units in each agency, the encouragement of congressional leadership, and direct pressure from the president, both through the media and on his own administration.

Privatization is a policy that should be attractive to both Democrats and Republicans. It represents the most efficient way of delivering services to taxpayers at least cost. It is the least painful way of making budget cuts. Moreover it is probably the only way of satisfying the increasing infrastructure requirements of the next decades.

Prospects are stronger for a more bipartisan approach to privatization in the next administration. Democrats in Congress are gradually abandoning their seemingly automatic opposition to all privatization proposals. According to an Ohio Democrat, Rep. Dennis E. Eckart: "We're not going to let the President sell the Post Office to Federal Express. But given the budget constraints we're under, given the demands that people make on government services, we ought to look at alternatives and better ways to provide them. The basic Democratic response until now has been 'Drop dead' but I think that's a mistake."

Congressional Democrats may be being influenced by the more positive attitude being taken by some Democrats at the state and local level. For example, Mayor Wilson Goode of Philadelphia has recently become cochairman of the Privatization Council, and he is a keen advocate of the contracting out of services to private enterprise. Governor Michael Dukakis has fostered the idea of public-private partnerships in Massachusetts. Auburn, Massachusetts mayor Jan M. Dempsey, despite describing herself as "an old-hat liberal Democrat," has become a privatization convert since the success of wastewater privatization in Auburn. "We think privatization is the way to go," she says.

Similarly, Republicans are taking a more open-minded attitude to privatization. There is growing recognition of the importance of the policy in all parts of the party. George Bush himself has said that even the U.S. Postal Service should be considered as a privatization candidate. The success of privatization abroad has elevated it to the position of a more mainstream issue in the United States.

Objective consideration of the merits of privatization by both Democrats and Republicans should lead to its adoption as a major theme of U.S. policy in the 1990s—and thus to the reversal of the creeping expansion of state power that has characterized the first nine decades of the 20th century.

16. The Drug Prohibition Problem
Jeff Riggenbach

Only a few years ago, it would have been difficult to find an informed and responsible person—whether scholar or journalist, policy analyst or politician—who would raise serious and fundamental questions about federal drug policy. In a nation where virtually every other public policy issue was hotly and vigorously debated, not only in Washington but on national television and in newspapers and magazines nationwide, there was striking unanimity of opinion on the drug issue. Individuals may disagree about military spending, deregulation, tax cuts, import restrictions, and abortion, but apparently they harbored no disagreements at all about illegal drugs. The dangers posed by such drugs, both to individuals and to society as a whole, seemed to most Americans to make it imperative that the federal government strictly prohibit their manufacture, possession, and sale. The only real debate was over how many resources should be devoted to enforcement of prohibition and what strategies should guide enforcement efforts.

Today, all this has changed. Suddenly, respected and influential scholars, journalists, politicians, and even law enforcement officials are openly questioning whether prohibition is really the best policy for the U.S. government to adopt toward psychoactive drugs such as marijuana, cocaine, and heroin. And a rapidly growing number of informed and responsible people are advocating a dramatically different drug policy for our nation—namely, legalization. The individuals advocating this change in national policy—or at least a serious national debate on the idea of legalization—are neither lunatic-fringe "crazies" nor self-interested "druggies" with a hidden (and personal) agenda. They are, on the contrary, such people as Baltimore mayor Kurt Schmoke; San Jose, California, police chief Joseph McNamara; Princeton University political scientist Ethan Nadelmann; Nobel laureate economist Milton Friedman; psychiatrist Thomas Szasz; and syndicated columnists William F. Buckley,

267

Jr., Richard Cohen, Stephen Chapman, and Doug Bandow. Under the influence of their ideas and arguments, at least four major metropolitan dailies—the *Detroit News;* the Orange County, California, *Register;* the *Tampa Times;* and the *Oakland Tribune*—have called for serious consideration of drug legalization. This is a step no major American newspaper would have considered taking, even as recently as, say, 1985. During the past year, *Time* and two of the commercial television networks—CBS and ABC—have devoted serious and respectful coverage to the growing legalization movement, and, in the process, have given even greater currency to its ideas and arguments. In September 1988 the House Select Committee on Narcotics, headed by Rep. Charles Rangel (D-N.Y.) held two days of hearings on drug legalization.

The proponents of legalization do not argue that drugs such as marijuana, cocaine, and heroin are harmless. Rather, they argue that the social problems associated with the use and abuse of these drugs pale beside the social problems created by prohibition of the drugs. The proponents claim that prohibition has not only failed to eliminate, or even to ameliorate, the problems associated with the use and abuse of these drugs, but has actually exacerbated the problems; that is, that our policy of prohibition has been not just ineffective but actually counterproductive, so that no policy at all might actually have been better.

The Goals of Drug Prohibition

To understand the position of the proponents of drug legalization, it is necessary to consider the goals that the policy of prohibition is meant to achieve. Federal and state laws prohibit the manufacture, possession, and transfer of marijuana, cocaine, and heroin because lawmakers hope thereby to eliminate, or at least reduce, the serious problems associated with their use. These problems are, on the one hand, ill health (often of so severe a character that it leads to joblessness, poverty, and death), and, on the other hand, increased crime (most notably murder, assault, thievery, abuse of family members, and prostitution).

Legislators have adopted a policy of prohibition toward the drugs associated with these problems because they reason that if such laws can prevent the manufacture, possession, and transfer of the drugs, the result will be to lessen the ill health and crime in the communities where the drugs are presently manufactured, used, bought, and sold. They reason further that even if the laws succeed only in reducing both the number of people who manufacture, use, buy, and sell the drugs and the quantities of drugs available in our cities, the result will still be a reduction in the incidence of ill health and crime.

For the current policy of prohibition to work, then—that is, for it to achieve its stated goals—it must succeed in either eliminating or reducing the incidence of drug abuse and drug trafficking in our society.

Has prohibition in fact done either of these things?

Unfortunately, it is impossible to answer this question with any substantial degree of confidence and certainty. We do know with certainty that prohibition has not eliminated the use of or traffic in cocaine; if it had, the seizures of cocaine by police officers, Drug Enforcement Administration (DEA) agents, Coast Guard officers, and Customs Service officials would have ceased. Since cocaine is still being seized, both at the borders and in U.S. cities and towns, it is obvious that the use of and traffic in cocaine are continuing despite the policy of prohibition.

But if one attempts to judge whether prohibition has reduced the use of cocaine or reduced the amount of cocaine on the market in this country, one begins running into serious methodological difficulties.

Of course, it is possible to determine exactly how much cocaine has been seized by law enforcement authorities in any given year. It is known, for example, that some 79,134 pounds of cocaine were seized by federal authorities in 1987.[1] But there is no way of knowing how much cocaine they failed to seize in that year—how much cocaine slipped past federal agents. Nor is there any way of knowing how many Americans use drugs, which drugs they use, or how often they use them. Of course, people can be polled on these questions. Such polls, at last word, showed that there are between 5 million and 6 million regular users of cocaine in the United States, around half a million regular users of heroin, and around 18 million

---

[1]Don Lattin, "Pot, LSD Coming Back—Harder Stuff Fading," *San Francisco Examiner*, May 31, 1988, p. 1.

regular users of marijuana (about 6 million of whom use marijuana on a daily basis).

But surely it is naive to believe that individuals engaged in criminal behavior that they know is punishable by heavy fines and lengthy prison terms are going to admit their involvement in such criminal activity to a stranger—even if they are promised anonymity. They know, after all, that undercover police officers and undercover DEA officers routinely make comparable promises of confidentiality for the specific purpose of winning the confidence of drug users and drug dealers to gather evidence that will be used to justify arresting and prosecuting those users and dealers at a later time. They know also that on occasion, undercover officers even offer drugs for sale (some of them genuine, some of them ersatz) to set up buyers for arrest. Drug users therefore cannot be relied upon to be candid about their drug use.

This makes it difficult to know what to make of the trend in recent years toward ever larger and more frequent seizures of cocaine along the U.S. borders. The trend may reflect nothing more than the increase during those years in the manpower and other resources being poured into the interdiction effort, both by the federal government and by state and local governments in coastal states. Or it may be that the large profits available in the cocaine trade have begun attracting more amateurs—smugglers whose methods are less sophisticated and who are therefore easier to apprehend. Or it may be that as the DEA has long insisted, it is seizing more and more cocaine because more and more cocaine is being brought into this country.

Certainly this last interpretation is given credibility by the anecdotal evidence supplied by police officers and others who have observed the cocaine marketplace in various U.S. cities firsthand. One fact this anecdotal evidence seems to prove is that the wholesale and retail prices of cocaine have dropped steadily over the past decade. A drop in price always signals either an increase in supply or a decrease in demand. And all the same anecdotal evidence suggests that demand for cocaine has been steadily increasing, rather than decreasing.

It is impossible to know, of course, what would have happened if the laws had been different. It may be that illicit drug use and the attendant ill health and crime would have grown even more rapidly had another policy been pursued.

270

The available data make clear, however, that our drug problem would probably not have been larger had government refrained from prohibiting the drugs in question. The data make clear, in fact, that our drug problem would probably have been smaller and less costly than it has been. In other words, the policy of prohibition seems not only to have failed to ameliorate our drug problem but actually to have exacerbated it, making conditions worse than they might have been had we done nothing at all.

Prohibition in the Past

Some of the data that support these conclusions are derived from study of the Prohibition era—the period between 1919 and 1933 in which alcoholic beverages were treated under federal law as cocaine, heroin, and marijuana are treated today. In studying this period, of course, one has to deal with many of the same methodological problems encountered when attempting to quantify the drug problem of today. Reliable figures on the production and consumption of alcoholic beverages during the 1920s are as hard to come by as reliable figures on the production and consumption of cocaine in the 1980s.

However, many historians of the Prohibition era believe that the use and abuse of alcohol not only failed to drop off but actually increased during the 1920s, when it was prohibited by law.[2] Indeed, the fact that alcohol was prohibited during the twenties seems actually to have played some part in making its use even more popular than it had been before. (Unquestionably, the adoption of the Eighteenth Amendment provided the irreverent and iconoclastic young people of the Roaring Twenties with one more icon to smash, one more rule to break, one more symbol of the old order to thumb their noses at. For many young people, of any and every generation, to be forbidden to have something is only to make it more attractive than when it was not forbidden.)

Since consumption of alcohol seems to have increased during the Prohibition era, the incidence of all the social problems associated with alcohol consumption must necessarily have increased along with it. Thus there were more cases of liver disease during the 1920s

[2]Thomas M. Coffey, *The Long Thirst: Prohibition in America, 1920–1933* (New York: W. W. Norton & Co., 1975), pp. xi and 187. See also John Kaplan, *Marijuana: The New Prohibition* (New York: World Publishing Co., 1970), p. 303.

271

than during previous decades, more cases of acute alcoholic poisoning, more injuries and deaths caused by drunken drivers and drunken operators of heavy equipment and machinery, more work-time lost to alcoholic dissipation, and more violent crimes committed by enraged drunks.[3] Furthermore, there were poisonings and deaths that wouldn't have taken place at all if alcoholic beverages had not been prohibited by law—poisonings and deaths caused by wood alcohol sold as whiskey by unscrupulous dealers, or by impurities and contaminants in the whiskey distilled by incompetents who had been drawn to bootlegging because it seemed to offer a quick and easy way to make money. All in all, Prohibition seems not only to have failed as a means of ameliorating the social problems associated with the use of alcoholic beverages but to have actually made those problems worse.

Another source of data useful to the student of contemporary American drug policy is the brief history of the black market in cigarettes that arose after World War II in and around various European cities. Cigarettes, along with other scarce goods, were tightly rationed during this period. In Germany, the ration was 40 cigarettes per month for each adult male and 20 cigarettes per month for each adult female. This ration was entirely adequate to satisfy the desires of some smokers, and it was, of course, more than adequate for nonsmokers. But for those who had been accustomed to smoking 20 or more cigarettes per day, in some cases for many years, the ration was utterly inadequate.

Predictably, a black market arose to supply these heavier smokers with the extra cigarettes they desired. Like all black marketers, those who dealt in illicit cigarettes charged exorbitant prices for their products. And the heavy smokers found ways to pay those prices. As Edward Brecher put it a quarter-century later in his authoritative Consumers Union study *Licit and Illicit Drugs*, "When the supply of cigarettes is curtailed, cigarette smokers behave remarkably like heroin addicts."[4] In Germany in the mid-1940s, heavy cigarette smokers went without food and health care to save their money to

[3]Kaplan, p. 342. See also Edward Brecher, *Licit and Illicit Drugs* (Boston: Little, Brown & Co., 1972), p. 265.
[4]Brecher, p. 226.

buy cigarettes. To raise the money to buy cigarettes, they committed muggings and burglaries and prostituted themselves.

There is no evidence to suggest that the overall consumption of cigarettes declined during the period of rationing. It therefore seems reasonable to conclude that there was no reduction in either of the two problems most commonly associated with cigarette smoking: the damage done to the health of smokers and the increased risk of fire that has long been linked with smoking of any kind. In fact, the evidence suggests that the rationing of cigarettes actually led to a greater impairment of smokers' health than had already existed during the years when cigarettes were widely and legally available at low prices. For, under the conditions imposed by rationing, smokers neglected proper nutrition and health care in an effort to devote more of their resources to the purchase of cigarettes.

At the same time, the rationing of cigarettes seems to have created at least one new problem of a kind not normally associated with cigarette smoking: an increase in the rate of crime, especially theft and prostitution. This increase in the crime rate seems to have been caused, not by the use of cigarettes per se, but by the rationing of cigarettes, which provided heavy smokers with a powerful incentive to do whatever was necessary, including the commission of crimes, to raise the funds they needed to pay the black market price of tobacco.[5]

Again, in the instance of postwar cigarette rationing in Europe, an attempt by centralized authority to reduce the available supply of a product not only failed to reduce either the availability of that product or the frequency of its use but actually exacerbated the problems associated with its use and created new problems that had not existed before. If the postwar rationing program for cigarettes was to be evaluated in terms of its success at reducing the problems associated with cigarette smoking (although, of course, it was not established to achieve that end), it would have to be judged—just as the U.S. government's experiment with alcohol prohibition in the 1920s must be judged—as not only ineffective but counterproductive.

[5]Ibid., pp. 226–27.

The Problems with Drug Prohibition

As noted, the use of such drugs as cocaine, heroin, and marijuana appears to have increased rather than decreased under prohibition. And if these drugs really are being used in larger quantities by larger numbers of people than before, the problems of ill health and crime associated with their use consequently must have increased. In other words, prohibition would seem to have failed to attain either any reduction in the use of and traffic in these drugs or any reduction in the associated problems.

Moreover, prohibition seems to have exacerbated the problem of ill health that is commonly associated with illegal drug use in much the same way that the postwar attempt to ration cigarettes in Europe exacerbated the health problems associated with cigarette smoking and in much the same way that alcohol prohibition in the United States in the 1920s exacerbated the health problems associated with alcohol consumption. By driving up the prices of drugs (in some cases to levels several thousand times higher than the prices on the legal market), prohibition provides drug users with a powerful incentive to neglect proper nutrition and health care to devote more of their resources to the purchase of drugs. In this way, prohibition helps to ensure that drug users will be even less healthy than they would have been otherwise.

Also, by turning the traffic in drugs such as cocaine, heroin, and marijuana over to organized crime, prohibition ensures that the drugs available to users will not be held to the standards of purity and truth-in-labeling that apply to products bought and sold on the legal market. By doing so, prohibition ensures that the number of poisonings and deaths caused by ingestion of impure and improperly manufactured drugs will be much larger than it would be otherwise—just as Prohibition caused an increase in the number of poisonings and deaths associated with the ingestion of impure and improperly distilled alcohol.[6]

The available evidence suggests that prohibition acts in a similar fashion to exacerbate the problem of drug-related crime. It is generally assumed that almost all drug-related crime is of three main types. First, there is violent crime (primarily murder and assault)

[6]F. R. Menue, "Acute Methyl Alcohol Poisoning," *Archives of Pathology* 26 (1938): 79–92.

274

committed by users as a direct result of their intoxication. Second, there is violent crime (primarily murder, assault, and armed robbery) committed by drug traffickers, mainly but not exclusively against other drug traffickers. This type involves disputes over "turf" (the right to monopolize the drug trade within a particular area), over unpaid debts, and over "rip-offs" (deliveries of drugs that turned out not to be what they had been represented to be in either content or weight). Third, there is the mostly nonviolent property crime (primarily burglary) committed by users to raise the money they need to buy drugs.

The first of these types of crime—violent crime committed by users because they are "hopped up" or "high"—is largely mythological. The nonpartisan Drug Abuse Council concluded in its 1980 final report, after more than five years of exhaustive research, that "alcohol and secobarbital—both legally produced psychoactive substances—are the drugs most likely to be involved with subsequent assaultive behavior," and that "there is no substantial evidence to link the use of any other drug, licit or illicit, with assaultive crime."[7] And no new evidence has come to light in the past decade that would justify either retracting or modifying that conclusion.

As to the second type of crime—the violent attacks perpetrated by drug dealers against their competitors—precisely the same kind of violence was commonplace in such big cities as New York and Chicago during the 1920s, when the trade in alcoholic beverages was dominated by men such as Al Capone and Bugsy Siegel. Today, when alcoholic beverages are sold by legitimate businesses in a legal market, rival liquor dealers no longer shoot it out in the streets. It is not the trade in drugs per se but the prohibition of that trade by law that causes most of the violent crime of this second type. Drug prohibition has placed the drug trade in the hands of professional criminals—men who are in the habit of using weapons to settle most if not all of their disputes, whatever they may be.

The third type of drug-related crime—the mostly nonviolent property crime committed by users—presents us with difficult (and possibly insoluble) problems of measurement and interpretation. It is known, for example, that at least 35 percent, and possibly as

[7]Drug Abuse Council, The Facts About "Drug Abuse" (New York: The Free Press, 1980), p. 83.

many as 70 percent, of those convicted of serious crimes are also users of illicit drugs. But it is not known what these figures signify. Do they mean that illicit drug use leads to serious criminal behavior, perhaps because illicit drug users have trouble raising the money to purchase the drugs they desire? Or does the statistical correlation between drug use and serious criminal behavior merely confirm what common sense would suggest? That is, because the only people who deal in drugs are criminals and criminals are more likely than most people to be acquainted with criminals, criminals are more likely than others to know where drugs may be bought and drug use is therefore generally more common among criminals than among the population at large.

It seems likely, given the inflated prices charged for drugs such as heroin by black-market dealers, that at least some heroin users do commit some property crimes to pay those prices. However, as the Drug Abuse Council concluded nearly a decade ago,

> while there is evidence to suggest that many heroin users may commit property crimes to support use, nobody really knows how much crime is actually committed to obtain money to support heroin habits. Police and court records do not contain this information, and estimates—which are not particularly reliable—vary, calling it anywhere from 10 to 50 percent of all revenue-producing crimes, depending upon the type of offense and the location.[8]

However, regardless of which estimate is accepted and how much property crime may actually be committed by heroin users who need money to buy drugs, it is evident that by driving up the price of heroin, prohibition dramatically increases the amount of money that users need to raise to feed their habit. And by doing so, prohibition virtually ensures that there will be a dramatic increase in the number of property crimes committed by users. More than one study has shown that when police beef up drug enforcement in an area, thereby reducing supply and increasing the risks faced by drug dealers, the result is that drug prices go up and there is an increase in property crime. Conversely, when police ease up on

[8]Ibid.

276

drug enforcement in an area, drug prices fall and the rate of property crime falls with them.[9]

Prohibition, in other words, has not only failed to reduce the number of people who abuse illicit drugs and the severity of the problems that commonly accompany such drug abuse; it seems to make matters worse by helping to bring about more ill health and more crime than drug abuse could produce on its own.

Prohibition Encourages Corruption and Organized Crime

Yet this is still not the most damning indictment that can be brought against our present drug policy, for all the available evidence suggests that prohibition has created a number of serious new problems—problems that would almost certainly not exist at all in the absence of such a policy.

First, by driving up the prices of illicit drugs, the current policy has made the drug trade immensely profitable. People can earn much more money today by dealing in cocaine than they could earn in the same amount of time by dealing in any legal commodity. They can earn even more if they can drive away competitors with acts and threats of violence, so that they can enjoy a monopoly over the sale of cocaine in a particular area. And they can earn still more if they can persuade law enforcement officers to look the other way or even help them put their competitors out of business. The economic incentive for drug dealers to attempt to bribe officers of the law is enormously powerful, thanks to prohibition. And because dealers are prepared to offer such hefty bribes to safeguard their enormous profit margins, the economic incentive for officers to accept bribes is also enormously powerful—again, thanks to prohibition and the effect it has on drug prices.

Even officers who refuse bribes often find it too attractive to resist the temptation to steal illicit drugs seized by their departments and to increase their incomes by selling them. In effect, prohibition has made it more difficult for police officers to remain honest. It has increased the likelihood of police corruption. And an officer who has once succumbed to the temptation of corrupt practices will find

[9]Lester P. Silverman and Nancy L. Spruill, "Urban Crime and the Price of Heroin," *Journal of Urban Economics* 4 (January 1977): 101. See also *Heroin Supply and Urban Crime* (Washington: Drug Abuse Council, 1976) and *The Facts About "Drug Abuse,"* pp. 85–86.

it much easier to do the same again and again. Why expose our society to a substantially increased risk of police corruption to continue a policy we know to be both ineffective and counterproductive?

Nor are officers of the law alone among Americans in being drawn by our drug laws into a criminal milieu that most of them would never have entered otherwise. Drug users are made to face a somewhat similar problem. Aside from their violations of the drug laws, most drug users are not criminals—at least in the beginning. Most of them are not even the kinds of petty scofflaws who routinely violate traffic regulations and leave parking tickets unpaid. Most of them are ordinary, law-abiding citizens with an ordinary law-abiding citizen's respect for law and order. The typical drug user is no different from the typical law-abiding solid citizen who wants to have a few drinks after work or a few beers while watching a ball game.

Current drug policy mandates, however, that while the drinker's favorite intoxicant is legally available at an affordable price, the marijuana smoker's or the cocaine user's favorite intoxicant is available only at an absurdly inflated price and at the risk of lengthy imprisonment. Moreover, the policy mandates that while the drinker may purchase his whiskey or beer publicly from a reputable retail business, the marijuana smoker and cocaine user must make their purchases in secret and from criminals.

In this way, the policy ensures that even those drug users—the majority of them—who give no evidence of a predisposition to criminal behavior will be brought into contact with criminals and the criminal subculture. In this milieu, among these people, even normally law-abiding citizens will not find it difficult to discover within themselves a new sympathy for the criminal element, a new disrespect for the law, and a new tendency to look upon other criminal behavior, behavior they would once have condemned, as no more heinous than drug dealing. It is particularly undesirable for teenagers and other young people to become familiar with the criminal subculture in this way and to develop such attitudes as these. The question we must face is this: Is it worth weakening our citizenry's respect for law and order just to preserve a policy that is both ineffective and counterproductive?

And why should we work to preserve a policy that only serves to strengthen one of our society's foremost enemies—organized crime? It is generally acknowledged that it was only the tremendous opportunities presented by Prohibition during the 1920s that enabled what had been a relatively weak and severely localized criminal syndicate to so enrich itself and consolidate its power that it could emerge in the 1930s as a powerful force of nationwide significance. Today, our drug laws are performing a similar service for gangsters of the same stripe. Thanks to these laws, which keep legitimate businesses out of the drug trade and ensure that one of the most lucrative businesses in America will be left in the hands of organized crime, the United States has recently been invaded by a powerful, violent, and unscrupulous new criminal enterprise based in South America. Is it not ridiculous to invest as heavily as we do in attempts to cripple organized crime, while at the same time pursuing a drug policy that only undermines whatever progress we make?

Nor should we forget that our drug policy also undermines other law enforcement efforts, though not in so direct a way. The resources—money, manpower, and time—that can be devoted to law enforcement, like the resources for anything else, are not infinite. The more we invest in drug enforcement, the less we can invest in the investigation and prosecution of violent crime and property crime. When then–attorney general Edwin Meese remarked last year that he and his department—the Department of Justice—devoted more time to the Reagan administration's War on Drugs than to any other single activity, he was telling us how little time he and his aides had left to devote to safeguarding the individual rights of American citizens.

Toward a Workable Drug Policy

What can be done to improve the effectiveness of our efforts to combat the problems associated with illicit drug use? Is there a policy that would combat these problems more effectively than prohibition, without either exacerbating them or creating new ones? The available data suggest that a policy of partial decriminalization of drugs such as cocaine, heroin, and marijuana, if combined with a policy of regulation and education, would constitute a major improvement in U.S. drug policy.

When advocates of fundamental change in drug policy make use of the term "decriminalization," they are often accused by defend-

279

ers of the status quo of advocating across-the-board legalization—
a state of affairs in which all individuals, irrespective of age, would
be free to buy whatever drugs they want in whatever quantities
they like. The "decriminalization" proposed here is not of this type.

The partial decriminalization proposed here would take the following form:

• The sale of drugs such as cocaine, heroin, and marijuana would
be permitted under conditions similar to those that now govern the
sale of alcoholic beverages. That is, only properly licensed retailers
would be permitted to deal in these drugs, and the licenses issued
would resemble current liquor licenses in being restricted to merchants who had proved themselves both responsible and prudent
in their marketing of potentially dangerous products. Also, like
today's liquor licenses, they could be speedily suspended or revoked
in the event of irresponsible or imprudent conduct on the part of
the licensees.

• Only adults (now defined as those over 21 years of age) would
be permitted to purchase drugs such as cocaine, heroin, and marijuana.

• Advertising of the decriminalized drugs would be limited or
possibly forbidden.

• Manufacturers would be held to federally mandated standards
of purity and would be required to print warnings on each package
concerning the possible hazards of using the product.

• The decriminalized drugs could be taxed, as tobacco and alcohol are today, and the tax revenues could be used to finance education aimed primarily at children and young adults and designed
to discourage drug use by future generations.

For such a policy as the one sketched above to become reality,
certain existing legislation would need to be repealed—specifically,
the Drug Abuse Act of 1970. This law, a legacy of the first Nixon
administration's war against the widespread use of drugs by the
hippies and student rebels of the 1960s, has been the basis of federal
policy on drugs such as cocaine, heroin, and marijuana ever since
its adoption by Congress two decades ago. Its repeal would pave
the way for substitution of a more judicious and less harmful federal
drug policy.

A useful adjunct to such a drug policy would be implementation
of a voucher or tax-credit system for primary and secondary edu-

cation. If all parents, not just those who are well-to-do, had the opportunity to choose which schools their children would attend, schools would be forced to compete for students not only by improving their performance as teachers of the basic academic subjects but also by excelling at providing a drug-free environment on their campuses.

It is important to note that the policy change advocated here—the adoption of a policy of partial decriminalization of the more popular and widely used recreational drugs—would not immediately and irrevocably eliminate all the many problems associated with the current policy of prohibition. It would be no panacea. But it would lead to significant improvement over the current situation. It would reduce drug-related street crime. It would reduce the extent to which drug use undermines the public health. It would reduce the extent to which scarce law enforcement resources are diverted from the investigation and prosecution of violent crime. It would cut off a major source of income for organized crime. It would make our cities safer places in which to live and work and play. It would be an important step forward in a field where, for far too many decades, our only steps have been backward ones.

17. Saving the Inner City
David Boaz

The past six years have been a time of great economic growth in the United States. The U.S. economy has produced 15 million new jobs since 1982, and a higher percentage of Americans are now employed than at any time in our history. Personal income per capita is up 12.3 percent.

Critics of the Reagan administration have been forced to reach for ways to explain away the success of the economy. Growth has been uneven, they say. The coasts are booming but not the heartland. The middle class is disappearing. The economy is like "a swiss cheese with lots of holes." These charges don't hold up under analysis. Consider just one indication, the condition of black Americans. In the last five and a half years, blacks have gained 15 percent of the jobs, though they account for only 11 percent of the working-age population. The black employment rate—the percentage of working-age people holding jobs—has risen to a record level of 56 percent. Black median income is up, the number of middle-class blacks has increased by a third since 1980, and black businesses have grown at an annual average rate of 7.9 percent since 1982 (compared with 5 percent for all businesses).[1] It would seem that President John F. Kennedy and Rep. Jack Kemp were largely correct when they defended their tax-cutting policies with the argument that "a rising tide lifts all boats."

Nevertheless, in the midst of the most affluent society in the history of the world, there is a poverty problem. It is difficult to assess the extent and severity of overall poverty. The poverty rate itself—13.6 percent in 1986—isn't very helpful in this matter. As Charles Murray has pointed out, aside from such problems as graduate students living—and even raising families—on incomes

---

[1]Joseph Perkins, "Boom Time for Black America," *Policy Review*, Summer 1988, pp. 26–28.

below the poverty line, the official poverty statistics probably over-estimate the incidence of real poverty in rural areas and small towns and among the elderly while they may undercount it in central cities.[2] And George Gilder has reminded us that official American poverty is not necessarily a life of grinding misery:

> Let us imagine a population of American poor who can feed themselves on less than one-fifth of their incomes, as other Americans do. . . . Let's give them twice as much housing space [as the Japanese]. Imagine further that home ownership is possible for the poor, and that perhaps two-fifths of them achieve it (well above the overall Japanese level). Imagine telephones and color televisions in more than four-fifths of their homes. . . . Imagine giving a car to virtually every poor person who is not perpetually drunk or in jail. Assume the poor achieve access to health care comparable to that of middle-class American families and assume further that their life expectancy at birth is over seventy years, and improving steadily. . . .
>
> What you have just imagined is the current condition of the population below the poverty line in the United States today.[3]

The Plight of the Underclass

But there are some of the American poor who truly live in wretched poverty. Beyond the material deprivation in their lives, they suffer an even worse deprivation of the spirit. They cower in fear of criminals in their neighborhood; they have no jobs and no hope of improving themselves; they don't expect their children to have a better life, and they impart to their children the kind of values that make those low expectations self-fulfilling. These are the people we call the underclass.

Where did the underclass come from? There have always been poor people, and if poverty is defined in terms of a relative lack of access to the standard of living in society, then, by definition, there will always be poor people. But the underclass seems to be something new since World War II or even since the 1960s. William Julius Wilson has described how "blacks in Harlem and in other ghetto

[2]Charles Murray with Deborah Laren, "According to Age," paper presented at the Working Seminar on the Family and American Welfare Policy, Washington, September 23, 1986, mimeo, pp. 65–66.

[3]George Gilder, "Welfare's 'New Consensus': The Collapse of the American Family," *Public Interest*, Fall 1987, p. 23.

neighborhoods did not hesitate to sleep in parks, on fire escapes, and on rooftops during hot summer nights in the 1940s and 1950s, and whites frequently visited inner-city taverns and nightclubs."[4] The increased crime rate in the inner city cannot be adequately captured in statistics; it is this kind of historical reflection that reminds us of how unlivable our inner cities have become in a generation.

Many theories have been advanced to explain the development of the underclass, especially racial discrimination and social-program budget cuts. To the extent that the inner-city underclass is predominantly black, it is hardly the case that there is more racism in society today than in the 1940s and 1950s. And there has certainly been no reduction in government aid to the poor; on the contrary, means-tested noncash assistance to the poor and the near-poor rose from $5.9 billion in 1965 to $21 billion in 1970 to $52 billion in 1983 (in constant 1984 dollars). Cash benefits added $29 billion more in 1983.[5]

Indeed, what cannot be denied is that the underclass has emerged simultaneously with the dramatic expansion of government programs designed to help the poor. These programs were begun with the best of intentions, at least in most cases. The slogan of the War on Poverty was "a hand, not a handout." Liberals called for new poverty programs that would permanently liberate people from the need for government assistance. Charles Frankel wrote in the *New York Times Magazine* that a liberal

> will not be content with attitudes of *noblesse oblige* or with policies that merely "take care" of the poor. . . . His ultimate test of a welfare program will be the effect it will have on producing individuals who, like Eliza Doolittle at the conclusion of "Pygmalion," are prepared to walk out on those who have helped them and to open competitive enterprises of their own.[6]

---

[4]William Julius Wilson, *The Truly Disadvantaged: The Inner City, the Underclass, and Public Policy* (Chicago: University of Chicago Press, 1987), p. 3.

[5]Working Seminar on the Family and American Welfare Policy, *The New Consensus on Family and Welfare* (Washington: American Enterprise Institute, 1987), p. 10 and Table A-6.

[6]Charles Frankel, "A Liberal is a Liberal is a Liberal—," *New York Times Magazine*, February 28, 1960, p. 21, quoted in Charles Murray, *Losing Ground: American Social Policy, 1950–1980* (New York: Basic Books, 1984), p. 22.

When President Kennedy proposed his first poverty program, the *New York Times* editorialized in the same spirit:

> President Kennedy's welfare message to Congress yesterday stems from a recognition that no lasting solution to the problem can be bought with a welfare check. . . . The dividends will come in the restoration of individual dignity and in the long-term reduction of the need for government help.[7]

Twenty-five years later, however, we find millions of Americans more or less permanently dependent on government assistance—a condition, Nick Eberstadt reminds us, that was once called "pauperism."[8] Pauperism, according to the *Oxford English Dictionary*, is "dependence upon public relief, as an established condition or fact among a people."

Poverty and Public Policy

The question of what public policies we might change in the area of welfare and poverty is not primarily an issue of cost to the taxpayers. Government expenditures on assistance to the poor in 1983—about $81 billion—amounted to less than 7 percent of total government spending in that year, less than social security, less than NATO, much less than education. The issue, therefore, is not whether welfare programs are bankrupting the taxpayers but what they are doing to the recipients.

We are slowly realizing that it is not really all that difficult to avoid poverty in the United States. As Charles Murray has written,

> The requirements for getting out of poverty in this country are so minimal that it takes a mutually reinforcing cluster of behaviors to remain in poverty, even if you are black and even if you are female. If you follow a set of modest requirements, you are almost surely going to avoid poverty.
>
> These requirements for a male, black or white, are to go to a free public school and complete high school. Get into the labor market and get a job, any job, and stick with the labor market.[9]

[7]"Relief is No Solution," *New York Times*, February 2, 1962, quoted in Murray, *Losing Ground*, p. 23.

[8]Nick Eberstadt, "Economic and Material Poverty in Contemporary America," paper presented at the Working Seminar on the Family and American Welfare Policy, Washington, April 30, 1987, p. 74.

[9]Murray, "According to Age," p. 89.

The Working Seminar on the Family and American Welfare Policy echoed this message:

.The probabilities of remaining involuntarily in poverty are remarkably low for those who
— complete high school
— once an adult, get married and stay married (even if not on the first try)
— stay employed, even if at a wage and under conditions below their ultimate aims.[10]

The question facing policymakers is, How can we encourage poor Americans, especially poor young people, to make the choices that will lead them out of poverty? As Murray has argued, in the 1960s "we"—the upper middle class elite—"changed the rules" for the poor. Opinion molders and policymakers, with the best of intentions, told the poor that their poverty was not their own fault. They made welfare easier to get. They made it more difficult to throw disruptive or uncooperative students out of school. They made it more difficult to put criminals in jail. And somehow, we ended up with more people mired in the welfare system, fewer students learning in the schools, and more crime.

By reducing society's disapproval of people who do not study, do not work, and do not meet their obligations, we took away the respectability formerly accorded those who do study, do work, and do meet their obligations. As Murray has said, the intelligentsia and the policymakers began treating the poor "in ways that they would never consider treating people they respected."[11] Being generous to the poor was equated with not holding them responsible for the consequences of their actions, a form of condescension that we would never accept from our peers nor show to those we respect.

These policies have created a class of people who take little responsibility for their own lives and find dependency a permanent way of life. Nearly three-fourths of all unmarried women who first join welfare rolls under the age of 25 spend at least five years on the rolls, with an average total stay of more than nine years.[12] But

---

[10]*The New Consensus on Family and Welfare*, p. 5.

[11]Murray, *Losing Ground*, p. 222.

[12]Kevin R. Hopkins, "A New Deal for America's Poor," *Policy Review*, Summer 1988, p. 70.

what can we expect? As Kevin Hopkins of the Hudson Institute has written:

> As long as work is seen as one of a number of options for self-support rather than as a social and economic necessity, welfare recipients will continue to work at far lower rates than necessary to provide for their families' needs. [And] as long as [Aid to Families with Dependent Children] exists and provides at least marginally adequate benefits, it will continue to serve as a means by which young . . . women [of low socioeconomic status] can bear a child outside of marriage without great fear of financial risk.[13]

What set of policies could break that cycle of dependency? Following is a five-part program.

1. Abolish Welfare for Working-Age People

At the end of *Losing Ground,* Charles Murray proposed a "thought experiment" about welfare:

> We have available to us a program that would convert a large proportion of the younger generation of hardcore unemployed into steady workers making a living wage. The same program would drastically reduce births to single teenage girls. It would reverse the trendline in the breakup of poor families. It would measurably increase the upward socioeconomic mobility of poor families. These improvements would affect some millions of persons.
>
> All these are results that have eluded the efforts of the social programs installed since 1965, yet, from everything we know, there is no real question about whether they would occur under the program I propose. . . .
>
> The proposed program, our final and most ambitious thought experiment, consists of scrapping the entire federal welfare and income-support structure for working-aged persons, including AFDC, Medicaid, Food Stamps, Unemployment Insurance, Worker's Compensation, subsidized housing, disability insurance, and the rest. It would leave the working-aged person with no recourse whatsoever except the job market, family members, friends, and public or private locally funded services. It is the Alexandrian solution: cut the knot, for there is no way to untie it.
>
> The prospective advantages are real and extremely plausible. In fact, if a government program of the traditional sort (one that

[13]Ibid., p. 72.

would "do" something rather than simply get out of the way) could *as plausibly* promise these advantages, its passage would be a foregone conclusion. Congress, yearning for programs that are not retreads of failures, would be prepared to spend billions."[14]

When Murray made his audacious proposal, he expected criticism, and he got it. He also expected better ideas, and he didn't get any. He assumed that someone, some expert somewhere, would be able to point to a program he had not considered, and he would then be able to agree that indeed there was a less drastic solution. In four years, however, no such expert has come forward with a workable welfare program.

Workfare is the latest idea. But

> a review of workfare programs with strong job-search components conducted by the Manpower Demonstration Research Corporation found employment gains among welfare participants generally no better than 10 percent. Even the administrators of Massachusetts' celebrated ET-Choices program could claim a net drop in the welfare rolls of only 4.5 percent from 1983 to 1986, a time of vigorous statewide economic growth. Similarly in New York, another state with extensive and highly touted job training and employment programs, the welfare caseload has fallen by a mere 4.5 percent over the same period.[15]

Murray himself, asked recently to name *some* poverty programs that have worked, replied, "I cannot think of a single large program, state or federal, that I consider to be a meaningful success."[16]

Whatever their costs in other ways, transfer programs for the elderly do not create a culture of dependency because the elderly are assumed to have completed their working and child-rearing lives. Also, social security is perceived to be an insurance program, something earned, rather than a handout. But transfer payments to people who could work give them an option not to work. Furthermore, because some unemployed people, especially the low-skilled, often view work as a hassle, they have little incentive to

[14]Murray, *Losing Ground*, pp. 227–29.
[15]Hopkins, p. 70.
[16]Charles Murray, "Aw, Never Mind," *Washington Monthly*, June 1988, p. 40. Murray spent 12 years as an evaluator of social programs before writing *Losing Ground*.

spend 40 or more hours a week plus transportation time to make only a little more money than welfare pays.

If we abolished welfare for working-age people, would there be real pain? Yes. Some people, especially older women after divorce or the death of a husband, use AFDC the way it was intended, as a temporary support while they work out a new way of supporting themselves. Without welfare, they would have to find other arrangements. But the very fact that they use AFDC only temporarily means that they are capable of finding jobs, new marriages, or other means of support.

The people whose lives would be most changed by a cessation of welfare are those who have come to depend on it, such as the young women whose average stay on AFDC is nine years. They are precisely the people who are being trapped in a web of dependency by the present system. Without welfare, their lives would be disrupted initially but improved in the not-so-long run by the need to take responsibility for themselves. Perhaps for the first time, they would have to find jobs or get help from relatives or from private charity.

Unemployment is now at a 14-year low. Employers are complaining about the difficulty of filling entry-level jobs. They are raising wages, offering transportation to workplaces, and hiring immigrants.[17] Immigrants, both legal and illegal, have been able to find jobs easily enough. More than 70 percent of both welfare mothers no longer on AFDC and inner-city black youth have told researchers that finding a job is not difficult.[18]

Jobs are available, and new jobs are being created every day. One of the most pernicious misunderstandings of the economy is the notion that there is a fixed supply of "jobs" sitting somewhere and that if someone gets a job the supply is reduced. In fact the supply of jobs is almost infinitely elastic, as the creation of 28 million new American jobs in the past 13 years ought to indicate. However,

[17]See William E. Schmidt, "Growing Job Problem: Finding People to Work," New York Times, October 28, 1984, p. 26; Dirk Johnson, "Labor Scarcity Is Forcing Up Low-Level Pay," New York Times, March 17, 1986, pp. B1–B2; Zita Arocha, "Illegal-Worker Ban Leaves Firms Hurting," Washington Post, June 6, 1988, p. 1.

[18]Lawrence M. Mead, "Work and Dependency, Part I: The Problem and Its Causes," paper prepared for the Welfare Dependency Project of the Hudson Institute, September 1986, p. 16 and generally pp. 8–17.

government regulations can interfere with the process of finding a job.

2. Abolish the Minimum Wage

Most inner-city teenagers and welfare mothers have very low skills, which are not worth much to an employer. They are the people for whom the minimum wage may be a real barrier to employment. By raising the cost of an employee above his value to an employer, minimum-wage laws prevent some people from getting jobs. There are other laws that contribute to this problem; social security taxes and unemployment compensation also add to the cost of hiring a new worker, for instance. But the clearest example of a law that throws the most-disadvantaged people out of work with the best of intentions is the minimum-wage law.

Countless studies have shown the counterproductive effects of such laws.[19] A recent analysis by economists Richard B. McKenzie and Curtis Simon estimated that an increase in the minimum wage to $4.65 by 1990 would cost 764,000 jobs by that year and 1.9 million jobs by 1995.[20] Rather than increase the minimum wage, the way to really help low-income workers—and current nonworkers—is to repeal the minimum-wage law and let more people get jobs.

Although it is true that a minimum-wage job doesn't pay very well—about $7,000 a year—only a few minimum-wage earners are heads of households and fewer still are supporting a family on just one income. More importantly, however, the only way to get a better job is to start with any job. This is the lesson that immigrants have been reminding us of. Until a welfare mother has had a minimum-wage job in which she learned basic job skills, she has no hope of getting a better job. To say she should hold out for a good job is to condemn her to a life of joblessness. Good jobs require skills, which are not developed on the welfare rolls.

[19]See Belton M. Fleisher, *Minimum Wage Regulation in the United States* (Washington: National Chamber Foundation, 1983); and Richard B. McKenzie, *The American Job Machine* (New York: Universe Books/Cato Institute, 1988), pp. 198–217.

[20]Richard B. McKenzie and Curtis L. Simon, *The Proposed Minimum Wage Increase: Associated Job Loss by State, Region, and Industry* (Washington: National Chamber Foundation, 1988).

3. Repeal Licensing Laws

More than 850 occupations are licensed by various governments. A potential worker has to have some kind of government permission to enter these trades. Now it is unlikely that many welfare mothers could hang out a shingle for a law practice in the absence of licensing laws, but they might become taxi drivers or hairdressers. In such cities as New York, Miami, Philadelphia, and Chicago, however, the price of a taxi license can be $15,000, $40,000, or even more. At one point in the 1970s a New York taxi license cost more than a seat on the New York Stock Exchange.

Licensing requirements are often unrelated to the ostensible purpose of protecting consumers. Many licensing examinations require that the applicants be able to speak, read, and write standard English so they can answer the questions, even though Spanish or nonstandard English might be perfectly adequate for communicating with their potential customers. In some states, beauticians are required to be high school graduates, barbers have to be able to name all the bones in the human hand, and applicants for many licenses have to have lived in the state for six months or a year. All such laws prevent people from getting jobs or from going into business; their impact is greatest on minorities and the poor.

4. Legalize Drugs

One of the biggest problems with our current drug culture is that drug dealing has become the most attractive career available to many inner-city young people. Drug prohibition reduces the supply of drugs, thereby pushing up prices. High prices mean high profits for dealers and enough money to support many layers of distribution. Preteen children get hired as runners, lookouts, and sellers. Teenagers buy BMWs with cash. Too many ghetto youths look around them and see three alternatives: welfare, which doesn't require working; a legal job, which probably means hard work and low pay; and drug dealing, which means a lot of money.

If drugs were legalized, playground pushers would be replaced by regulated stores. Just as there are no teenagers today buying luxury cars with the proceeds of liquor dealing, there would be no teenage drug millionaires under drug legalization. The best long-term choice for underclass teenagers to make is to stay in school, get a job—even a low-paying job—and learn the skills that will lead to better jobs. But to make this choice seem attractive to people who have trouble looking 10 years into the future, we need to take away the seductive alternatives of welfare and drug pushing.

One thing we have learned from the rise of drug dealing in the ghetto is that inner-city youth lack neither the ambition nor the ability to be entrepreneurs. If that entrepreneurial drive could be channeled into legitimate enterprises—as it would be if legalization took the phenomenal profits out of drug dealing and if repeal of licensing laws opened up more opportunities—we could expect to see flourishing businesses rising out of the wasteland of our inner cities.

Another benefit to inner-city communities of drug legalization, of course, would be crime reduction. More than half of the violent crime in major cities is attributed to junkies seeking money to pay for a habit that is made needlessly expensive by drug prohibition. This crime, and that committed by warring dealers, would cease with the end of prohibition.

5. *Allow Educational Choice*

Another major factor that keeps people trapped in the underclass is poor education. The national statistics on educational decline—SAT scores fell from 978 in 1963 to 890 in 1980—don't begin to capture the depths of the problem of inner-city schools. A better indicator is the Washington, D.C., valedictorian who was refused admission to George Washington University because he scored only 600 on the SAT. Like so many other urban teenagers, he had been conned into thinking he was getting an education. Urban schools are a nightmare of violence, drugs, gangs, and very little learning. A recent *Washington Post* series described life in a Washington high school. Students were casual at best about attendance, homework, and class behavior, and teachers were resigned to the situation. Getting through a class without violence seemed to be the goal.[21] As Phil Keisling has written, inner-city youth are "consigned to lives of failure because their high school diplomas are the educational equivalent of worthless notes from the Weimar Republic."[22]

---

[21]Athelia Knight, "Pursuing the Legacy: A Year at McKinley High School," *Washington Post*, September 13–16, 1987.

[22]Quoted in Lucy P. Patterson, "Department of Education," in *Agenda '83*, ed. Richard N. Holwill (Washington: Heritage Foundation, 1983), p. 115.

293

We have had 10 years of the Department of Education and 5 years have elapsed since a blue-ribbon commission reported on the disastrous state of American education. There has been little improvement. How many more generations of inner-city youth must leave school uneducated while administrators say, "Give us just a little time"? Around the country, private schools are educating inner-city children; it's just the politicized, bureaucratized monopoly government schools that can't do it. What inner-city parents need is choice and power. Education vouchers or tax credits would turn them from hapless recipients of government services into valued customers. Educational choice plans would let parents choose the schools their children will attend—public or private. With all parents able to afford nongovernment schools, alternatives would spring up. There would be church-run schools, storefront academies like Harlem Prep, traditional schools like Marva Collins's Westside Prep, Montessori schools, even profit-making schools. All of them would know that if they failed to provide better education than their competitors, they would go out of business.

Not all inner-city parents would make good choices, of course. Some would still leave their children in rotting public schools (though even public schools would probably get better under the pressure of competition), and some would choose ineffective schools. But this only means that some inner-city children would still get the poor education that most get today. Educational choice would mean that many minority teenagers would graduate from high school with a real education—and the lifelong benefits of that are incalculable.

Conclusion

This is a radical program. But deep-rooted problems require radical solutions. And this program has the advantage that it will work. The most tragic and divisive problem America faces is that some of our citizens are trapped in poverty and dependency in the midst of an economic boom in the richest society in history. Our deepest emotions are touched by the sight of fellow Americans for whom the American dream is not even imaginable.

For 20 years we have tried flooding the poor with money and social programs. That approach has not only failed to eliminate poverty, it has created a seemingly intractable problem of dependency. Our goal now must be to destroy the culture of dependency. We can do that by making honest work the best alternative for welfare mothers and inner-city teenagers. The elimination of non-work and drug dealing as better alternatives will accomplish that.

It is time to grant the poor respect, to acknowledge that they are responsible for their own lives. When we treat them as responsible citizens, I believe they will act as such. Their lives may be hard; the combination of hard work and low pay may at first be harder than a life on welfare. But the benefits would be clear: transforming many of the hard-core unemployed into steady workers, dramatically reducing unwed teenage motherhood, bringing back the family in the inner city, moving the underclass into the lower middle class and beyond. All it requires on the part of upper middle class policymakers and opinion molders is the willingness to judge a poverty program by its effects on the poor rather than its effects on our own psyches.

18. Draining the Agricultural Policy Swamp

James Bovard

Federal farm policy is trampling individual rights, sacrificing the poor to the rich, and giving congressmen and bureaucrats vast arbitrary power over American citizens. For almost 60 years, the U.S. government has devotedly repeated the same agricultural policy mistakes. Unfortunately, the federal safety net is slowly strangling American agriculture.

Farm subsidies—roughly $25 billion a year in federal handouts, plus $10 billion more in higher food prices—are the equivalent of giving every full-time subsidized farmer a new Mercedes each year.[1] Annual subsidies for each dairy cow in the United States exceed the per capita income for half the population of the world.[2] With the same $160-plus billion that government and consumers have spent on farm subsidies since 1980, the U.S. government could have bought every farm, barn, and tractor in 30 states.[3] The average American head of household now works almost one week a year simply to pay for welfare for less than a million farmers.[4]

Federal farm policy has been a Sisyphean struggle against the gradual, inevitable decline of crop prices. Wheat, corn, oats, and cotton prices have been declining in real terms for over a hundred

---

[1]There are roughly 300,000–400,000 full-time subsidized farmers; a new Mercedes can be procured for $30,000.

[2]The total cost to consumers and taxpayers of the dairy program is between $6 and $7 billion, and there are about 10 million dairy cows in production; thus the subsidy per cow is around $600–700. According to the World Bank, China's per capita income is $325, India's is $290, and Vietnam's is less than $450. See World Bank, *World Development Report* (Washington, 1988), p. 222.

[3]James Bovard, "Farm Subsidies Stifle Agriculture," *New York Times*, May 29, 1988, p. F2.

[4]The average family income is about $30,000. The $35 billion in annual farm subsidies works out to roughly $140 a person, or $560 for a family of four.

years, and crop prices have nose-dived in comparison to the units of labor required to purchase them.[5] Crop prices have declined because the cost of production has steadily declined, thanks to new farm machinery, new seed varieties, better fertilizers, and so forth. Yet, politicians perennially proclaim that the fact that wheat prices are now lower than they were 10, 20, or 30 years ago proves that society is treating farmers unfairly and that farmers deserve recompense. Politicians have long misunderstood this economic trend and have cited the decline in crop prices as proof of market failure and of the need for political intervention.

The Federal Takeover of the Farm Sector

It is difficult to understand the current farm policy quagmire without examining the origin of current programs in the 1920s and early 1930s.

The federal takeover of American agriculture began in 1929, when the Federal Farm Board attempted to corner the wheat and cotton markets to drive up prices and enrich American farmers. The invention of tractors had greatly lowered wheat production costs around the world during the 1920s, thereby encouraging farmers to boost production; as a result, wheat prices trended downward. Even though prices were lower, many American farmers were prospering: total farm income in the 1920s was almost as high as it had been during the farmers' golden days before the outbreak of World War I. Yet, congressmen, looking only at the wheat price per bushel, announced that a crisis existed.

The Federal Farm Board succeeded in temporarily driving American wheat and cotton prices above world prices, but exports fell as a result. The board responded to plummeting exports by urging American farmers to cut back their plantings and abandon all aspirations to export. The board also sought to completely separate U.S. farm prices from world farm prices, primarily because politicians felt that world farm prices were unfair to American farmers.

Franklin D. Roosevelt became president on March 4, 1933, and the *New York Times* reported a few days later that farm leaders (including future secretary of agriculture Henry Wallace) were urg-

[5]See Julian Simon, *The Ultimate Resource* (New York: Universe Books, 1982), p. 75.

298

ing him to appoint a "farm dictator."[6] The Agricultural Adjustment Administration (AAA), created in 1933, proceeded to set U.S. crop prices far above world crop prices. Although U.S. exports of automobiles rose 110 percent, iron and steel product exports increased 125 percent, and fruit and nut exports increased 10 percent, between 1932 and 1934, exports of major farm commodities collapsed.[7] In five years the United States went from being one of the world's largest wheat exporters to being a net wheat importer. Agricultural economist O. B. Jesness summed up the government's attitude toward crop exports: "It has been common among representatives of the AAA to express the view that foreign markets are gone and that all we can do is mourn their loss."[8] Agricultural economist B. H. Hibbard reported in the Nation in 1934 that the AAA "put a thousand times as much effort into reduction of output at home as they put into the effort to restore foreign trade during their first year in control."[9]

Government first wrecked the agricultural export market and then used the decline of exports to justify imposing controls on American farmers. As Assistant Secretary M. L. Wilson observed, "Concerted cooperative crop control for American agriculture just now is necessary to compensate for the virtual loss of the foreign market."[10]

The destruction of export markets is the key to understanding New Deal farm policy, as well as all subsequent farm policy. This pattern of overpricing farm products and then controlling farmers has been repeated time and time again since the 1930s.

Farm programs in the 1930s were based on parity. Parity is the ratio of purchasing power of farm prices with nonfarm prices compared to the ratio of farm and nonfarm prices from 1910 to 1914. Parity assumes that the ratio between farm and nonfarm prices was

[6]New York Times, March 12, 1933, p. 1.

[7]Joseph Davis, Wheat and the A.A.A. (Washington: Brookings Institution, 1936), p. 3.

[8]O. B. Jesness, "Validity of the Fundamental Assumptions Underlying Agricultural Adjustment," Journal of Farm Economics (February 1936): 32.

[9]B. H. Hibbard, "First Year of the Agricultural Adjustment Act," Nation, July 4, 1934, p. 257.

[10]M. L. Wilson, "Validity of the Fundamental Assumptions Underlying Agricultural Assessment," Journal of Farm Economics (February 1936): 19.

"fair" in the years preceding World War I and that current prices can be "fair" only insofar as they correspond to the price ratio existing 75 years ago. But the parity formula was designed by the U.S. Department of Agriculture (USDA) in such a way as to greatly understate farm income—and thereby create a need for vastly more government intervention. Even though more than 25 percent of farmers had off-farm jobs, parity disregarded farmers' off-farm income in comparing farm and nonfarm income. The parity formula assumed no change in the productivity of machinery that farmers purchased, even though a 1935 USDA publication admitted that "engineers have estimated the wearing quality and capacity of 25 items of farm machinery in 1932 average about 170% of pre-war. This means that the prices in recent years represent machines of greater producing capacity than in the pre-war years."[11]

Since the New Deal the federal government has solidified its control over the agriculture sector through the introduction of a number of additional programs. USDA has become one of the largest, most powerful, and most expensive cabinet departments. As a result, modern American farmers often must pay closer attention to the maneuverings of politicians and USDA bureaucrats than they pay to the weather, improved farm technologies, and changing market conditions combined.

A USDA Honor Roll

Farm programs have different goals, different means, and different results.

Acreage-reduction programs are the foundation of federal grain programs. Congress sets federal price support and target prices higher than market-clearing levels; farmers respond to high prices by producing surpluses; and then USDA responds to the surplus by rewarding farmers for reducing their production. In 1988, USDA rewarded farmers for not planting on 78 million acres of farmland— an area equivalent to the entire states of Indiana and Ohio, plus much of Illinois. It shut down some of the best American farmland in an effort to drive up world wheat and corn prices. Acreage set-aside programs are based on the "America is OPEC" model—a

[11]"Index Numbers of Prices Paid by Farmers for Commodities Bought" (Washington: U.S. Department of Agriculture, 1935), p. 123.

300

blind faith that the United States can dominate world crop prices solely by increasing or decreasing its crop output. However, during the 1980s, as USDA paid more and more American farmers to take vacations, foreign farmers continually expanded their output.

Each year, USDA marketing orders force farmers to waste or squander roughly 500 million lemons, 1 billion oranges, 70 million pounds of raisins, 70 million pounds of almonds, and millions of plums and nectarines. USDA gives a majority of growers of several kinds of fruits and nuts the power to outlaw competition and to force other growers to abandon much of their crop. To preserve federal control, USDA effectively bans new technology that would boost fruit sales and benefit both growers and consumers. USDA assumes that farmers gain more from the higher prices than they lose from abandoning part of their harvest (many California citrus and almond farmers vehemently disagree).

The dairy program personifies Congress's disregard for efficiency. By 1985 the federal government had accumulated three billion pounds of surplus dairy products in its warehouses and underground vaults. In 1986–87 the federal government spent almost $2 billion paying farmers to slaughter over a million cows to reduce the dairy surplus. Yet, simultaneously with the "Bossie Massacre," Congress maintained dairy price supports far above market-clearing prices—thus perpetuating the dairy surplus. The Dairy Termination Program failed to reduce milk production. New dairy growth hormones are boosting milk production per cow by up to 30 percent, thereby opening up the possibility for a radical fall in dairy prices. Yet, several congressmen have denounced the new technology for destabilizing the government dairy program. As Rep. Steve Gunderson (R-Wis.) declared, "The dairy industry needs more productivity, more milk like a drunk driver needs another drink."[12] In the halls of Congress, higher productivity is seen as a problem rather than as an opportunity.

The sugar program restricts sugar imports to boost domestic prices and provides a price support for American sugar production. Sugar is one farm commodity in which the United States is manifestly uncompetitive: U.S. farmers have a far greater cost of pro-

[12]House Agriculture Committee, *Review of Dairy Program Issues*, June 11, 1986, p. 32.

duction for sugar than do Latin American farmers because the U.S. climate is not suited for efficient sugar production. Because federal sugar price guarantees have been so high in recent years, U.S. sugar growers have boosted production, which has required repeatedly slashing the import quota for foreign sugar. Since 1981 the federal government has reduced sugar imports by 75 percent, thereby forcing the shutdown of 10 domestic sugar refineries and destroying thousands of American jobs. The United States now imports less sugar than it did 75 years ago. The Department of Commerce estimates that the sugar program costs consumers over $3 billion a year in higher sugar prices,[13] and the State Department estimates that reduced sugar imports have cost U.S. allies such as Costa Rica, the Dominican Republic, and the Philippines $800 million a year.[14] Federal subsidies to sugar growers amounted to over $250,000 a year per sugar grower during the mid-1980s.[15]

Federal agricultural credit programs have destabilized farmers' finances and, by helping drive up farmland values, have undercut American competitiveness. The Farmers Home Administration was created to help the struggling family farmer, and ended up bankrolling John DeLorean's Deluxe Motor Car Factory, providing $50 million to a single California farm (now bankrupt), and giving almost $1 billion in subsidized credit to already bankrupt farmers in 1985 alone. The General Accounting Office concluded that receiving too many subsidized loans was a major cause in the bankruptcy of 25 percent of Farmers Home borrowers.[16] With each federal farm credit disaster, government dominance of agriculture credit has increased, and the federal government now effectively controls half of all farm debt.

USDA provided over $6 billion in export subsidies and credits in 1987. It spent three times the world price to dump American sugar and butter on world markets and four times the world price for

[13]"Commerce Department Study Shows High Cost of Sugar Program," *Journal of Commerce*, May 17, 1988, p. 14.

[14]Clifford Krauss, "U.S. Sugar Quotas Hurt Latin American Farmers," *Wall Street Journal*, September 26, 1986, p. 1

[15]Public Voice for Food and Health Policy, *A Consumer's Guide to Sugar Prices* (Washington, 1985), p. 7.

[16]General Accounting Office, *Farmers Home Administration—Problems and Issues Facing the Emergency Loan Program* (Washington, November 1987), p. 39.

each additional hundredweight of rice exported in 1986.[17] The federal government is paying American farmers $4.35 a bushel to grow wheat—and then subsidizing the sale of wheat to the Soviets for $1.75 a bushel. Under the Targeted Export Assistance Program, USDA is paying for foreign advertisements for Samuel Adams beer, Paul Newman gourmet sauces, Moyle Mink furs, and Chateau San Michel wine.[18] USDA's Foreign Agriculture Service is paying export promotion subsidies for several commodities—such as oranges, almonds, and raisins—for which USDA's Agricultural Marketing Service restricts exports.

The 1988 Drought Bill: Farm Policymakers in Action

The 1988 drought provided a good case study of congressional agricultural policymaking. For approximately the last 10,000 years, drought has been considered a normal risk of farming. The federal government offers farmers subsidized crop insurance that fully protects them against any loss due to severe weather. Farmers voluntarily bought crop insurance for over 50 million acres of farmland in 1988. Yet, Congress insisted on bailing out the farmers who failed to protect themselves against bad weather. As one former USDA official put it, "It's a real shame that we had a drought and an election in the same year."

USDA programs discouraged farmers from taking normal precautions against bad weather in 1988. Lavish federal subsidies for wheat production encouraged North Dakota farmers to grow wheat instead of sunflowers, even though sunflowers are far more drought-resistant and better suited for North Dakota's climate. Although some varieties of corn are much more drought-resistant than others, the vast majority of farmers use only the highest-yield seed varieties, in that USDA pays them according to their yield (bushels per acre)—or their expected yield, in case of drought.

Farmers as a class may actually wind up profiting from the 1988 drought. Even if crop yields were 20 percent or 30 percent below normal, farmers may still do very well because prices were already 40 percent, 50 percent, or even 100 percent higher than in 1987.

[17]James Bovard, "Put Agricultural Policy Out to Pasture," *Wall Street Journal*, February 4, 1988, p. 26.

[18]James Bovard, "TEA Parity: Export Subsidy at Its Most Absurd," *Wall Street Journal*, August 12, 1988, p. 28.

Many farmers were little affected by the drought but profited greatly from the higher prices. As USDA economist Richard Kodl has noted, "In several recent droughts, farmers as a group were more than compensated for lower crop yields by higher market prices."[19]

Congress rushed to provide drought relief in the summer of 1988, long before the final effects of the drought were clear. The drought-relief bill was a huge pork barrel. In the first week of congressional consideration, for example, members of Congress attached almost a hundred amendments to the legislation, with most amendments providing special benefits to their home-state constituents.[20] The drought-relief bill included a federal decree effectively raising retail milk prices by eight cents a gallon from April to June 1989. Although milk production was breaking all records earlier in 1988, and American dairy cows are now more productive than ever before, Congress justified raising federal milk-support prices by claiming that there might be a milk shortage unless Congress again drove up milk prices.

The final drought-relief bill also provided over $100 million in subsidies to corporations producing ethanol. The federal government is willing to subsidize corn purchases by corporations (such as Archer Daniel Midlands) that produce ethanol. Yet, even with low-price corn, ethanol still costs more than twice as much per gallon as gasoline, and ethanol often damages car engines as well. The total cost of the drought-relief bill was between $5 and $6 billion.[21]

Rhetoric and Reality in Rural America

The farm lobby has persuaded the public that the vast majority of farmers are needy, and that the vast majority of farm products are totally dependent on government aid. These two ideas are the foundation of the public support of agricultural welfare.

Nevertheless, the median farm family income has exceeded aver-

---

[19]Interview with author, July 3, 1988.

[20]Ward Sinclair, "Drought Relief Turns into Pork Barrel," *Washington Post*, July 17, 1988, p. A3.

[21]*Wall Street Journal*, July 29, 1988, p. 38.

age American family income every year since 1964.[22] The average
full-time commercial farmer earned over $80,000 in 1986, and the
average full-time farmer's net worth is 10 times higher than the
average American family's net worth. Even though farmers as a
class are rich, because Congress has provided so many tax breaks,
farm operations as a class pay no income taxes. In 1983, when net
farm income was $12 billion nationwide, farmers and farm investors
claimed a net loss of $9.3 billion for tax purposes.[23]

Federal farm aid goes largely to wealthy farmers. In 1986 the
largest farmers received 150 times as much in handouts per farm as
the smallest farmers.[24] Even more important, federal aid goes to a
minority of crops and farm products produced in the United States.
The farm problem is not so much a farm problem as a wheat, dairy,
corn, cotton, rice, tobacco, and peanut problem. The only crops
that have been perennially in surplus and in need of federal "aid"
have been those crops that politicians have sought to manage.

Over 90 percent of the 400-plus farm products produced in the
United States receive no federal subsidy, and farmers who produce
unsubsidized crops and livestock have had far higher (presubsidy)
profits than farmers of politically favored crops. There is no rhyme
or reason to the distribution of federal farm benefits: dairymen are
subsidized heavily, while cattlemen receive almost nothing from
the federal government. Corn growers are treated royally by USDA,
while soybean growers have been hurt by the side effects of other
federal farm programs. Peanut growers are guaranteed a good
income, while pecan growers have prospered without any federal
aid.

Federal farm programs cost taxpayers far more than they benefit
farmers. Citing a USDA study of farm program effects, the Council
of Economic Advisers concluded:

> For every dollar of net cash income transferred from consumers
> and taxpayers to farmers, an extra $4.25 would be incurred because
> of [farm] program provisions that inhibit the efficient operation of

[22]Lloyd D. Tiegen, *Agricultural Parity: Historical Review and Alternative Calculations*
(Washington: Department of Agriculture, 1987), p. 37.

[23]General Accounting Office, *Tax Policy—Economic Effects of Selected Current Tax
Provisions on Agriculture* (Washington, August 1986), p. 6.

[24]Department of Agriculture, *Economic Indicators of the Farm Sector, National Financial Summary, 1986* (Washington, December 1987), p. 50.

farm operation of farm markets. Much of the $21 billion consumer and taxpayer expenditure would go not to farmers but would be dissipated throughout the agricultural industry in the form of higher input prices (including land) and increased profits to suppliers of materials and services to farmers.[25]

Ending the Farm Policy Tangle

The best solution to most farm problems is to abolish the USDA program that causes the problem. Most of American agriculture is healthy and relatively uncontrolled by politicians. The key to a prosperous agriculture is to stop disrupting the unhealthy sector so that it can become as strong as the uncontrolled sector.

Abolishing farm programs is not as imposing a task as it may seem. The sugar program was abolished in 1974 but Congress reestablished it in 1977. The House of Representatives voted to abolish both the peanut and sugar programs in 1981, and the Senate came within a few votes of abolishing the tobacco program in 1983. Congress has come within striking distance of emaciating dairy subsidies on several occasions.

The new administration should take the following steps:

- Abolish all programs that reward farmers for not working. Paying farmers not to work will always make the United States a poorer place. Acreage set-asides have always presumed that USDA has a special ability to foresee the future and plan accordingly. Yet, USDA's set-aside programs are ridiculed each year by the weather, by scientific breakthroughs that boost yields, and by farmers' ingenuity in circumventing USDA restrictions. Once set-aside programs are abolished, there will be no way to restrict wheat and corn production. This will effectively destroy politicians' ability to set price supports above market-clearing levels. Once politicians take their foot off the brake (acreage-reduction programs), they will be forced to take their foot off the accelerator (price supports above market-clearing levels).

- Terminate all marketing order supply controls. Marketing order supply controls are a crime against Mother Nature, and farmers will be better off selling their entire harvest rather than being restrained according to the paternalistic dictates of USDA

[25]*Economic Report of the President*, 1986, p. 155.

306

bureaucrats. A few cooperatives such as Sunkist and the California Almond Growers Exchange, which have used federal controls to cartelize their industries, will suffer, but the most efficient, productive farmers will be better off than before.

- Abolish the daily program. There is no good reason why butter and cheese should cost three times more in the United States than on the world market. Calcium is the nutrient that low-income Americans lack most. What justification is there for sacrificing 25 million poor people to benefit slightly more than 100,000 dairymen? With the advent of new technology and the coming explosion in dairy production, the federal government will finally be forced to concede to lower milk prices. Wisconsin's member of Congress will need to find some other ways to buy reelection, but otherwise the nation will not be damaged.

- Abolish the sugar program. There are only 11,000 farmers growing sugar cane and sugar beet in the United States. The average sugar cane grower is a millionaire, and every sugar beet grower could switch to other crops. There is no more reason for the United States to produce its own sugar than there is for it to produce its own bananas. Further, it is ridiculous to allow a small band of farmers to hold U.S. foreign policy hostage.

- Abolish all credit subsidies for farmers. There is an old saying, "One farmer's fortune is his neighbor's misfortune." There is no justice in having the federal government annually bail out one farmer while his neighbor must compete against him. The abolition of the Farmers Home Administration (FmHA) would be a giant step toward reducing unfair competition in farming. FmHA-subsidized loans have driven up farmland values, thereby making it more difficult for unsubsidized young farmers to survive and prosper. FmHA should cease making all new loans, and should transfer its authority to collect old loans to private loan-collection agencies. The more incompetent farmers that FmHA keeps on the land, the less stable American agriculture will be. Instead of losing $100,000 a year farming, many FmHA borrowers should be earning $25,000 a year painting houses, selling cars, or repairing vacuum cleaners.

- Abolish all export subsidies. Once government stops driving up crop prices, it will no longer need to provide export subsidies to lower prices for foreign buyers. Many export subsidies are created to "compensate" for other USDA programs that drive U.S. prices above world market prices. The main achievement of export subsidies is to camouflage the damage federal agricultural policy does to American farmers' competitiveness. If American farmers cannot sell at a profit, then they should not be producing crops.

Free-market agriculture in the United States is the biggest threat to the European Community's Common Agricultural Program. If the United States would only unleash the full efficiency of the American farmer, the battle for exports would be over. The European Community has tottered on the edge of bankruptcy almost every year since 1981, and it has been saved in large part because of massive American set-asides. The United States lacks the power to set world crop prices, but it can make it very expensive for other countries to continue subsidies after the United States has abandoned its own subsidies. The more the United States hobbles American farmers, the easier it is for foreign governments to pamper their farmers. Abolishing all set-aside programs and restrictions on output would have a deep psychological effect on foreign politicians.

Conclusion

There are no easy ways to drain the agricultural policy swamp, which has been festering for 60 years. But the abolition of federal farm programs could reduce the federal deficit by $20 billion or more a year, and thus would be an excellent place to begin meeting the goals of the Gramm-Rudman-Hollings balanced budget act. Federal agricultural programs are among the most flagrant examples of wasteful spending in existence, and if Congress and the new president cannot harvest massive budget savings here, then there is little hope of meaningful budget reform. The failure to control agricultural spending was one of Reagan's worst budgetary failures, and a new president must avoid the same pitfall.

Many members of Congress claim that the federal government owes farmers compensation for the end of government handouts. The federal government has spent the equivalent of over $200,000 on every full-time farmer since 1981. What sense does it make to force the average taxpayer to compensate someone worth 10 times as much as himself for the abolition of annual subsidies that often exceed that taxpayer's salary? Inequities should be abolished, not gradually phased out over 20 years. The first premise of any solution to the agricultural crisis is that taxpayers owe farmers nothing except a fair price in the marketplace. And the best definition of fairness is a price on which a buyer and seller can voluntarily agree.

There are no neat and clean solutions to a 60-year tangle of federal policies. When farm programs are abolished, there will be dislocation, there will be pain, there will be winners and losers. But the fact that a tiny minority of Americans may be less well off is not an excuse to continue handicapping the American economy, bloating the federal budget deficit, and effectively mandating malnutrition among many low-income Americans.

19. Protecting the Environment

Terry L. Anderson

When we entered the 1980s, there was reason to think that natural resource and environmental policy would change. Former president Jimmy Carter had published his hit list of water reclamation projects that should not go forward because they did not make economic or environmental sense or both. The Sage Brush Rebellion against federal control of western lands combined with President Reagan's appointment of James Watt as secretary of the interior was seen by many as the first step toward massive privatization of the public domain. The President's Commission on Americans Outdoors (PCAO) was appointed to examine prospects for more private-sector involvement in outdoor recreation. And the appointment of Anne Gorsuch as head of the Environmental Protection Agency signaled an indication that the Reagan administration was going to relax environmental regulatory standards to the detriment of air and water quality and rely more on market-like concepts such as effluent charges and transferable discharge permits.

However, an examination of the record of the Reagan administration reveals that it has been business as usual in Washington. The pork barrel for water projects remains full in spite of a reorganization of the Bureau of Reclamation. Although a few hundred acres of the public domain have been sold, the total size of the federal estate has grown. The PCAO has paid lip service to the private sector but has also called for a billion-dollar trust fund to purchase lands for public recreation and greater regulation of waterways and of private property along "scenic byways." At EPA, effluent charges and transferable discharge permits have been given little consideration.

On the brighter side, however, environmentalists seem more aware of the failures of government resource management and more receptive to free-market alternatives. Alston Chase's book, *Playing God in Yellowstone,* disclosed many examples of bureaucratic

311

mismanagement of the crown jewel of the national park system, and the recent fires in that area have driven home the problems associated with "natural" ecosystem management. The discovery that agricultural pollutants were destroying the Kesterson Wildlife Refuge led the Environmental Defense Fund to propose water marketing as a solution to this environmental atrocity. Ducks Unlimited has continued to raise funds to purchase duck habitat, and the Nature Conservancy has expanded its private holdings to over three million acres in the United States.

The only instance in which the Reagan administration gets high marks for examining innovative solutions to resource and environmental management is in the publication of the 1984 report of the President's Commission on Environmental Quality (CEQ). The report documents such examples of private-sector environmental protection as oil exploration in harmony with the environment on privately owned Audubon Society preserves; nearly three million acres of privately owned forests managed for recreation and traditional uses by North Maine Woods, Inc.; and the success of the Hawk Mountain Sanctuary Association, which began as a private effort to preserve hawk habitat in Pennsylvania and has expanded to raptor research and other educational programs.

Changing the trend away from traditional political control of natural resources and the environment in the 1990s will require a more careful construction of the intellectual foundation for free-market environmentalism and the development of additional evidence such as that in the 1984 CEQ report arguing that private alternatives can work.

The Analytical Framework

The traditional way we think about natural resource and environmental policy has been conditioned by welfare economics, which emphasizes market failure and suggests that planning can be substituted for the market process. Although this way of thinking emphasizes the trade-offs inherent in resource allocation, it cannot and does not tell managers what trade-offs to make or what values to place on resources. Welfare economics leads to the conclusion that there is a "social optimum" that can be known and implemented by the scientific manager who is supposed to be "always analytical. . . . Always, the economist's reasoning, his *analytical* framework . . . and his conclusions are exposed forthrightly to the examination and criticism of others. In these ways, *scientific objectivity* is actively sought."[1]

The problem with this approach is that it fails to consider the incentives of scientific managers in the political sector. Political intervention is justified by the argument that markets fail to provide the optimal amount of environmental amenities because costs and benefits are not internal to decisionmakers. Therefore the argument is that too much pollution will be generated through voluntary transactions; in other words, because the polluter does not have to pay for his garbage disposal, he disposes of more than the optimal amount.

The problem with government intervention, however, is that the political process functions by externalizing or diffusing costs and concentrating benefits. Consider externality reasoning applied to the management of politically controlled lands. When the scientific manager diverts amenity production to lumber production, there is an opportunity cost associated with the reallocation. If he owned the land and had to forgo the value of the amenities (either because he could enjoy them himself or because he could market them), this cost would have to be considered. The bureaucratic manager, however, can ignore such opportunity costs because they are externalized to the general taxpayer. The tendency for special-interest groups to dominate politics is a classic example of this; government allocation creates externalities by allowing users to enjoy the benefits of resources without having to pay the costs. The likely result is that we will get too much wilderness land, too many clear-cuts, too much pollution control, too much spent on toxic-waste reduction, and on and on.

The new resource economics (NRE) offers an alternative way of thinking that emphasizes the importance of individual incentives generated through private property rights and liability rules. At the heart of all voluntary, noncoerced interaction between individuals is the exchange of property rights—the rights to take specific actions regarding specific physical objects. For voluntary exchange or markets to function, property rights must be well-defined, enforced, and transferable. Definition requires that the physical attributes of

[1]Alan Randall, *Resource Economics* (Columbus, Ohio: Grid Publishing Co., 1981).

resources be specified in a clear and concise manner; they must be measurable. Property rights also must be enforced, in that scarcity generates physical incompatibility. Finally, property rights must be transferable if voluntary exchanges are to create gains from trade and force existing owners to take into account alternative human values.

Traditional resource economics has focused on cases in which the costs of defining, enforcing, and transferring property rights are high, and it has referred to these costs as externalities or market failure. In the case of air pollution, for example, the suggestion is that if property rights to air cannot be well-defined and enforced, external (or social) costs will arise and generate market failure. The problem with this approach is that ignores the evolution of property rights.

First consider the incentive to define and enforce property rights. The existence of alleged externalities means there are potential resource values up for grabs. If property rights can be established, these values are internalized. When the cattlemen entered the Great Plains in the 19th century, the prospect of enforcing property rights by fencing the land was as remote as fencing the air. Land was abundant and traditional wood and stone fencing materials were nonexistent. However, as land values rose, effort was put into defining and enforcing property rights. Human fences known as line camps—in which cowboys rode along boundaries and ensured that cattle stayed in their pastures—provided an initial solution. Eventually an entrepreneur greatly reduced the cost of enforcing property rights with the invention of barbed wire.

In a more modern context, suppose that individual A wants to build a structure that obstructs the view of individual B. In this case the air space and its ability to create a view or living space is a scarce resource that—depending on the costs of defining and enforcing property rights—may be worth owning. It could be that individual B, desiring to maintain a view, could purchase a covenant from A precluding A from building any upper floors that would obstruct B's view. Or perhaps an entrepreneur recognizing that views are valuable would purchase a large tract of land, place building restrictions on each parcel, establish view rights, and capture the value in land prices. If an entrepreneur can establish property rights that internalize costs, he can capture the value of these rights. Hence, externalities provide the incentive for individuals to search for ways to define and enforce property rights.[2]

Because values depend on information related to "the particular circumstances of time and place"[3] it is resource users who are most likely to realize the benefits and costs of defining and enforcing property rights. If fact, since most resource values are time- and place-specific, making centralized decisions about the appropriate property rights becomes impossible. For example, defining property rights to air space in 1840 would not have made good sense in that no one could know that such rights would become valuable. Only as the knowledge from the particular circumstance of time and place evolved spontaneously could individuals realize these values.

Several examples illustrate the ability of entrepreneurs to establish property rights. Migratory wildlife such as deer and elk have long been considered an example of a resource to which property rights cannot be established. However, as hunting on public lands has become more and more crowded, entrepreneurs have organized hunting on private ranches throughout the West. Where individual landholdings are large (for example, 50,000 to 300,000 acres), establishing property rights has been easy. But for smaller parcels, it has taken innovative efforts to bring landowners together. Greyson Creek Meadows Recreation, Inc., a group of 45 sportsmen in Montana, for example, has leased more than 30,000 acres owned by 12 individuals for hunting, fishing, and family recreation. In addition to an annual lease fee, the landowners receive $100 per elk killed on their property and are relieved of the burden of having to manage the hunters. Although the wildlife is not owned, the control of access provides some opportunity to manage the quality of the recreational experience. Similar organizations are springing up around the country as the values of recreation resources rise and the possibilities for establishing property rights are recognized.

The Nature Conservancy provides an example of how the establishment of property rights is promoting environmental preservation. In Montana the Nature Conservancy purchased an area known

[2]Terry L. Anderson and P. J. Hill, "The Evolution of Property Rights: A Study of the American West," *Journal of Law and Economics* 18, no. 1 (April 1975).

[3]F. A. Hayek, "The Use of Knowledge in Society," *The American Economic Review* 35, no. 4 (September 1945): 522.

as the Pine Butte Swamp, the last prairie habitat of the grizzly bear in the lower 48 states. The area had been eyed by state and federal fish and game officials, but they did not have the money to purchase the private property. The Nature Conservancy raised the funds through both large and small donations and purchased the property, which it now manages. In addition it has obtained conservation easement on surrounding lands to help control the habitat. It performs controlled prairie grass burns, plants flora to enhance the habitat, uses cattle to simulate grazing by bison, conducts tours, and operates a guest ranch. Fees from some of the services help pay management expenses. The primary goal of the Nature Conservancy—grizzly bear habitat preservation in this case—has been achieved through private ownership of land where access is controlled and in some cases charged for. Other entrepreneurial efforts by the Nature Conservancy have generated similar success stories.

It is the combination of the incentive to establish property rights and the information about the costs and benefits of doing so that leads individuals to invest in the definition and enforcement of property rights. Even so, this does not necessarily mean there is no role for government in the definition and enforcement process or that property rights will always take all costs and benefits into account. The costs of establishing property rights are positive and potentially can be reduced through government institutions such as courts. At the same time, however, political institutions should not stand in the way of the spontaneous evolution of property rights through private contracting.

Toward New Environmental Policies

Two particularly important implications for natural resource and environmental policy derive from the new resource economics. The first is that well-defined and enforced property rights offer a mechanism for harnessing the productive and innovative capacity of individuals. Motivated by gains from trade, owners of resources have an incentive to act in ways that are consistent with good resource stewardship and environmental quality.

The second implication is that in cases in which the costs of defining, enforcing, and exchanging property rights are high enough to suggest market failure, we cannot immediately conclude that government intervention will result in an improvement. Govern-

316

ments evolve (at least in part) as a social institution to enable individuals to overcome the free-rider problems. However, as the new resource economics reminds us, government itself creates a free-rider problem because the contributions from citizens as a whole for the provision of public goods are not necessarily related to their consumption. Through government, benefits can be concentrated while costs are diffused. Checks and balances in the democratic political process are aimed at reducing this possibility, but they are by no means perfect. Therefore, government is not a perfect alternative to an imperfect market.

There are a number of areas in which a new administration could make a fresh start in environmental policy by acting on the insights of the new resource economics. The following proposals are not an exhaustive list but deal with some of the more important policy areas.

- Make polluters liable for hazardous-waste cleanup.

Superfund has been called a "hazardous waste of taxpayers' money" because it breaks the link between authority and responsibility. All producers of hazardous waste are required to pay into the fund, which is then used to clean up waste sites. This arrangement removes part of the incentive for individual waste producers to carefully assess the risks and alternatives for waste disposal. The government can and does play an important role in recording who is using which sites, and legislation could strengthen the liability requirements that are an important part of property rights. If the government must stay involved in the cleanup as with "orphan sites," it could "privatize" them by selling them—that is, by paying the lowest bidder to take responsibility for them.

An example of the efficacy of liability rules comes from the now infamous Love Canal.[4] Hooker Chemical, the company responsible for the initial disposal in the canal, took extreme care to ensure that chemicals would not leak from the clay-lined canal because it knew it could be held strictly liable for environmental damages. In fact, the techniques the company used in the late 1940s and early 1950s met EPA standards in place when the site was inspected in the 1960s. Leaching from the site occurred only after the site was sold to the city of Niagara Falls for $1 under threat of condemnation.

[4]Eric Zuesse, "Love Canal: The Truth Seeps Out," Reason, February 1981.

The city irresponsibly built a school on the site, moved dirt from the site, and dug a sewage-line trench through the impervious clay. Neither city officials nor the city in general were held liable for their actions. This misreported and misunderstood example provides an excellent case in support of liability rules (an important component of property rights) as a solution to hazardous-waste disposal problems.

• End federal water projects and allow the sale of water rights to conserve and clean up water.

Great progress has been made in improving water allocation through water marketing. The Bureau of Reclamation has been reduced in size, but it could be eliminated. Public construction of dams should be a thing of the past. At least water from existing Bureau of Reclamation projects should be made private so that owners, mostly farmers, can trade the water rights in accordance with market prices.

Unfortunately, many of the impediments to water marketing exist at the state level. States should make every effort to reduce the transaction costs of buying and selling water and allow new private rights to develop for instream flows. Perhaps the greatest threat to efficient water allocation is the public trust doctrine that makes state governments trustees for certain values—recreational, navigational, and environmental, for example—of the water without specifying exactly who is the trustee responsible and which public values are to be protected. As a result the public trust doctrine has become a mechanism for taking property without compensation to meet the demands of special-interest groups.[5]

Two examples suggest that water marketing can reduce the need for enormous public expenditures and reduce environmental problems. First, a proposed trade between the Imperial Irrigation District (IID) and the Municipal Water District of Southern California would encourage the IID to conserve irrigation water, which would be transferred to municipal use. Bureau of Reclamation rules that prevented farmers from profiting from water sales initially restricted the potential for water trading, and now bargaining over the terms

[5]For additional information on the public trust doctrine, see James L. Huffman, "The Public Trust Doctrine: Trampling on Property Rights While Harming the Environment," in *PERC Viewpoints*, no. 5 (Bozeman, Mont.: Political Economy Research Center, July 1988).

of trade has restricted progress of the transaction. Nonetheless, such potential gains are producing pressures to relax water-marketing restrictions.[6] The second example emanates from the Kesterson Wildlife Refuge where pollution from Westlands Water District irrigation drainage was killing wildlife. Zach Willey of the Environmental Defense Fund has estimated that if farmers were allowed to sell their water for a profit, they could economically clean up the drainage water.

• Privatize the national parks to avoid politicization.

The massive fires that have burned more than 50 percent of Yellowstone National Park's forestlands have brought the problems of political management of national parks to the headlines. Since the publication of *Playing God in Yellowstone,* environmentalists and policymakers have not been able to ignore the fact that politics rather than science dominates park policy. It has always been assumed that the elite corps of National Park Service employees are guarding our national treasures. However, even Yellowstone is facing significant environmental degradation owing to politics: raw sewage has been dumped into lakes; traffic congestion is significant; grizzly bears have been managed to near extinction; and enormous elk populations have overgrazed the range and decimated the aspen trees, thereby resulting in erosion.

Privatization of national parks should be considered, possibly with covenants placed on the property rights. Each park could be managed by a trust established with the specific charge of enhancing the values of the park. Trustees would have clear agent responsibilities to be overseen by Congress.[7] Receipts from entrance fees should be left to each park trust for reinvestment in the park. This would provide a price signal for park managers regarding what consumers want.

• Privatize political lands.

By referring to lands under the control of the federal government as political lands, the true nature of the management is made clearer. Scientific managers are continually subject to special-interest pres-

[6]See Terry L. Anderson and Donald R. Leal, "Going with the Flow: Expanding the Water Markets," Cato Policy Analysis no. 104 (Washington: Cato Institute, April 26, 1988).

[7]See Richard L. Stroup and John A. Baden, "Endowment Areas: A Clearing in the Policy Wilderness," *Cato Journal* 2, no. 3 (Winter 1982).

sures and almost never face the opportunity costs of their decisions. The Forest Service, for example, continually engages in below-cost timber sales, arguing that it is creating jobs and managing forest resources but ignoring environmental and recreational opportunity costs. The best solution would be to completely privatize the commodity-producing lands of both the Forest Service and the Bureau of Land Management. Short of this, political lands should be corporatized, following the New Zealand example of creating for-profit state-owned enterprises.[8] Wilderness lands should also be privatized by giving them in fee simple with covenants to environmental groups. Again, a second-best solution would be to establish "wilderness endowment boards" as trustees of wilderness lands.

• Leave management of energy resources to the private sector.

Conflict over oil leases on the outer continental shelf are typical of political battles that pit environmentalists against energy developers. Off the California coast, for example, only one new lease went through the entire regulatory process during the period from 1981 to 1986, and no offshore lease sales have taken place since 1984.[9] A majority of Californians oppose offshore development because they believe that oil and the environment do not mix.

The reason there is so much opposition to energy development on public lands is that no one owns the resource and therefore no one has an incentive to consider trade-offs between the environment and energy production. This problem is particularly evident in terms of the environmentally sensitive Alaska National Wildlife Reserve, where environmentalists oppose any development because of potential damage to tundra lands and wildlife. The environmentalist position on issues like this is that the environment should not be compromised. However, the experience of the Audubon Society on its privately owned preserves suggests that the environment and energy development need not be totally incompatible and that such organizations are willing to consider trade-offs if they can capture benefits from the sale of reserves.[10]

[8]For additional information on the idea of corporatization, see Randal O'Toole, *Reforming the Forest Service* (Washington: Island Press, 1988).

[9]See Ronald Brownstein, "Where Coastal Could Tar GOP," *Wall Street Journal*, September 14, 1988.

[10]For a discussion of the Audubon Society's Rainey Preserve, see Richard L. Stroup and John A. Baden, "Saving the Wilderness," *Reason*, July 1981.

To remove the conflict between environmentalist groups and energy developers, the management of energy resources should be left entirely to the private sector. Subsidies for developing energy resources should be eliminated along with all restrictions on oil exports and imports. Politically controlled energy resources such as coal deposits and offshore oil lands should be privatized through sale or lease of mineral rights. Ownership of leases should not be restricted to oil and gas companies that are willing to develop them; conservation organizations interested in preservation should also be encouraged to bid on the resources. If areas are particularly environmentally sensitive, the tracts of land with energy potential could be donated to environmentalist groups willing to manage them. This ownership would generate the incentive for both sides to negotiate development that is sensitive to environmental concerns.

- End farm subsidies and land use controls to protect agricultural land.

Agricultural subsidies have been responsible for a great deal of environmental degradation. Examples include dams for delivering subsidized water; extensive use of water that leaches salts from the soil and pollutes streams and lakes; and crop price subsidies that encourage the use of pesticides. By removing subsidies, allowing water marketing, and removing land use controls, farmers will discontinue some environmental degradation and have an incentive to consider possible alternative land uses. For example, Oregon rancher Dayton Hyde has created a private organization called Operation Stronghold to encourage ranchers to preserve environmental qualities. When he successfully created nesting habitat for rare birds, however, the federal government tried to regulate his land use, thus discouraging his production of environmental goods. Such intervention should be eliminated.[11]

Similarly, without crop subsidies, farmers and ranchers will consider using their land for nontraditional "crops" such as recreation. Legislation should be passed to allow landowners to charge access fees and capitalize on recreational land uses. In this way, wildlife that is most often considered a liability because it consumes crops

[11]For further information, consult President's Council on Environmental Quality, *Environmental Quality, 1984: 15th Annual Report* (Washington: Government Printing Office, 1984).

and attracts hunters can be converted to an asset that can be husbanded.

- Give Indians control of their lands.

It is well-known that American Indians face some of the worst socioeconomic problems of any minority group in the country even though they have considerable amounts of resources. For example, the Crow tribe in Montana has some of the richest coal reserves in the United States, yet the Crows remain among the poorest of American Indians. Part of the problem is that the Bureau of Indian Affairs is the trustee or agent for the Indians' resources. In this trustee relationship, the BIA is not directly responsible to its Indian principals. As a bureaucracy it responds more to political pressures in Washington than to the well-being of Indians. There may have been a valid argument in the 19th century for "protecting" Indians in an alien society, but that time has surely passed. Indian resources should be released from the trust status and turned over to the individual tribes.

Conclusion

The above examples provide a brief survey of possible policy reforms that would allow free-market environmentalism to flourish, but they are not meant to imply that all problems can be solved without collective action. If (and I emphasize "if" because there is disagreement in the scientific community) coal-fired generating facilities are responsible for acid rain, transaction costs will almost certainly preclude a market solution, given current technology. Similarly, nonpoint sources of pollution, ozone depletion, preservation of migratory fish and wildlife, and groundwater contamination from multiple sources are problems not easily remedied by market forces. By harnessing market forces for the easier problems, we can concentrate government efforts on the tougher problems.

In using utilitarian arguments to defend the use of the coercive powers of government to improve upon voluntary exchange, we always confront the fundamental dilemma of political economy: How can government be granted the coercive power to carry out its role of enforcing property rights without that power being used to prey on private rights? In a free society, natural resource and environmental policy must be formulated with this dilemma in the forefront. In instances in which private property rights are not well-defined and enforced, government policies should focus on how property rights can be solidified. Efforts should be made to avoid policies such as the public trust doctrine, zoning, and public land ownership, which undermine private property rights and effectively promote the transfer of resources from one group to another. Secure private property rights to natural resources and the environment can unleash the powerful forces of the market process to promote good resource stewardship, environmental quality, and economic growth. Such possibilities provide the seeds for generating coalitions among conservationists, fiscal conservatives, and individualists that will make the necessary policy reforms possible. The new administration has a historic opportunity to put together such a coalition in support of a new approach to environmental protection.

PART IV

THE CONSTITUTION AND LIBERTY

20. Judicial Choice and Constitutional Order

James A. Dorn

> It is sufficiently obvious, that persons and property are the two
> great subjects on which Governments are to act; and that the
> rights of persons, and the rights of property, are the objects, for
> the protection of which Government was instituted. These rights
> cannot well be separated. The personal right to acquire property,
> which is a natural right, gives to property, when acquired, a right
> to protection, as a social right.[1]
>
> —James Madison

A fundamental problem facing any constitutional democracy is
how to safeguard individual freedom while providing for representative government. The potential for abuse in majority rule places
a great responsibility on the judiciary to act as a bulwark against
the political branches, especially in the American system where the
Supreme Court is the final arbiter of our constitutional order. In
fulfilling this duty, however, the justices must follow a legitimate
method of constitutional interpretation, one that will guide them
when the text is broad or silent. Finding such a method requires an
understanding of the history and structure of the Constitution, as
well as its moral underpinning. What is clear from the Constitution's historical foundations is that the Framers viewed the document as a charter for limited government. Moreover, they viewed
rights to life, liberty, and property as natural rights antecedent and
superior to rights created through legislation.

Laws protecting persons and property, overseen by a vigilant

---

[1]"Speech in the Virginia State Convention of 1829–30, on the Question of the Ratio
of Representation in the Two Branches of the Legislature," December 2, 1829. In
James Madison, *Letters and Other Writings of James Madison*, vol. 4, 1829–36 (Philadelphia: J. B. Lippincott and Co., 1865), p. 51.

judiciary, lay the basis for a just government and permit the spontaneous emergence of both social and economic coordination. Because the protection of property, liberty, and contract is at the core of a free market system, constitutional order is a prerequisite for economic order, which in turn is an important determinant of economic prosperity and the liberty it affords. Judicial choices, therefore, help shape the socioeconomic system and affect the range of individual choice. The judiciary thus plays a critical role in the maintenance of a free and prosperous society.

Judges can depart from the Framers' "Constitution of liberty," as F. A. Hayek put it,[2] either through misguided judicial activism or restraint. Constitutional confusion and even chaos can then result as the preferences of either judges or special interests substitute for the Framers' rule of law and a background jurisprudence of natural liberty.

The importance of judicial choice and interpretation for constitutional order points in turn to the importance of selecting judges who recognize the constitutional principles of the Framers and hence what Edward Corwin called "the 'higher law' background" of the Constitution.[3] Over the last half-century our judiciary has largely lost sight of those principles and that background, especially in its failure to protect property rights and economic liberty. The challenge facing the new administration, therefore, is to restore the Framers' constitutional vision by appointing judges who practice a *principled* activism, protecting liberty in every sphere, including the economic. Before meeting this challenge, however, the administration will have to familiarize itself with the substance of the Framers' Constitution, rethink the interrelation between judicial interpretation and constitutional order, and acknowledge the failure of both the liberals' doctrine of judicial activism and the conservatives' doctrine of judicial restraint. This chapter considers each of these areas and offers several policy recommendations for putting the nation back onto the path of judicial integrity and constitutional order. With the bicentennial of the Supreme Court and the Bill of

---

[2]Friedrich A. Hayek, *The Constitution of Liberty* (Chicago: University of Chicago Press, 1960).

[3]Edward S. Corwin, *The "Higher Law" Background of American Constitutional Law* (Ithaca, N.Y.: Great Seal Books, Cornell University Press, 1955).

Rights approaching, it is an appropriate time to reconsider the role of the judiciary in protecting our rights.

Restoring the Constitution of Liberty: A Principled Judicial Activism

If we are to restore the Framers' Constitution of liberty, the Court will have to reestablish itself as the guardian of both economic and noneconomic rights. To do so, however, the Court will have to return to what Stephen Macedo has termed "a principled judicial activism,"[4] that is, an activism designed not to further the personal agendas of judges or the will of the majority, which usually means the will of concentrated special interests, but to restore the higher-law principles of the Framers' Constitution.

Because many of these issues were drawn to public attention during the recent confirmation hearing of Judge Robert H. Bork, it would be useful to focus upon Bork's intellectual odyssey by way of further developing them.

Early in his career, Bork was on a path toward a principled judicial activism. Along the way, however, he was sidetracked by his increasing preoccupation with majoritarian government. This distraction, a focus on states' rights, and a legitimate distaste for the liberals' "living Constitution" led him to adopt a sort of legal and constitutional positivism, and an attendant moral skepticism, thus rejecting a constitutional theory based on the natural rights doctrine that was widely accepted by the Framers.

He thus moved away from his original principled approach to constitutional interpretation and toward judicial restraint. Bork's failure to continue his search should not lead us to conclude, however, that there is no principled path between the conservatives' judicial restraint and the liberals' judicial activism, a path that returns the Court to actively enforcing those principles of limited government and individual rights that are at the root of the higher-law Constitution. Such a balanced approach to judicial choice in reviewing cases that come before the Court will serve to reestablish the Court as the cornerstone of our constitutional democracy, ensuring liberty and justice for all.

[4]Stephen Macedo, *The New Right v. The Constitution* (Washington: Cato Institute, 1986), ch. 5.

Bork's Wrong Turn

Writing in 1968 Bork called for a "legitimate judicial activism" as opposed to the activism practiced by liberal judges—an activism he labeled "the jurisprudence of interest voting."[5] The activism he proposed was to be in accordance with the Madisonian tradition, which "assumes there are some aspects of life a majority should not control, that coercion in such matters is tyranny, a violation of the individual's natural rights." Since Bork at the time thought that "the definition of natural rights cannot be left to either the majority or the minority," he argued that "it is precisely the function of the Court to resolve this dilemma by giving content to the concept of natural rights in case-by-case interpretation of the Constitution."[6] For the early Bork, three conditions were required for legitimate activism: (1) "a warrant for the Court to move beyond the limited range of substantive rights that can be derived from traditional sources of constitutional law"; (2) "construction of a two-level theory of constitutional freedoms, the first tier consisting of freedoms that are primarily political, the second of all other claimed rights"; and (3) a theory of government to determine when coercion is justified.[7]

With regard to the first condition, Bork believed "the idea of deriving new rights from old is valid and valuable." Taking the "general set of natural rights" explicit in the Bill of Rights as "the givens" or "starting point," Bork would have applied common law reasoning to derive "new natural rights." With regard to the second and third conditions, he concluded that in cases where "the danger of being wrong seems roughly equal in either direction, the Court has no basis for setting aside political judgment" and "must then decide in favor of the governmental action." According to Bork, the best strategy for implementing a jurisprudence of legitimate activism is for the Court to continue "practicing restraint for the most part, but cautiously and experimentally working out the principles of legitimate activism."[8]

---

[5] Robert H. Bork, "The Supreme Court Needs a New Philosophy," *Fortune*, December 1968, p. 178.

[6] Ibid., p. 168.

[7] Ibid., pp. 170, 174.

[8] Ibid., pp. 170, 174, 177.

Although Bork appears to have been on the right path in 1968, his theory was both incomplete and inconsistent. In particular he never systematically attempted to lay the foundation for a rational theory of rights, much less to use such a theory to derive a consistent set of rights; nor did he fully realize that this foundation was to be discovered in the Framers' general acceptance of the theory of natural rights. Finally, although his division of rights into political rights and nonpolitical or natural rights was justified, his ranking of the former over the latter was inconsistent with the Framers' belief that an individual's natural rights take precedence over his politically determined rights when the two come into conflict.

More generally, however, Bork's nascent majoritarianism nipped in the bud his attempt to formulate a legitimate judicial activism. Indeed, he perhaps unwittingly predicted the route he himself would follow in his jurisprudential odyssey. Remarking that for the Court to practice a legitimate activism, it must "have, and demonstrate the validity of, a theory of natural rights," he went on to conclude that "a Court without such a theory should candidly admit its lack, eschew policy questions, and practice restraint. Otherwise it will inevitably deny the majority some of its legitimate power to rule."[9]

By 1986 it was abundantly clear that Bork would not be the leader of any judicial revolution designed to restore the Constitution of liberty, given his narrow understanding of the higher-law roots of the Framers' Constitution. In an interview that year, he stated, "The effort to create individual rights out of a general, abstract, moral philosophy, I think, is doomed to failure from the beginning because I don't think there is any version of moral philosophy that can claim to be absolutely superior to all others." The Framers, according to Bork, "didn't sit down and work out a utilitarian philosophy or a contractarian philosophy or something of that sort." Rather, their intent, as Bork saw it, was "to leave large areas of life to the democratic process."[10] Bork seems to have come to the conclusion that in framing the Constitution, Madison and his colleagues had no moral theory to inform their political judgments, or

[9]Ibid., pp. 169–70.

[10]Quoted in Patrick B. McGuigan, "An Interview with Judge Robert H. Bork," *Judicial Notice* 3 (June 1986): 4.

perhaps that their moral theory held that rights were grounded in democratic theory. Yet there is a preponderance of evidence to the contrary, showing that the Framers widely accepted the natural rights doctrine and the Lockean concept of limited government. The justification for the American Revolution, in fact, rested on the colonists' belief that England had violated not only their rights as Englishmen but their natural rights, especially the right of autonomy. As such, the Declaration of Independence is best viewed as a declaration of rights, widely regarded as self-evident. Indeed, as Carl Becker observed: "The philosophy of Locke seemed to Jefferson and his compatriots just 'the common sense of the matter.' "[11]

If Bork wanted a "starting point" for a theory of natural rights, all he had to do was to look to the self-evident truths of the Declaration of Independence. To reiterate: Individual rights predate government; the legitimate basis of government is individual consent (that is, unanimity); and a just government is one that protects life, liberty, and property. From these givens, a set of individual rights can be derived that are consistent with the basic right to liberty or noninterference and with the Lockean concept of limited government. That Bork failed to acknowledge this possibility points to his preoccuption with majority rule and his willingness to ignore the higher-law background of the Constitution, a posture that is regrettably evident throughout the judiciary. Likewise, by choosing to ignore the higher-law Constitution, Bork and the contemporary Court have chosen to cut the Framers' constitutional rights fabric in half—affording economic rights virtually no standing in the pro-

[11]Carl L. Becker, *The Declaration of Independence: A Study in the History of Political Ideas* (New York: Vintage Books, 1958, reprint of 1922 edition), p. 72. On the prevalence of the natural rights doctrine in colonial America, see Terry L. Anderson and Peter J. Hill, "Constraining the Transfer Society: Constitutional and Moral Dimensions," *Cato Journal* 6 (Spring/Summer 1986): 331–33. They note that

> One of the distinguishing features of colonial America was the general acceptance of the Lockean concept of natural rights. This concept provided the colonists with a generally understood common point for determining the origin and sanctity of rights. . . . The general acceptance of the concept of natural rights was found in everything from colonial education to religion to politics.

See also James A. Dorn, "Public Choice and the Constitution: A Madisonian Perspective," in James D. Gwartney and Richard E. Wagner, *Public Choice and Constitutional Economics* (Greenwich, Conn.: JAI Press, 1988); Roger Pilon, "On the Foundations of Economic Liberty," *The Freeman* 38 (September 1988): 338–45.

cess of judicial review while elevating First Amendment rights, such as freedom of religion, to the status of "fundamental" rights, a distinction that was unbeknown to the Framers.[12]

Further evidence testifying to the influence of the natural rights doctrine on the Framers' constitutional vision recently emerged in the form of a handwritten draft of the Bill of Rights.[13] The proposed first amendment provided for a "living constitution" in the sense that it regarded individuals as having "an inherent and unalienable right to change or amend their political Constitution," since legitimate government power is derived from the consent of the people. The proposed second amendment explicitly recognized that "people have certain natural rights which are retained by them when they enter into Society. Such are the rights of Conscience in matters of religion" and "of acquiring property. . . . Of these rights therefore they shall not be deprived by the Government of the united States." In the proposed eighth amendment, the Madisonian property right was further affirmed, in that "Congress Shall not have power to grant any monopoly or exclusive advantages of commerce to any person or Company; nor to restrain the liberty of the Press."[14] Although the final Bill of Rights did not incorporate all the draft provisions, the newly discovered document sheds important light on the higher-law background that helped shape the Framers' constitutional vision.

By giving up before he really started, Bork took a wrong turn at the constitutional crossroad, moving away from a legitimate judicial activism and toward a flawed jurisprudence of judicial restraint and majoritarian dominance, all grounded, purportedly, in some "original intent." As Edward H. Crane pointed out in this regard, the major problem with Bork's adherence to original intent rests "not so much in the oft-noted difficulty in determining intent . . . as it does with the sleight-of-hand invocation of the framers' intentions

[12]See Gordon Crovitz, "Constitution Protects Life, Liberty *and* Property," *Wall Street Journal*, October 8, 1986, p. 34. According to Crovitz, "There was no original intent by the Founders that there be any such system of gradations in the level of judicial review. Instead these distinctions are best explained as reflecting the personal preferences of judges."

[13]Herbert Mitgang, "Handwritten Draft of a Bill of Rights Found," *New York Times*, July 29, 1987, pp. A1, C21.

[14]Ibid., p. C21.

and simultaneous rejection of their philosophy."[15] In defense of a legitimate judicial activism, Crane wrote: "The point is, judicial activism in the name of what the Constitution says is not only commendable, it is a moral and legal imperative. And the Lockean principles that underlie the work of the framers dictate no less respect for property and economic rights than they do [for] such fundamental rights as privacy and free speech."[16]

Toward a Principled Judicial Activism

Attorney General Edwin Meese criticized the liberals' version of judicial activism as "a chameleon jurisprudence" and called for a "jurisprudence based on first principles," which "is neither conservative nor liberal, neither right nor left."[17] Yet Meese's "Jurisprudence of Original Intention" is itself without any ultimate principle except that of deferring to majority rule whenever uncertain about individual rights. That presumably is why Bork contended that constitutional law currently exhibits a "theoretical emptiness at its center." At the same time, Bork's moral skepticism led him to reject "abstract and philosophical" approaches to the law because "they always lack what law requires, democratic legitimacy." But here Bork was confusing law with legislation; and although he was certainly correct to attack the "new theories of moral relativism and egalitarianism" that now dominate "constitutional thinking in a number of leading law schools," his blanket condemnation places him in the same moral relativist camp he criticizes.[18]

In the absence of any significant developments in constitutional law theory, at least any consistent with a truly free society, it is time to ask if we cannot do better. The answer, as heard from scholars such as Chicago's Richard Epstein and Harvard's Stephen Macedo, is a resounding Yes. Both agree that the theory must start with the plain constitutional text and then proceed to an inquiry as

[15]Edward H. Crane, "The Soul of a Congressman," *Wall Street Journal*, September 14, 1987, p. 24.

[16]Edward H. Crane, "When Judicial Activism Is No Vice," *St. Louis Post-Dispatch*, December 21, 1986.

[17]Edwin Meese III, Address before the D.C. Chapter of the Federalist Society Lawyers Division, November 15, 1985, pp. 13–14; available from the U.S. Department of Justice.

[18]Robert H. Bork, *Tradition and Morality in Constitutional Law*, the Francis Boyer Lectures on Public Policy (Washington: American Enterprise Institute, 1984), p. 6.

334

to its meaning within the moral framework shaping the Framers' constitutional vision.

In his search for a theory of constitutional interpretation that is true to the limited-government view of the Framers, Epstein turned to the eminent domain clause and to the Lockean view of government and rights as that influenced the Framers. By refining this theory, he developed a systematic approach to determining the limits of the Leviathan, an approach that is entirely consistent with the Framers' natural rights philosophy and their concept of limited government.[19] Criticizing both the liberals' "living constitution" and the conservatives' practice of judicial restraint, Epstein argued:

> A sound theory of original intention . . . makes it indefensible to assume that modern zoning, landmark preservation and rent-control statutes, or collective bargaining and minimum-wage laws are beyond constitutional review simply because none was heard of in 1791. Rightly understood, original intention demands that judges articulate and apply general constitutional language to novel legislation. The fashionable conservative view of judicial restraint often wrongly assumes that the presumption of judicial restraint obviates that need. Judicial restraint may call for inaction when the Constitution is silent. But that silence cannot be simply presumed, but must be demonstrated by close textual analysis.[20]

According to Epstein, "too much attention" has been focused "on the abstract debate between judicial activism and judicial restraint," and "too little concern" has been shown for "the substantive theories of governance on which the Constitution rests." In particular, he emphasizes that "the conservative insistence on judicial restraint, exemplified by Mr. Meese, has left the liberals with a free field over substantive theories." In Epstein's judgment, this "monopoly is best countered not with the unyielding assertion that the courts should not (or hardly ever) override the political branches of government." Rather, "it can and should be attacked as inconsistent with the constitutional means selected by the framers to ensure a just and stable society." What is clear is that "the Constitution rests on a political theory of limited government,"

[19]See Richard A. Epstein, *Takings: Private Property and the Power of Eminent Domain* (Cambridge, Mass.: Harvard University Press, 1985).

[20]Richard A. Epstein, "Needed: Activist Judges for Economic Rights," *Wall Street Journal*, November 14, 1985, p. 32.

which "deserves public defense and judicial fidelity." For Epstein, "it is the disregard of that substantive principle that discredits Justice Brennan's brand of judicial activism" as well.[21]

Epstein's approach to judicial interpretation of constitutional provisions is consistent with Macedo's principled judicial activism, an activism that is gaining greater support as the theoretical vacuum of both the liberal and the conservative jurisprudential positions is becoming more and more apparent. In *The New Right v. the Constitution*, Macedo exposed the shortcomings of the jurisprudence of original intent and offered a "rights-based jurisprudence," one that traces back to Bork's original call for a "legitimate judicial activism."[22] But where Bork failed to connect fully with the natural rights tradition inherent in the Framers' Constitution, Macedo took that tradition as the only justifiable basis for judicial activism. According to Macedo, "For the people who drafted and ratified the Constitution, legitimate government depended not only on the document's origin in popular consent, but also on its conformity with certain principles of justice and 'unalienable Rights,' which were held to be 'natural' or of higher moral standing than the will of any majority"[23]—an insight that apparently is escaping the attention of most conservative judicial passivists.

Given the inherent weaknesses of the current approaches to judicial interpretation of constitutional provisions, Macedo has seen the "need for a constitutional vision with a robust conception of judicially enforceable rights grounded in the text of the Constitution, in sound moral thinking, and in our political tradition." He believes that such a "principled judicial activism would overcome the incoherence of the modern Court's double standard" (that is, treating personal liberties as "fundamental" and separate from economic liberties, which are offered only minimal judicial protection).[24]

A principled judicial activism is also a balanced approach to

[21]Ibid.

[22]See also Macedo, "The Endangered Branch: The Judiciary Under Reagan," in David Boaz, ed., *Assessing the Reagan Years* (Washington: Cato Institute, 1988); Roger Pilon, "On the Foundations of Justice," *The Intercollegiate Review* 17 (Fall/Winter 1981): 3–14.

[23]Macedo, *The New Right v. The Constitution*, p. 18.

[24]Ibid., p. 43.

judicial choice and constitutional interpretation because, as Epstein pointed out, it recognizes two types of judicial error: (1) the error of misguided judicial activism, that is, the error of intervening when the Court should stand still; and (2) the error of misguided judicial passivism, that is, the error of standing still when the Court should intervene. In both cases, to act or not to act, the Court will be guided by its constitutional vision. Thus, conservatives have tried mostly to minimize the first type of error while liberals have focused on the second type. The ideal for Epstein is to "minimize both types of error."[25] To do so, however, requires moving from the defective conservative and liberal visions to a principled judicial activism.

By creating an artificial and historically untenable division of the rights fabric, and reserving the term "fundamental" only for those personal rights deemed inviolable by the Supreme Court, the texture of the Framers' Constitution of liberty has been all but forgotten. Within this distorted constitutional environment, it is no wonder that it now appears radical for anyone to call for the restoration of substantive due process protection for private property and freedom of contract.[26] The fact is, however, that the principled judicial activism advocated by Epstein, Macedo, and others would simply return us to the substantive vision of the Framers, who, though revolutionaries, justified their revolution on rational grounds— supported by the doctrine of natural rights and justice under a rule of law limiting the powers of government to the protection of life, liberty, and property. As such, Gordon Crovitz has recommended that conservatives who favor a truly free society and a jurisprudence based on the Framers' original intent "should relax" in that "it requires no inappropriate activism for judges to read the text of the Constitution, which explicitly protects economic rights, and adjudicate accordingly."[27]

[25]Richard A. Epstein, "Judicial Review: Reckoning on Two Kinds of Error," in *Scalia v. Epstein: Two Views of Judicial Activism* (Washington: Cato Institute, 1985), p. 15.

[26]See, for example, Charlotte L. Allen, "The Lone Voice Acquires a Chorus," *Insight*, August 1, 1988, pp. 50–51. In referring to principled judicial activism she observed that "there is a new radical kind of conservatism afoot . . . that is concerned less with judicial restraint than with protecting individual freedom from government interference" (p. 51).

[27]Crovitz, "Constitution Protects Life, Liberty *and* Property," p. 34.

The intent of conservatives such as Bork and Meese who have tried to come up with a legitimate approach to judicial interpretation of constitutional provisions may be good, but the substance is lacking. A full-fledged theory of judicial choice and constitutional interpretation requires more than the conservatives' jurisprudence of original intent has to offer. The recognition of this fact, together with an understanding of the higher-law background of the Constitution, implies that there is no need to be discouraged in the search for first principles; they are already evident in the natural law/limited-government framework of the Constitution, understood as a rule of law. Within this context the duty of the judiciary is clear and simple: Uphold the "supreme Law of the Land" and act as a bulwark against the political branches in the protection of individual rights, both personal and property rights, in the spirit of the Framers' Constitution of liberty.

To guide the Court in the direction of "liberty and justice for all," what needs to be done is to work out the full implications of a principled judicial activism, so that any new rights derived are consistent with the Framers' first principles and the basic right to liberty or noninterference. In addition to the work of Epstein and Macedo, significant progress in this direction has been made by legal philosopher Roger Pilon. His work shows that the broad rights of the Constitution can be given a rigorous, logical justification, as against the skeptical claims of the legal realists, and can be articulated to yield a far-reaching and powerful theory of rights capable of assisting judges in their work of constitutional interpretation.[28]

[28]See especially Roger Pilon, "Ordering Rights Consistently: Or What We Do and Do Not Have Rights To," *Georgia Law Review* 13 (Summer 1979): 1171–96; idem, "Corporations and Rights: On Treating Corporate People Justly," *Georgia Law Review* 13 (Summer 1979): 1245–1370; idem, "On Moral and Legal Justification," *Southwestern University Law Review* 11 (1979): 1327–44; idem, "On the Foundations of Justice," pp. 3–14; idem, "Capitalism and Rights: An Essay toward Fine Tuning the Moral Foundations of the Free Society," *Journal of Business Ethics* 1 (February 1982): 29–42; idem, "Property Rights, Takings, and a Free Society," *Harvard Journal of Law and Public Policy* 6 (Summer 1983): 165–95; and idem, "Legislative Activism, Judicial Activism, and the Decline of Private Sovereignty," *Cato Journal* 4 (Winter 1985): 813–33.

Mention should also be made of Randy Barnett's work dealing with judicial interpretation and the Ninth Amendment. In particular, see Randy E. Barnett, "Foreword: Judicial Conservatism v. A Principled Judicial Activism," *Harvard Journal of Law and Public Policy* 10 (Spring 1987): 273–94; and idem, "Why the Ninth Amendment?" *Humane Studies Review* 5 (Winter 1987/88): 1, 6–9.

Likewise, the pioneering work done by Bernard H. Siegan in helping to restore economic liberties to their rightful place in the constitutional order has laid the basis for a resurgence of interest in this aspect of our rights structure.[29] Consequently, more and more attention is being focused on what Bork early on referred to as the "irrational discrimination" between economic and noneconomic freedoms.[30]

In sum, if the Court elects to enforce the Constitution of liberty and protect property, in the Madisonian sense, constitutional order and economic stability will ensue. But if the Court continues to split the Framers' constitutional fabric and to ignore the higher-law background, constitutional uncertainty and chaos will increasingly come to dominate. The restoration of a principled judicial activism, resting on first principles widely accepted by the Framers, will put the judiciary back on the path to being what the Framers intended, namely, "an impenetrable bulwark" against the politicization of our rights and freedoms.

Recommendations for Restoring Constitutional Order

Both liberals and conservatives have an interest in maintaining the intellectual and political capital they have invested in their pet theories of judicial interpretation. Both can therefore be expected to resist any change toward a principled judicial activism. But those at the margin may be swayed by rational argument, and as the defects of the status quo become more and more apparent, the margin may move toward a more balanced approach to constitutional interpretation—an approach based on the Framers' first principles, not on the preferences of judges or the sentiments of roving majorities. That is why it is important to set the intellectual framework for a restoration of the Framers' Constitution of liberty. With the erosion of the economic constitution and the uncertainty surrounding personal liberties, it is an appropriate time for the Court to follow Bork's earlier advice and begin "working out the principles of legitimate activism." For, as Bork observed in 1968, "Law grows by trial and error, through generalizations tried, refined, and, if

[29]Bernard H. Siegan, *Economic Liberties and the Constitution* (Chicago: University of Chicago Press, 1980).
[30]Bork, "The Supreme Court Needs a New Philosophy," p. 170.

need be, relinquished. There is nothing improper in that if the Court is candid about its real operative principles and prepared to abandon its mistakes."[31]

Three interrelated tasks must be accomplished if constitutional order is to be restored:

- First, judicial integrity must be restored so that judges once again become the guardians of the Framers' higher-law Constitution.
- Second, judges must be appointed who practice a legitimate, principled judicial activism and restore constitutional order.
- Third, a constitutional ethos of liberty must be established so that citizens understand the importance of the Constitution as a charter for limited government and individual freedom.

These recommendations, if followed, will put us back on the road toward the truly liberal republic envisioned by the Framers.

Restore Judicial Integrity

If it is to regain the respect due it in a constitutional democracy, the judiciary must reestablish itself as the guardian of the Framers' first principles and act as a bulwark against political opportunism by maintaining constitutional order. It can do this by following a balanced approach to constitutional interpretation—a principled judicial activism designed to restore economic liberties to their proper place in the constitutional order and to protect the private domain in line with the higher law of the Constitution. Following this route will help promote both economic and social order as individuals exercise their freedom to choose under a stable rule of law.

Before judges can move toward a principled judicial activism, however, they must first regain a proper perspective of the Constitution and Bill of Rights, especially the economic constitution and the forgotten Ninth Amendment. The Ninth Amendment is more than an "inkblot," as Bork described it during his confirmation hearings; it is a reminder of the natural rights tradition that underlies the constitutional text and a reminder that the Framers established a limited government, not an unlimited democracy. Unfortunately the Court has indeed treated the Ninth Amendment as an "inkblot." If the Court is to restore its integrity and rebuild the

[31]Ibid., p. 177.

Framers' constitutional order, it will have to make whole the natural rights fabric of the higher-law Constitution. The right to property and the right to privacy will both have to be woven back into the Supreme Court's constitution if the gap between constitutional law and the Framers' Constitution of liberty is to be closed. In any decision regarding new rights, however, the Court will have to be guided by the rational test of consistency, in that any derived rights will have to conform with the Framers' first principles.

Treating individuals as equal before the law of liberty and protecting their natural rights as a whole, without discriminating against either economic or noneconomic rights, will help restore respect not only for the Constitution as the "supreme Law of the Land" but for its judicial guardian as well. We may then once again say, as A. V. Dicey did in another era, that "to the judiciary in short are due the maintenance of justice, the existence of internal free trade, and the general respect for the rights of property."[32]

Appoint Principled Judicial Activists

Appointing judges who are friendly to the text and structure of the Framers' Constitution and knowledgeable about its higher-law background will enhance the reputation of the judiciary as an institution committed to "right reason" and justice. With the probable appointment of three new justices to the Supreme Court over the next four years and a host of appointments to the federal judiciary at lower levels, definite criteria should be established to ensure the selection of individuals who have a commitment to individual rights and are not afraid to use judicial review as a device to strike down both economic and social legislation that intrudes on the private domain.

The judicial selection process, especially for Supreme Court justices, can provide a useful forum for public debate over the role of the judiciary in a constitutional democracy. Unless the appointed judges are those who have a firm commitment to individual rights, the Court will continue on its present course, shifting between a rootless activism and a misguided restraint. The judicial function in protecting our substantive rights is too important to be left either to the subjective preferences of liberal activists or to the timidity of

[32]A. V. Dicey, *Introduction to the Study of the Law of the Constitution* (Indianapolis: Liberty Classics, 1982, reprint of 1915 edition), p. 91.

conservative passivists—and thereby to legislators and the uncertainty of majority rule. Appointing justices who take a balanced approach to constitutional interpretation by practicing a principled judicial activism will serve to reinforce both the country's moral strength and its international respect as a nation ruled by law, not by men.

Establish a Constitutional Ethos of Liberty

Both the direction and speed of judicial and constitutional reform will depend to a large extent on public, and therefore political, sentiment. If the public at large recognizes the importance of the rule of law and a principled judicial activism, the climate will be set for establishing a constitutional ethos of liberty, encompassing respect for both economic and noneconomic rights. But if the public is ignorant of the higher-law background of the Constitution—that is, perceives the Constitution primarily as a blueprint for majoritarian government—and is disrespectful toward the judiciary, little progress will be made in restoring the Framers' Constitution, at least as long as the Court is politically sensitive. That is why Justice Scalia, in the debate over restoring substantive due process protection to economic liberties, called for a "constitutional ethos of economic liberty" as a necessary condition for restoring the parity of economic rights. In his opinion, "constitutionalization," by which he apparently meant the Court's upholding of first principles, can help "society to preserve allegiance" to such principles. But for Scalia, "the allegiance comes first and the preservation afterwards." Thus, as a justification for not restoring judicial protection to substantive economic rights, Scalia argued: "I do not detect the sort of national commitment to most of the economic liberties generally discussed [presumably private property and freedom of contract] that would enable even an activist court to constitutionalize them. That lack of sentiment may be regrettable, but to seek to develop it by enshrining the unaccepted principles in the Constitution is to place the cart before the horse."[33]

The emphasis placed by Scalia on public allegiance to constitutional principles is certainly warranted. Such allegiance is a necessary condition for the survival of a constitutional democracy and a

---

[33]Antonin Scalia, "Economic Affairs as Human Affairs," in *Scalia v. Epstein: Two Views on Judicial Activism* (Washington: Cato Institute, 1985), p. 7.

free society. But one must distinguish between choices at the constitutional and post-constitutional stages, and the role of the judiciary in each. At the constitutional stage, Scalia is quite right. It was the general acceptance of the natural rights doctrine and the Lockean concept of limited government that provided the allegiance necessary for establishing a Constitution of liberty and a Supreme Court to enforce it. At the post-constitutional stage, however, Scalia fails to be convincing. Indeed, he distorts the Framers' constitutional vision by elevating popular sentiment and majoritarianism above individual rights, which a just government and a responsible judiciary were entrusted to safeguard. In the post-constitutional world, therefore, the preservation of constitutional principles comes first and popular sentiment with respect to those principles comes second.

It is precisely because the contemporary Court has failed to place principles before sentiment that it has eroded our economic liberties over the past 50 years and kept our personal freedoms in a state of flux. Public appreciation of constitutional principles is important, but that appreciation must itself be nurtured by a Court exhibiting a constitutional ethos of liberty. Allowing activist liberal judges and legislators to set the tone for an ethos of redistribution can only serve to fuel the welfare state and undermine the constitutional basis for a free society.

If popular sentiment concerning private property and privacy diminishes, the proper route for the Court is to uphold these principles, not to either stand idly by or to actively assist in the effort. That is to say, in the post-constitutional world the judiciary's role is to be the final arbiter and guardian of the Framers' Constitution, and thereby set a precedent for lower courts and the nation as a whole. In this fashion, judges as principled judicial activists could act as an effective bulwark against those who might otherwise try to undermine the rights of persons and property.

Thus, when the Court practices a principled judicial activism, its example will also help establish a constitutional ethos of liberty in the public at large. But the problem, of course, is who will monitor the monitor? Here it is important to note the role of general education. For if the public does not accept the principles underlying the Constitution of liberty and prefers instead to place democracy above freedom, it will be impossible to preserve the very freedom that makes democracy possible. We will then move more and more toward what Terry Anderson and Peter J. Hill have called the "transfer society."[34]

That educational effort is imperative and must take place at various levels—within the judiciary itself and the public at large—becomes obvious even from a cursory look at the current state of constitutional awareness. The following examples suffice to illustrate the dismal state of the Framers' Constitution:

> When asked during his tenure as assistant attorney general for civil rights what he was doing to safeguard economic rights, William Bradford Reynolds (a staunch conservative) answered that he had "never thought of private property rights as civil rights."[35]
>
> In a survey by the Hearst Corporation regarding the public's understanding of the Constitution, 45 percent of those interviewed thought that the Marxist phrase "from each according to his ability, to each according to his need" was part of the Constitution.[36]
>
> In an interview at the Manhattan Institute, Judge Robert Bork, when asked if he might support Epstein's call for a change in Court policy toward the protection of economic liberties, replied that he was "not hostile to economic liberties, constitutionally enforced, *provided you can show me that that is what the framers intended.* . . . If Prof. Epstein has historical evidence that justifies what he is suggesting, that's fine" [emphasis added].[37]

The principles that were once self-evident and common sense are obviously no longer so. The puzzling question is, Why?

Perhaps it is because public education has failed to instill what James M. Buchanan has called a "constitutional attitude," namely, a long-run perspective that considers the role of stable institutions in promoting social and economic order.[38] It is the loss of this

[34]Terry L. Anderson and Peter J. Hill, *The Birth of a Transfer Society* (Stanford, Calif.: Hoover Institution Press, 1980).

[35]Quoted in Gordon Crovitz, "Is the New Deal Unconstitutional?" *Wall Street Journal*, January 13, 1986, p. 24.

[36]Hearst Corporation, *The American Public's Knowledge of the U.S. Constitution*, A Hearst Report (New York: The Hearst Corporation, 1987), p. 13.

[37]Quoted in Daniel Schuchman, "Persuadable on Economic Rights," *Wall Street Journal*, September 14, 1987, p. 24.

[38]James M. Buchanan, *Freedom in Constitutional Contract: Perspectives of a Political Economist* (College Station: Texas A & M University Press, 1977).

constitutional perspective and ignorance of the concept of spontaneous order that may help explain both the erosion of the economic constitution and the uncertain state of the Framers' Constitution of liberty. In Buchanan's words, "The present situation in the United States" is "one of 'constitutional anarchy.' The effective constitution has been allowed to erode to the extent that the predictability that should be inherent in a legal structure is seriously threatened." As such, the time may be ripe for "genuine constitutional revolution," which would restore the "constitution of freedom." But this will require taking on a "constitutional attitude," that is, "an appreciation and understanding of the difference between choosing basic rules and acting within those rules."[39]

If a "constitutional revolution" is to occur, then the Court is in the best position to lead it; and the president, by his nominations to the Supreme Court and lower federal courts, is in a position to bring the debate over judicial choice and constitutional order to the public. Indeed, the president should use the influence of his office to foster a constitutional ethos of liberty. By pointing to the importance of a stable government by law and a vigilant judiciary—protecting both economic and noneconomic rights—the president can help restore confidence in the Lockean property right. His success in constraining the growth of government and protecting individual rights will largely determine whether we remain in a state of constitutional chaos or restore the Framers' vision of constitutional order and freedom.

[39]Ibid., pp. 296–98.

21. Liberty Is Destiny

George Gilder

As we approach the 21st century, we are entering the quantum era of economics and technology. Quantum physics is a complex and elaborate theory of the nature of physical reality. But it can be summed up in a simple proposition: the overthrow of matter. In quantum theory, the materialist superstition—the belief that all reality can be explained by the interplay among material particles—has collapsed at the heart of matter itself. The most important intellectual event of our century, this development is now transforming global economics and geopolitics.

The previous theory—Newtonian physics—had enthroned matter. All Newtonian reality consisted of "hard impenetrable particles of mass," such as the solids perceived by human senses. Quantum theory shows that Newton's massy particles spring from a further domain in which Newton's laws are inapplicable and sensory evidence is irrelevant. The irreducible atom of quantum theory is not a "massy particle" but a quantum of information—a probability amplitude. It defines the likelihood of finding a quantum entity at any particular point. But that entity can also appear simultaneously at another point. Nonlocal, and interfering like a wave at impact rather than colliding like a particle, a probability amplitude is less a thing than a thought; it takes physics beyond the sensory domains of the materialist superstition.

The overthrow of Newton's opaque solids represented a Copernican moment in modern history. In the early 16th century, Copernicus displaced the earth from the center of the universe. Early in this century, quantum physics displaced human senses as the central test of reality. Newtonian physics was intelligible to human beings, but it rendered the solid state unintelligible and opaque. The paradoxical propositions of quantum theory are utterly unintelligible to the human sensory system, but they do render the inner space of matter intelligible.

347

The overthrow of matter in physics made possible the overthrow of material limits in technology. At the heart of the quantum economy is the transistor. Although the first transistor radios 30 years ago used far less efficient and versatile transistors that cost some $9 apiece, transistors now are invisible and virtually free. The fantastically shrinking transistor now costs only a few ten-thousandths of a cent, and some of the latest chips contain literally millions of such devices. These chips cost between $0.80 and $2 each to produce and can contain all the logic in what once was called a giant computer, costing millions of dollars. The compounding of such benefits is the chief source and secret of the creation of wealth in the quantum economy.

Throughout all previous human history, the creation of wealth depended upon the extraction, transport, manipulation, and modification of heavy materials against the resistance of gravity, the demands of entropy, and the constraints of time and space. Slaves sweated in galleys, and regimented workers imitated machines, performing routine physical labor. States grew powerful by accumulating physical wealth and territory, slaves and armies. Atlas and Sisyphus groaning under the load of a material globe symbolized the human predicament.

Today, new wealth is chiefly created by reaching beyond mass into the quantum domain and manipulating matter from the inside. This real world is called solid state. Yet the crucial insight of solid-state physics is that nothing that humans conventionally call solid is actually solid at all. The floor beneath one's feet consists of atoms that are more than 99.9 percent space. In proportion to the size of its nucleus, the atomic system is as empty as the solar system.

Such propositions seem amazing only from the viewpoint of the materialist superstition, in which we imagine that our senses are central. In a mind-centered system, modern physics is more practical and realistic than the deterministic materialism of the old physics. By conquering the imagined limits of conventional time and space, mankind has vastly enlarged the dimensions of human life. It has opened a continent far more capacious than Columbus's America or the wastes of loss and entropy beyond the planets. Indeed, by opening inner space, man has gained the technologies that have made possible the human exploration of outer space and the creation of a global ganglion of cables and satellites that transmit information at near the speed of light. From the silicon in grains of sand, the transistor generates imperishable gains of knowledge that grow as they are shared, and that overcome all the dismal sciences of limited growth.

Technology Is Liberation

It was once imagined that giant computers could simulate a market economy and thus make socialist planning possible. Contrary to these predications, however, computers make socialism totally futile and obsolete. By their very nature, computers distribute power rather than centralize it. At the heart of every computer is a chip or set of chips. In volume, anything on a chip is cheap. But moving up the hierarchy from the chip to the circuit board to the network and to the telecommunications system, interconnections between components grow exponentially more expensive and less efficient. A first law of the technology is to concentrate components and connections—and thus computing power—on single chips. The evolution of the industry therefore constantly increases the power of the individual workstation, based on a single chip, in relation to any large computer attempting to control it through a network.

The International Business Machines (IBM) Corp. at first thought that the proliferation of personal computer networks would increase sales of mainframes to manage them. Instead, peer networks arose and soon outperformed centralized mainframe networks. The 32-bit personal computers of the late 1980s are over 90 times more cost-effective (in millions of instructions per second per dollar) than supercomputers.

Concentrating components on a chip not only enhanced their speed and effectiveness but also vastly dropped their price. Finally, in the form of the microprocessor, the computer on a chip cost a few dollars and outperformed the computer on a pedestal. Rather than pushing control to Big Brother at the top as the pundits predicted, the technology by its very nature constantly pulled power down to the people. The ultimate beneficiary—the individual with a personal computer or workstation—gained powers of creation and communication far beyond those of the kings of old.

The individual was not only the heir to the throne of the technology; he also was its leading creator. Although made possible by hardware innovations from around the world, the move to small computers was chiefly an American revolution, driven by the invention of new software. As fast as the Japanese and others could expand the capacity of computer memories, American entrepreneurs filled them with useful programs. Some 14,000 new U.S. companies, many of them led by teenagers and college "hackers," launched a vast array of software packages, and they changed the computer from an arcane tool of elites to a popular appliance. As a result of this software, ranging from spreadsheets and word processors to data bases and video games, the United States pioneered and propagated the use of small computers. As the 1990s approached, the United States had an installed base of small computers 11 times larger than Japan's, and the U.S. share of the world software market had risen from under two-thirds to more than three-quarters.

Once believed to be a bastion of bureaucratic computing, IBM itself has become a prime source of the redistribution of computer power. As IBM's machines become smaller and cheaper and more available to the public, they also become more effective and more flexible. The trend will continue. The basic limit on the speed of computers is size: an electron can move nine inches in a billionth of a second. This constraint dictates that supercomputers of the future will be concentrated into a space of three cubic inches. Unlike the industrial revolution, which imposed economies of scale, the information revolution imposes economies of microscale. Computer power continually devolves into the hands and onto the laps of individuals.

Technology Disperses Power

The advance into the microcosm is now accelerating. Propelling it are three major and convergent developments in the industry, once again dispersing power rather than centralizing it.

The first is artificial intelligence, giving to computers rudimentary powers of sight, hearing, and common sense. Computer technology has long been essentially deaf, blind, and dumb. Reachable only through keyboards and primitive sensors and programmable only in binary mathematics, computers have remained mostly immured in their digital towers. Artificial intelligence promises to vastly enhance the accessibility of computers to human language, imagery, and expertise. Taking input by voice, computer systems can collapse to the size of chips and spread human intelligence through

350

the human environment. Continuing to leave ivory towers and data processing elites behind, the computer can open itself to the needs of untrained and handicapped individuals, even allowing the blind to read and the disabled to write.

The second major breakthrough is the silicon compiler. Just as a software compiler converts high-level languages into the bits and bytes that the computer can understand, the silicon compiler converts high-level chip designs and functions into the intersecting polygons of an actual chip layout. This technology makes possible the complete design of integrated circuits on a computer, from initial concept to final silicon.

To understand the impact of this development, imagine that printing firms essentially wrote all the books. This has been the situation in the computer industry: to "write" a chip, one essentially had to own a semiconductor manufacturing plant—in effect, a silicon printing press—that cost between $50 million and $200 million to build on a profitable scale. But with silicon compilers and related gear, any computer-literate person with a $20,000 workstation can create a major new integrated circuit precisely adapted to his needs. If mass production is needed, semiconductor companies around the globe will compete to print one's design in the world's best clean rooms.

In a prophetic move, however, a few firms are now even introducing forms of silicon desktop publishing. A firm called Actel has created a way not only to design but also to create and test major microchips on a desktop device that costs some $20,000. Contrary to the analysis of the critics, the computer industry is not becoming more capital-intensive. Measured by the capital costs per device function—the investment needed to deliver value to the customer—the industry is becoming ever cheaper to enter. The silicon compiler and related technologies move power from large corporations to individual designers and entrepreneurs.

The third key breakthrough is the widespread abandonment of the long-cherished von Neumann computer architecture with its single central processing unit, separate memory, and step-by-step instruction sets. Replacing this architecture is a massively parallel system with potentially thousands of processors working at once.

This change in the architecture of computers resembles the abandonment of centralized processing in most large companies. In the past, users had to line up outside the central processing room, submit their work to the data processing experts, and then wait hours or days for it to be done. Today, much of the work is dispersed to thousands of desktops and performed simultaneously.

The new architecture of parallel processing breaks the similar bottleneck of the central processing unit in every computer. It allows the computer itself to operate like a modern corporate information system, with various operations all occurring simultaneously, rather than like an old mainframe with people constantly queuing up for access to the central processor. Parallel processing promises huge increases in the cost-effectiveness of computing. It will bring super-computer performance of specific tasks to individuals with specific needs.

Any one of these breakthroughs alone would not bring the radical advances that are now in prospect. But all together, they will increase computer efficiency by a factor of thousands. Carver Mead of the California Institute of Technology, a pioneer in all three of these new fields, predicts a 10,000-fold advance in the cost-effectiveness of information technology over the next ten years. The use of silicon compilers to create massively parallel chips to perform feats of artificial intelligence will transform the computer industry and the world economy.

An exemplary product of these converging inventions is speech recognition. Kurzweil Applied Intelligence, a small firm in Waltham, Massachusetts, has introduced voicewriter technology that commands available vocabularies of hundreds of thousands of words, active vocabularies in the tens of thousands of words, learning algorithms that adapt to specific accents, and operating speeds of over 60 words per minute, faster than most people can compose. To achieve this speed and capacity on conventional computer architectures would require some 4,000 MIPS (million instructions per second). Yet, the new speech-recognition gear will operate through personal computers and will cost several thousand dollars. That is just $1.50 per MIPS. IBM mainframes charge some $150,000 per MIPS, and the most efficient general-purpose small computers charge some $3,000 per MIPS. By using massively parallel chips adapted specifically to process the enigmatic onrush of human speech, these machines can increase the cost-effectiveness of computing by a factor of thousands.

The talkwriter is only one of hundreds of such products. They use these technologies to increase the efficiency of computer simulation by a factor of thousands, to radically enhance the effectiveness of machine vision, to create dramatically improved modes of music synthesis, to provide new advances in surgical prosthesis, to open a world of information to individuals anywhere in the world—all at prices unimaginable as recently as three years ago. As prices decline, the new information systems inevitably will become personal technologies, used and extended by individuals with personal computers.

With an increasing stress on software and design rather than on hardware and materials, the computer industry symbolizes the quantum era. The real power and added value in the modern age is not in things but in thoughts. The chip is a medium—much like a floppy disk, 35-millimeter film, phonograph record, video cassette, compact disk, or even a book. All of these devices cost a few dollars to make; all sell for amounts determined by the value of their contents—the concepts and images they bear. What is important is not the medium but the message.

Knowledge Is Power, Knowledge Is Freedom

Microchip entrepreneur Jerry Sanders once declared that semiconductors would be "the oil of the eighties." Some analysts now fear that giant companies will conspire to cartelize chip production as OPEC once monopolized oil. They predict that by dominating advanced manufacturing technology and supplies, a few firms will gain the keys to the kingdom of artificial intelligence and other information technologies.

Unlike oil, however, which is a substance extracted from sand, semiconductor technologies are written on sand and their substance is ideas. To say that huge conglomerates will take over the world information industry because they have the most efficient chip factories or the purest silicon is like saying that Kodak will dominate the movie industry because it makes the best film or that the Canadians will dominate world literature because they have the tallest trees.

Contrary to all the fears and prophecies, the new technologies emancipate entrepreneurs to economize on capital and enhance its

353

efficiency: mixing sand and ideas to generate new wealth and opportunity for men and women anywhere in the world.

The chief effect can be summed up in the simple maxim that knowledge is power. Most people agree that this statement conveys an important truth. Today, however, knowledge is not simply a source of power. It is supremely the source of power.

The other things that no longer confer power—or do so radically less than before—include all the goals and dreams of all the tyrants and despots of the centuries: power over natural resources, territory, military manpower, national taxes, trade surpluses, and national currencies.

In an age when men can inscribe new worlds on grains of sand, particular territories have lost their economic significance. Not only are the natural resources under the ground rapidly declining in relative value, but the companies and capital above the ground can rapidly leave. Capital markets are now global; funds can move around the world, rush down fiber-optic cables and bounce off satellites at near the speed of light. People—scientists, workers, and entrepreneurs—can leave at the speed of a 747, or even a Concorde. Companies can move in weeks. Ambitious men no longer stand still to be fleeced or exploited by bureaucrats.

The old industrial technologies favored control. The new technologies favor freedom. Governments cannot take power by coercing people or raising taxes, by mobilizing men or heaping up trade surpluses, by seizing territory or stealing technology. In the modern world, even slaves are useless; they enslave their owners to systems of poverty and decline. The new source of the wealth of nations is the freedom of creative individuals in control of information technology.

This change is not merely a gain for a few advanced industrial states. All the world will benefit from the increasing impotence of imperialism, mercantilism, and statism. All the world will benefit from the replacement of the zero-sum game of territorial conflict with the rising spirals of gain from the diffusion of ideas.

Ideas are not used up as they are used; they spread power as they are shared. Ideas begin as subjective events that always arise in individual minds and ultimately repose in them. The movement toward an information economy necessarily means a movement toward a global economy of individuals and families. Collective

354

institutions will survive only to the extent that they can serve the men and women who comprise them.

All the theories of the computer as an instrument of oppression misunderstand these essential truths of the technology. In the information age, nations cannot gain strength by controlling and taxing their citizens. To enhance their international stature, governments must reduce their powers and emancipate their people on the frontiers of a new age of freedom.

Contributors

Terry L. Anderson is a senior associate of the Political Economy Research Center and a professor of economics at Montana State University.

Doug Bandow is a senior fellow of the Cato Institute.

David Boaz is vice president for public policy affairs of the Cato Institute.

James Bovard is an associate policy analyst of the Cato Institute and author of *Farm Fiasco*.

Ted Galen Carpenter is director of foreign policy studies of the Cato Institute.

Edward H. Crane is president of the Cato Institute.

James A. Dorn is editor of the *Cato Journal* and associate professor of economics at Towson State University.

Pete du Pont is the former governor of Delaware.

Catherine England is director of regulatory studies of the Cato Institute.

Peter J. Ferrara is a professor of law at George Mason University and a senior fellow of the Cato Institute.

George Gilder is the author of *The Spirit of Enterprise* and the forthcoming *Microcosm*.

Christopher Layne is an adjunct scholar of the Cato Institute.

Daniel J. Mitchell is director of tax and budget policy of Citizens for a Sound Economy.

William A. Niskanen is chairman of the Cato Institute.

Earl C. Ravenal is Distinguished Research Professor of International Affairs at the Georgetown University School of Foreign Service and a senior fellow of the Cato Institute.

Jeff Riggenbach is executive producer of the Cato Institute's "Byline" radio program.

Fisher Simons is the pseudonym of a prominent Washington tax policy analyst.

Fred L. Smith, Jr., is president of the Competitive Enterprise Institute.

Alan Tonelson is a project director for the Twentieth Century Fund.

Peter Young is on the staff of the Adam Smith Institute.

S. David Young teaches accounting and finance at the A. B. Freeman School of Business at Tulane University.

Cato Institute

Founded in 1977, the Cato Institute is a public policy research foundation dedicated to broadening the parameters of policy debate to allow consideration of more options that are consistent with the traditional American principles of limited government, individual liberty, and peace. Toward that goal, the Institute strives to achieve a greater involvement of the intelligent, concerned lay public in questions of policy and the proper role of government.

The Institute is named for *Cato's Letters*, pamphlets that were widely read in the American Colonies in the early 18th century and played a major role in laying the philosophical foundation for the revolution that followed. Since that revolution, civil and economic liberties have been eroded as the number and complexity of social problems have grown.

To counter this trend the Cato Institute undertakes an extensive publications program dealing with the complete spectrum of policy issues. Books, monographs, and shorter studies are commissioned to examine the federal budget, Social Security, regulation, NATO, international trade, and a myriad of other issues. Major policy conferences are held throughout the year, from which papers are published thrice yearly in the *Cato Journal*.

In order to maintain an independent posture, the Cato Institute accepts no government funding. Contributions are received from foundations, corporations, and individuals, and other revenue is generated from the sale of publications. The Institute is a nonprofit, tax-exempt, educational foundation under Section 501(c)3 of the Internal Revenue Code.

CATO INSTITUTE
224 Second St., S.E.
Washington, D.C. 20003